FLORA TRISTAN'S PEREGRINATIONS

FLORA TRISTAN (1803–1844)

PEREGRINATIONS OF A PARIAH

FLORA TRISTAN

TRANSLATED BY

CHARLES DE SALIS

INTRODUCTION BY

JOANNA RICHARDSON

LONDON

THE FOLIO SOCIETY

1986

Pérégrinations d'une Paria, by Flora Tristan, was first published in France in 1838.

Set in 12 point Old Style spaced one point and printed by Butler & Tanner Ltd, Frome, on Wentworth Opaque paper. Bound by Butler & Tanner in cotton buckram and printed lithographically with a contemporary engraving of Arequipa

PRINTED IN GREAT BRITAIN

CONTENTS

LIST OF ILLUSTRATIONS

(Except where otherwise indicated, all the illustrations are taken from and reproduced courtesy of the Canning House Library)

TRANSLATOR'S NOTE

This translation is based on the Maspero text of *Pérégrinations d'une Paria*, published in 1980, which was abridged to about three-quarters of the original text. Flora Tristan had a tendency to repeat herself, so the abridgement seemed to the translator to offer a racier, more readable account, while losing nothing of great value. For the sake of continuity the cuts have not been marked in this edition, and anyone interested should consult the Maspero edition.

Most of the information contained in the translator's footnotes has been taken from *Gauguin's Astonishing Grandmother*, by C. N. Gattey.

INTRODUCTION

In 1789 a young French *émigrée,* Thérèse Laisnay, found herself in Spain. She was no doubt an attractive young woman, for she settled in Bilbao with Don Mariano de Tristan Moscoso: a Spanish colonel of dragoons, a Knight of the Order of St James, and nephew of the Archbishop of Granada. Don Mariano came from an ancient noble family in Aragon, which had long been settled in the Spanish colony of Peru. He and his mistress had a daughter, Flora, who was born in 1803, and a son. No doubt Thérèse would have liked to marry her constant lover, the father of her children; one can only assume that Don Mariano was afraid of his family's displeasure: they expected him to make a grand alliance. Perhaps they had even put financial pressure on him to ensure that he did not commit himself unwisely. He and Thérèse remained man and wife in everything but name.

In 1802 they had settled in Paris. In 1806 Don Mariano bought a splendid *hôtel,* le Petit Château, in the Grand-Rue de Vaugirard; it stood in extensive grounds, which were shaded by centennial trees, and peopled by tasteful classical statues. This privileged life did not last for long. In June 1807 Don Mariano died very suddenly of apoplexy.

Thérèse had not only lost her lover; she soon lost all material comfort. In September 1808, after the Spanish rebellion against Napoleon, the property of all Spaniards who were living in France was sequestered. Thérèse tried in vain to keep le Petit Château, but in 1817, after ten years' struggle, judgment was finally given against her.

During these ten years she had sunk deeper and deeper into poverty, and her young son had died. In her despair she asked for help from Don Mariano's family in Peru. They knew that she had not been married to Don Mariano, and that she had no legal claim upon them. They did not even answer her letters. Thérèse did not tell her daughter that she was illegitimate; although the Tristan Moscosos rejected her, she continued to fire the girl's imagination, and tell her of the antiquity and distinction of her father's family. They were said to be descended from Montezuma, the Aztec emperor. Facts might be embroidered with fiction, but that only made them more appealing.

In 1818 Thérèse and Flora settled in a squalid, ill-famed *quartier* of Paris, near the place Maubert. Flora suffered less from the poverty, the neighbourhood of beggars, thieves and prostitutes, than she did from the humiliation. She tried to earn money colouring lithographs in the studio of André-François Chazal. He was a talented lithographer; he was also an ardent young man, and, inevitably, he fell in love with his beautiful assistant. Thérèse was more aware than most of the benefits of marriage, and she urged her daughter to exploit the situation. The Chazal family recognised already that the girl was wayward, given to wild fancies, and that she would never be a good wife and mother. Their counsels were of no avail. André Chazal and Flora were married early in 1821.

Flora was still dreaming of the Tristan Moscosos, and, no doubt, of the great Montezuma. Chazal could never hope to please the descendant of an emperor. It was apparent from the first that the marriage was disastrous. Flora resented domestic bonds, and her mediocre life. She despised her husband increasingly. Two children were born; in 1825, when she was once again pregnant, she escaped Chazal, and secretly gave birth to her daughter Aline. Chazal was not to see the child for years. Thérèse, ever patient, took charge of all three children, and for a considerable time Flora disappeared from the records.

She tried her hand once again, it is said, at colouring lithographs; she worked behind a counter in a confectioner's shop; she became a lady's maid in an English family. She travelled not only to England, but to Switzerland, Spain and Italy, and even – legend goes – as far as India, where she stayed for a while in Calcutta. It was during a break in this odyssey, in 1829, in a lodging-house in Paris, that she met a naval captain by the name of Chabrié. As fate would have it, he had just returned from Peru; and he confirmed all the stories that her mother had told her. He talked for hours about the distinction of the Tristan Moscosos. If there had been any prospect of a peaceful life for Flora, it had now irretrievably vanished. Chabrié revived her regret for what she considered to be her lost fortune. She wrote to her father's younger brother, Don Pio, sometime viceroy of Peru, to tell him of her misfortunes, and to ask for his justice and protection.

Don Pio was well aware that she had no legal rights. He merely gave her 3000 piastres and an annual income of roughly the same amount. However, he had gravely misjudged her character. She now had the funds to go to Peru to claim her father's inheritance. In 1833, she went to Bordeaux and embarked in Captain Chabrié's brig *Le Mexicain*, bound for America.

She was the only woman on board: a romantic adventuress in the best style. She was beautiful, sad, unprotected, and mysterious. Chabrié fell inescapably in love with her. He was an honourable man, and he proposed to her. It would have been simpler to tell him the truth, but Flora did not want to spoil her romantic interlude. It would no doubt have destroyed her image to confess that she had deserted a husband and three children, that she was a social outcast, a pariah, in France. So the romance continued, and she was obliged to invent countless stories and stratagems in order to avoid this impossible marriage. The journey did not only play havoc with her emotional life – and with that of Captain Chabrié – it did not solve her acute financial problems. When she reached Peru, Don Pio greeted her warmly, but he showed no charity, no compassion, no sense of moral obligation. He would only continue to give her a small pension.

She felt herself an outcast in the Old World and the New; but there remained one tangible result of her enterprise. Her journey inspired her to write her *Pérégrinations d'une Paria (1833–4)*. Two volumes (she had planned to write four) were published in 1838. They were lively, not entirely honest, but very self-revealing, as Charles de Salis's excellent translation makes clear. *Peregrinations of a Pariah* has the charm of a period piece. It has a slight early Victorian flavour. It is demure and dashing, romantic and eminently practical. It combines the Bohemian with a strict regard for convention. No one can say that the author deserves affection or esteem. She is selfish to the point of ruthlessness. She shows no real concern for other people's feelings (witness her behaviour to Chabrié); she shows little concern for her abandoned children, or for her impoverished mother, who is keeping them. She is bent on a romantic quest; she is always the heroine of the story. But a romantic quest it is, however material its purpose; and we may be grateful that she set it down.

Her journey to Peru had not been the only drama in the family. Her desertion had been a terrible blow for the wretched Chazal, and with time it had developed into an obsession. He had become half-deranged. In 1835 he had kidnapped his daughter Aline; and, after incredible dramas, she had been rescued and despatched to a boarding-school for safety. Soon afterwards her father had kidnapped her again, and taken her off to the slum in Montmartre where he was living. The child escaped; once more he had regained possession of her, on this occasion by legal means. However, it was alleged that he had sexually abused her, and the horrified girl, who was only twelve, went back to her mother. Chazal was arrested, and imprisoned in Sainte-Pélagie.

Even this was not the end of the melodrama. Incest could not be proved, and Chazal was therefore set free, while his wife asked for a judicial separation. In March 1838, thirteen years after she had left him, judgment was finally given against him. Chazal was not exactly placated by the publication of *Pérégrinations d'une Paria*, in which his former wife described their marital problems. A few weeks after it appeared, he procured pistols and bullets; he prowled around Flora's lodgings in the rue du Bac, and, on 10 December 1838, he found his opportunity and shot her.

She was severely wounded in the chest, but she survived to become the heroine of the moment. She was not averse to the part. This *crime passionnel* became the talk of Paris, and on 31 January 1839 Chazal was brought to trial. He had, he said, only one regret: that he had not killed his wife. He was finally sentenced to twenty years' imprisonment.

Chazal disappeared from history without trace, and

Flora changed her children's surname to Tristan. At the age of thirty-six, she embarked on a new life as a *femme de lettres*. She contributed to the fashionable magazine, *L'Artiste*, she published a novel, *Memphis*, and she frequented writers, philosophers and artists. It was now, as Jules Puech observed in his massive biography of Flora Tristan, that she became 'the ancestor of the feminist movement and of working-class socialism'.

From 1838 she affirmed women's right to happiness, and she called for the return of divorce, which had not been legal since 1816. She made contact with social reformers, notably Fourier and some of the Saint-Simonians. Their social philosophy appealed to a Romantic like herself, with her utopian dreams and her life-long sense of social injustice. But Fourier's co-operative system, which implied emancipation and free love for women, appealed to her less, perhaps, than the Saint-Simonian creed: the introduction of social equality and the disappearance of the exploited classes, the furtherance of education, and the emergence of what, in modern parlance, is called a meritocracy.

In 1839, soon after her husband's trial, she returned to London, this time to study working-class conditions. The result appeared in 1840: *Promenades dans Londres*.

Rarely has a book been written with such blatant *parti-pris*. Flora sets out, deliberately, to counter the anglomania so prevalent in France at the time. From the first paragraph it is clear that we can expect no balanced view.

What a vast city London is! This grandeur, out of all proportion to the area and population of the British Isles, immediately recalls to mind the oppression of India and the commercial superiority of England! But the wealth which is derived from the triumph of arms and cunning is of an ephemeral nature. It cannot last without reversing the universal laws which decree that, when the day arrives, the slave will break his chains, the subjugated nations shake off their yokes, and knowledge which is useful to man will be spread abroad so that ignorance, too, will be set free.

This ranting, violent tone never changes; everything that is English arouses Flora's hostility. There is more here than a desire for social reform, more than a fit of French anglophobia: there is a violence of almost manic proportions. The chapter on the English climate is all that can be expected. To Flora the age of coal and steam is the devil's doing. Her observations on English *spleen* are comical.

The Ocean mists leave a constant pall hanging over the British Isles; in English towns, there is also the heavy, mephitic atmosphere of the Cyclops's cave. Forests no longer feed the domestic hearth, it is the fuel of hell, torn from the bowels of the earth, which replaces them; it is burning everywhere, filling countless furnaces, it replaces horses on the roads, and winds on the rivers and seas which lap about the empire . . .

In London, you breathe in sadness; it is in the air, it enters you through every pore. Ah! nothing is more lugubrious, more spasmodic [*sic*], than the sight of this city on a day when there is fog, or rain, or dark and cold! When this affects you, your head is heavy and aching, your stomach finds it hard to function, breathing grows difficult, because of the lack of pure air, you feel an overwhelming lassitude – and then you are overcome by what the English call *spleen*! . . . On days like this, London has a terrifying appearance! You imagine that you are wandering in the necropolis of the world, you breathe in its sepulchral air, the light is wan, the cold is damp; and those long lines of uniform houses . . . seem like two rows of tombs stretching out into infinity, with corpses wandering among them, waiting for the hour of their burial.

Nothing in London could ever satisfy Flora Tristan. The Parisians were, she said, 'vivacious, communicative, open and brave, and the Londoners serious, unsociable, mistrustful and frightened, running like hares in front of the *policemen* who are armed with little batons'. As for the rest of the country: 'I have made several excursions into the English countryside . . . The appearance of the landscape is overwhelming in its uniformity.'

Yet, even in this extraordinary book, Flora's megalomania does not prevent her, occasionally, from being logical. When she considers the best way for the working-class to improve their condition, she decides that it is to form 'a solid, compact, indissoluble union'. She set down her theses in *L'Union ouvrière*. This book appeared in 1843, while she was campaigning actively among the workmen of Paris. She had come to regard her struggle on behalf of the oppressed classes as a sort of apostolic mission. She pursued it with all the ardour which she had once shown when she had sailed half across the world to seek her long-lost fortune. In 1844, although she was far from well, she set out on a long propaganda tour round France. In Bordeaux she was struck down by congestion of the brain; and in Bordeaux – where she had once embarked for Peru – she died on 14 November.

On Flora Tristan's death, her daughter Aline was nineteen. She was amazingly unaffected by her troubled youth. She became a *modiste* and then, on 15 June 1846, she achieved what neither her mother nor her grandmother had achieved: she was very happily married. Her husband was Clovis Gauguin. In 1847 they had a daughter, Fernande; in 1848 they had a son. Paul Gauguin, the future painter, was born in the Paris of the barricades. In many ways he was to resemble his grandmother, Flora Tristan. He had her passion, her taste for independence, and her energy. He also had some of the megalomania, some of the romanticism, the audacious love of colour, of the author of *Peregrinations of a Pariah*.

JOANNA RICHARDSON

I

THE *MEXICAIN* SAILS FROM BORDEAUX

Our departure date, the 7th of April 1833, was also my birthday. I had been in such a state of agitation as the day drew near that for three nights I had hardly slept. I felt exhausted; however, I rose at dawn in order to have time to finish all my preparations. This activity calmed the feverish emotions engendered by my thoughts. At seven o'clock M. Bertera* came to fetch me by cab; we drove, with the rest of my belongings, to the river steamer. What thoughts crowded through my brain as we drove the short distance from my house to the port! The morning bustle was beginning in the streets; I leant out of the window, eager to take a last look at the beautiful city where I had once spent so many peaceful days. The warm breeze fanned my cheeks; I was conscious of the abundance of life out there, whilst I myself was in the grip of sorrow and despair. I felt like a condemned criminal on the way to execution; I envied the women who were coming in from the country to sell milk, the workers on their way to work; I seemed to be watching my own funeral, and knew that I might be seeing these working people for the last time. We passed by the public park, and I said goodbye to its fine trees; how I remembered walking beneath their

* *Translator's note:* Felipe de Bertera was Peruvian Consul in Bordeaux. He acted as agent for Flora's uncle, Don Pio de Tristan, of Arequipa, with whom Flora had been in correspondence, and who had sent her money. Flora had now discovered that her father's property in Peru, worth at least a million francs, had been transferred to her uncle as next of kin, and it was in the hope of gaining possession of this that she was embarking on this journey.

shade! I dared not look at M. Bertera, for fear he would read my agony in my eyes. When we reached the river steamer my emotion was intensified by the sight of the crowd, some of whom had come to say goodbye to their friends whilst others were good-humouredly heading for destinations in the nearby countryside. The fatal moment had come: my heart beat so fast that for a moment I doubted my ability to remain standing. God only knows how I summoned up the strength to resist the wild temptation to say to M. Bertera: 'In heaven's name, save me! For pity's sake, take me away from here.' Again and again as we waited, I was on the point of grasping his hand and making this entreaty. But the crowd itself reminded me of that horrid spectre, Society, and of how it had rejected me.* As I remembered this, my tongue clove to my palate, I was bathed in a cold sweat, and with all the strength that I could muster I prayed fervently that God would grant me my death, the only remedy for my woes.

The signal for departure sounded and those who had come to say goodbye to their friends went on shore. The boat lurched and set off: I was alone, down in the saloon; all the passengers were on deck, waving goodbye. Suddenly, I felt angry, and anger gave me strength. Going over to a porthole, I cried aloud in a choking voice: 'Fools! I pity you, but without hatred; your scorn hurts me, but leaves my conscience untouched. The same laws and the same prejudices which victimise me fill *your* lives with bitterness; since you have not the courage to fling off their

* *Translator's note:* Flora's feeling of rejection was due to her precarious situation. She had left her husband who had ceased to earn enough to support her and had become a gambler; there was no divorce under French law, and her husband had automatic custody of her children. After a struggle she had allowed him to have the boy Ernest, but was determined to keep her seven-year-old daughter Aline. For six months she had moved about France with Aline under an assumed name, trying to evade pursuit. She had now left Aline (who was to become the mother of Paul Gauguin) with a kindly woman who kept a boarding school at Angoulême. Flora's fight against unjust laws thus began when she found herself a victim of them, a 'pariah' through no fault of her own.

yoke, you become their accomplices. Ah! if this is how you treat those high-souled natures and generous hearts who devote themselves to your cause, I prophesy that you will long remain in your grievous state.'

This outburst restored my courage and I felt calmer. The officers of the *Mexicain* came into the saloon: M. Chabrié,* the captain, was the only one who appeared moved; great tears rolled down his cheeks. I looked at him sympathetically and he came over to me, saying: 'It needs courage to leave one's country and one's friends, but I trust, mademoiselle, that we shall see them all again.'

By the time we reached Pauillac, I had regained an outward calm. I spent the evening writing my last letters and on the following morning at about eleven I went on board the *Mexicain*.

She was a new brig of about two hundred tons, of a design which promised good sailing. Her accommodation was quite comfortable, but very limited in size. The saloon was about sixteen to seventeen feet long by twelve feet wide: it was fitted up with five cabins, four of which were minute, and the fifth, at the far end, was larger and belonged to the captain. The first mate's cabin was outside the saloon, near the entrance. The poop deck was crowded with hencoops, baskets and all kinds of provisions, leaving very little space for standing. M. Chabrié, the captain, M. Briet, the first mate and M. David shared the ownership of the vessel, and most of the cargo belonged to them too. The crew consisted of fifteen men: eight sailors, a carpenter, a cook, a cabin-boy, a boatswain, a second mate, a first mate and the captain. All these men were young, strong and capable: except the cabin-boy, whose laziness and dirtiness were a constant irritation on board.

* *Translator's note:* Flora had met Chabrié in 1829 at a pension in Paris where she was staying with her daughter Aline, then aged four. She was posing as a widow. Chabrié had given her information about her uncle Pio de Tristan, and this had led to her getting in touch with the latter. It was by coincidence that she was to travel on his ship to Peru; but before sailing she had met him in Bordeaux, when she had asked him to forget that they had met before and that she had a daughter, and always to address her as Mlle Flora de Tristan.

The ship was generously provisioned, and our cook was excellent.

We were but five passengers: the first was an old Spaniard, a retired officer who had fought in the war of 1808 and had been settled in Lima for ten years. This good man had wished to see his native land once more before his death and was now on his way back to Peru. He had brought his nephew with him, a remarkably intelligent boy of fifteen. The uncle's name was Don José, and the nephew's, Cesario. The third passenger, a Peruvian, a native of the City of the Sun (Cuzco), had been sent to Paris at the age of sixteen for his education. He was now twenty-four. He was accompanied by his cousin, a young Basque of seventeen. The Peruvian was called Firmín Miota and his cousin simply Don Fernando; neither he nor the first two passengers were ever known by their surnames. Of these four, only M. Miota spoke French. I was the fifth passenger on board the *Mexicain*.

The captain, M. Zacharie Chabrié, was aged thirty-six, a native of Lorient. His father, an officer of the royal navy, put him into the same career and he received a naval education. After the events of 1815, M. Chabrié left the state service to try his luck in the hazardous merchant marine. I have no idea why he made this decision.

M. Chabrié was very different from the typical captain of a merchant vessel, usually excellent men who have started on the lower deck and worked their way up through their intelligence and good behaviour. M. Chabrié had plenty of native wit, and was a master of repartee and of remarks which showed both naivety and originality; he had a bluntness which came as much from frankness as from the habit of command. The two most remarkable things about him were his extreme good nature and his exalted imagination. But he had the worst temper that I have ever known in any man: he was intolerably touchy, irritated by the least thing; and became so surly and angry when he was in a bad humour that all traces of his good nature disappeared. Unrestrainedly he would wound his friends with the bitterness of his sarcasm and torture them pitilessly, seemingly rejoicing in the pain he was inflicting. And these bouts often continued, in my opinion, far too long.

One's first impression of him was that he was very ordinary, but after a few moments' conversation one soon realised that he was a man of breeding. He was of medium height and must have had a good figure, before he put on weight. He was almost entirely bald, and the whiteness of his crown contrasted oddly with his ruddy complexion. His small blue eyes, affected by the sea, had an indefinable expression combining mischievousness, impudence and tenderness. A slightly crooked nose and thick lips – ugly in anger but charming when laughing his childlike laugh – gave his whole countenance an air of frankness, good nature and audacity. His teeth were remarkably good: to use his own expression, he had a 'model set'. He was a man of strange contrasts in everything. His voice affected the ear in two different ways: when he spoke, no sound could be more hoarse, more raucous, more discordant. But when he sang a piece by Rossini, one of those we associate with the singer Nourrit, or a yodelling song or a sentimental ballad, oh! then the effect was divine. His pure, sweet voice and his expressive artistry were deeply moving. One was thrilled, shot through with pleasurable emotion. Captain Chabrié had missed his vocation, like so many others in our nonsensical society: he was born to sing at the Opéra. His fine tenor voice would have delighted a vast audience, and he could have held them in a state of bliss for six hours at a time, like the great Nourrit himself. To complete this portrait I should add that he was very particular in his dress, even dandified. But he took the greatest care of his health, and, sensitive to cold ever since he felt the first pangs of rheumatism in one leg, he piled one garment on top of another in the most absurd manner, as a protection against cold and damp.

The first mate, M. Louis Briet, also from Lorient and the same age as M. Chabrié, had been an imperial guardsman in 1815. When the emperor's fall deprived him of his fine horse, his gorgeous uniform and the chance of becoming a field-marshal, he was broken-hearted. Disappointed in his hopes of glory he went off to seek his fortune in the Spanish colonies. He had become a sailor, had risen to the rank of captain, and sailed on his own account or for an owner. In character he was more a soldier than a sailor, orderly in all things, which sailors are not; everything he did was cleanly and expertly done, and in addition he was completely sober. He spoke little, worked hard, and gave his orders in the cold, crisp tones of an officer commanding a battalion or a squadron, without appearing to have the sailor's anxiety about their prompt execution. His education had been neglected, but his natural good sense was such that this did not become apparent.

M. Briet was very tall and handsome, with a good figure and fine distinguished features. It was not in his character to be considerate or gallant towards ladies, but he always behaved with great politeness and correctness to everyone on board.

M. Alfred David, born in Paris, was thirty-four years of age. He was typical of those Parisians who have travelled much abroad. When he left the Collège Bonaparte at the age of fourteen, his parents put him on a boat to India, in order to toughen him up. The captain put him ashore at Calcutta, having had quite enough of his bad behaviour. There, the young rascal, who was wild but courageous, determined to be independent – and succeeded. He was first a sailor, then a language teacher, then a commercial traveller, and so on, staying in India for five years. He returned to France and began looking for a job, but after being let down by the sort of promises that abound in Paris he decided to try his luck again in some industrial career and went to Peru. At Lima he met M. Chabrié, they became friends and returned to France together in 1832, by which time M. David had been away for eight years.

He was self-educated, and, without being an expert on anything, he had a very wide knowledge of a number of subjects. He was active, enterprising, tireless, pleasure-seeking, always cheerful and insensitive to pain. He also had, to an extraordinary extent, that tendency to disparage other people which the author of *Candide* made fashionable towards the end of the last century. He always saw the bad side of the human race: obstinate in his opinions, he disagreed with everyone, criticised and quibbled about everything, and, naturally argumentative, would rush boldly into a discussion that he was unable to sustain, because he was incapable of any profound thinking or long concentration. When he became entangled in his own arguments he would have recourse to some silly joke, which, by making his audience laugh, would cause the subject of the discussion to be forgotten. However little he knew about anything M. David could discourse upon it with a self-assurance which would have disconcerted even its inventor. From a tender age, left to fend for himself against poverty, he had studied human nature in the raw; early disappointments had freed him from illusions. He hated mankind and regarded humans as wild beasts, ever ready to tear each other to pieces, and, having suffered himself from such treatment, he was constantly on guard against attack. He had never loved anyone and no one, not even a woman, had ever shared his sorrows. His heart had hardened: the only pleasure of which he was capable was complete self-indulgence. The soul, deprived of its gentler emotions, had been stifled in him before it had a chance to develop; physical sensations reigned supreme and the soul no longer existed. He loved good food passionately, was ecstatic about a good cigar, and tickled his fancy by dreaming of the pretty women of any colour whom he might find in any port he might enter. These were the only loves he knew.

M. David was very good-looking, tall and slim – even thin – but enjoying excellent health. His regular, well-cut features, pale complexion, black whiskers and shiny jet-black hair, his sparkling eyes and readily-smiling lips all combined in contrasting harmony to give an appearance of gaiety and happiness which he was far from feeling. He was what the world calls 'a pleasant fellow', talkative, full of eloquence and gaiety and the amiable qualities which women admire. Moreover, he was a dandy who wore silk stockings when going round Cape Horn, shaved daily, perfumed his hair, recited verses, spoke English, Italian and Spanish, and was never known to fall over, however heavily the ship was rolling! Such were the people who had gathered together on the *Mexicain*.

Once on board each one of us set to in an effort to get settled into our little holes as best we could. M. David helped me do so, explaining, in the light of his experience of sea voyages, how best to avoid the worst inconveniences.

I began to be seasick an hour after coming aboard our floating home. This condition has been described so often by its many sufferers that I shall avoid tiring my readers with yet another account of it. I shall only say that seasickness is quite unlike any other malady, in being a permanent agony, a suspension of life. It has the horrible power of depriving the unfortunate sufferer of his intellectual faculties and the use of his senses. People of a nervous disposition experience the cruel effects of this illness more intensely than others. I suffered from it so constantly that there was not one single day, during the one hundred and thirty-three of the voyage, that I did not vomit.

Our ship lay at anchor at the river mouth. The weather was evidently not favourable to sailing out into the dangerous Bay of Biscay: nevertheless, at about three o'clock, the captain gave orders for the anchor to be weighed. The heavy ship, riding the waves as light as a feather, came out into the vastness of sea and sky and, obeying man's command, set off on its course.

We were hardly out in the bay when a shrill wind and rough seas warned that a storm was at hand. It broke soon afterwards in full force with a terrifying roar. This was a new experience for me; I was present but could see nothing. I should have enjoyed watching it if I had had the strength to do so, but seasickness dominated my whole being: I was only conscious of the convulsions which ran through my body and which I was convinced were harbingers of death. It was a dreadful night. The captain was lucky to be able to re-enter the estuary. One wave had washed away the sheep, another our baskets of vegetables; and our poor little ship, so right and tight the day before, was badly damaged. The captain, though tired out, went on shore to buy fresh sheep and replacements for the vegetables. In his absence the carpenter repaired the damage caused by the storm and the sailors restored order, so essential on shipboard.

The first attempt did not make us any the wiser, and we straightway exposed ourselves to undoubted perils which nearly proved fatal, all on account of a false pride which only too often causes sailors to run pointlessly into danger, risking the lives of men and the safety of ships in their care. Next day, the 10th of April, although the sea continued rough, our masters – being prudent – rightly decided that they should keep the pilot on board until the weather was good enough to allow them to send him ashore without risk. Two other ships, however, which had left Bordeaux on the same day and for the same destination, were anchored close to us – the *Charles Adolphe* and the *Flétès* – and the latter, no doubt out of bravado, dropped its pilot and set out to sea, while the other, not wishing to be left behind, followed suit. The gentlemen on the *Mexicain* began by deploring this imprudence but – although of course not easily influenced by other people's example – they changed their minds for fear of being thought cowardly. At about four o'clock the pilot was dropped and we moved into angry waters: the waves towered over the ship like high mountains; we were but a speck on the ocean, and if two waves had met we should have been swamped.

It was three days before we could leave the bay, during which we were continually beaten by the storm and in a critical situation. All our men, either from sickness or exhaustion, were incapacitated. During these long days of agony our good captain never left the bridge. He told me afterwards that our frail brig was a number of times on the point of being dashed against the rocks or swallowed up by the waves. With God's help we escaped, but experiences such as these should surely make seamen think again, before they court such dangers.

Between two and three in the afternoon of the 13th, our captain, dog-tired and as wet as if he had fallen overboard, came down to the saloon, which he had not entered for three days. Seeing all the cabins closed, and no sign of life, he called out in his strong hoarse voice: 'Hey, passengers! Are you all dead?'

No one answered his friendly question. He then opened my cabin door a crack, saying in a voice of such kindness that I shall never forget it: 'Mademoiselle Flora, I understand from David you have been very ill. Poor lady! I deeply sympathise, for I too was once a sufferer from seasickness. But cheer up, we are now out of the narrow waters and on the high seas. Can you not feel how the horrible convulsions that shook us have now become a gentle roll? The weather is splendid. If you are strong enough to get up and come on deck, it would do you good. There is a pure and gentle air which is delightful.'

I thanked him with a silent look, being too weak to speak.

'Poor lady,' he said, full of goodness and compassion. 'This weather will allow you to sleep. I too shall sleep, I certainly need it.'

And indeed we all slept for twenty-four hours. I was wakened by M. David, who noisily opened up all the cabins, to find out, he said, whether all the passengers were stone dead. We were not dead, but Lord! what a state we were in! M. Chabrié, too noble a man to exploit his position as captain, treated crew and passengers alike as a friend rather than as a commander. During the storm, his role was that of first seaman and he at all times showed a benevolent interest in the well-being of those on board. He now invited us to rise, so that fresh linen could be provided, to go up on deck and above all to partake of a little hot soup. I was willing, but asked to be allowed not to eat. They were kind enough to have a bed made up for me on the poop deck. It took all my courage to get up and dress, and without their help I could not have reached the deck.

For the first fortnight on board I was insensible, except for a few short intervals of consciousness. From dawn until six o'clock in the evening I felt so ill that I could hardly think at all. I was indifferent to everything around me; I hoped that death would soon end my suffering; even though an inner voice told me that I would survive.

When we were close to the Canary Islands, we realised that the ship was taking in water and it was decided to call at the nearest port, which was Porto Praya in the Cape Verde Islands, for caulking. We had only been at sea for twenty-five days. So long had this seemed to me, for life on board had been so burdensome, that when I was told I should soon see land, my delight was such that my sickness disappeared: I was completely well again. Oh land! so often cursed by those who tread you, you yet seem like paradise to anyone who has spent a few months at sea, where there are no cool shades nor flowering meadows, and where one can meet neither relatives nor friends.

We were all on deck, keen to discover this land that we had garlanded in the colours of our imagination: our hearts beat fast as we swung round the cape at the end of the tongue of land which forms the bay of La Praya. What awaited us? It was at this anchorage that I experienced the first disappointment of my voyage. I was not good at geography, and never having read a description of La Praya, I had made one up in my head. I thought that an island called 'Cape Verde' should show a verdant landscape when seen from the sea; if not, how did it get its name? I did not realise that many place-names have been given in curious circumstances which bear no relationship to the places themselves. At Cape Horn the Land of Fire is more like a Land of Ice, but whoever discovered it thought it was on fire through some optical illusion or other, and named it as he saw it. Valparaiso, the Valley of Paradise, was named by the Spanish sailors who sailed into its bay; after so long and hard a voyage they would have given the name 'paradise' to the most arid coast, the most terrible country, provided it was *land*. Land is man's paradise: but it is up to him to plant the vine and the olive tree, and to uproot the thorns and brambles.

This black, entirely arid land is so monotonous that the sight of it is painfully depressing. The whole bay is ringed by rocks of varying height, against which the waves break thunderously. In the middle of the bay a high rocky headland stands out, shaped like a horseshoe. On the flat top of this stands the town of La Praya.

From a distance, the town is most impressive. On the round end of the horseshoe there is a battery of twenty-four large calibre guns; it is guarded by soldiers who are passably well equipped. On the left is a pretty church, newly built; on the right is the house of the American consul, topped by a little belvedere used for observing ships at sea. Here and there one can see clumps of banana trees, and groups of sycamores or other trees of the broad-leaved type.

II

LA PRAYA, CAPE VERDE ISLANDS

As soon as we had anchored, we saw a good deal of movement in the artillery battery. A few minutes later, a small boat came out towards us, rowed by four almost naked negroes. In the stern, holding the rudder, sat a cocky little man with enormous whiskers, whose swarthy complexion and curly hair indicated that he did not belong to the Caucasian race. His wore nankeen trousers dating back in style to 1800, which must have had a long and varied history before reaching him; a white quilted waistcoat; an apple-green frock-coat of coarse cloth, and a very long red scarf with white spots which did duty as a cravat, its ends waving gracefully in the wind: the whole was set off by a large straw hat, gloves that had once been white, and a fine yellow scarf which he held in one hand and used as a fan. He kept the sun off with a large umbrella, striped in sky-blue and pink, of a type that was common thirty years ago. When he reached our ship, he declaimed his various functions for our benefit: he was both harbour-master of La Praya and secretary to the governor; moreover, he was a merchant, both wholesale and retail, and so on and so forth. Evidently no law against plurality of functions had penetrated as far as the coast of Africa. This harbour-master was Portuguese; he explained that the island was the property of Don Miguel, his illustrious master, and in pronouncing his name, the comic creature raised his hat. He discoursed on politics, and tried to draw us on the subject. He accepted our brandy and our biscuits, made me pompous compliments in Portuguese, and after a long stay on board, of which the intention was to spy rather than to fulfil his official functions, he re-embarked, striking the pose of a captain-pasha taking his fleet out of Alexandria.

Whilst the little Portuguese was discoursing on the deeds of his great master, two other persons came on board who were no less remarkable in their clothes and their manners. One was captain of an American brig, the other commanded a schooner from Sierra Leone: the latter was an Italian and informed us on arrival that his wife was a Parisian from the rue St Denis. The good man, whose name was Brandisco, pronounced the name of that street with all the pride of a Roman patrician of Caesar's time declaring that he lived on Capitol Hill.

Our captain, the mate and M. David decided to land at the same time as the harbour-master, in order to call on the governor, regularise the ship's papers and find workmen to come as soon as possible to help our carpenter repair the damage to the ship. Since I am determined to tell the whole truth, I admit the pride I felt when I compared our longboat and its crew with the three other miserable little craft manned by negroes or poor American sailors. What a huge difference! Our boat was so spruce, so jaunty! Our sailors looked so fit! M. Briet held the rudder: his noble bearing worthily exemplified the French navy, and our captain, with his polished boots, his white drill trousers, his dark blue jacket, his black cravat in grained taffeta, and his fine straw hat adorned with a black velvet band drawn through a small buckle, was equally representative of the merchant marine. As for our M. David, he was every inch a dandy. He wore grey suede boots, grey twill breeches, and a short jacket in green Russian cloth, much braided; he wore no waistcoat, but a madras scarf in small check that was knotted casually round his neck; a small purple velvet cap was tilted over his right ear. He stood in the middle of the boat, waving at me and roaring with laughter, probably at the comic appearance of the personalities of the port of La Praya. In 1833 I was still a long way from having the ideas which I have since developed. At that time I was very exclusive: my country took more place in my thoughts than the whole of the rest of the world, and it was against the ideas and customs of my country that I judged the ideas and customs of other countries. The name of France and everything to do with it had an almost magical effect on me. I thought of an Englishman, a German or an Italian simply as a foreigner; I did not see that we are all brothers and that the world is our common fatherland. I was therefore still far from realising the interdependence of nations, the fact that the whole of mankind is affected by the good or ill fortune that befalls any one of them. But I here recall my impressions as I experienced them, when I saw our superiority over the people of other nations represented at La Praya.

The officers were a long time on shore; they returned only at dinner time, about five o'clock. During their absence we spent the time in conjecturing what the town of La Praya might have to offer. M. Miota intended to put up at a hotel, so as to escape from life on board during our stay in port. Cesario and Fernando planned to leave each day with the lieutenant and the cook when they went on shore to buy provisions. The two young Spaniards were keen to go shooting, to run across the plain, to eat fruit, to ride – in short, to get the exercise which is so necessary at their age and which their stiff limbs so craved for. I too worked out a plan for the length of our stay: I wanted to go and live in a Portuguese house, so as to be able to study the customs and habits of the country, to see everything and make careful notes on whatever I considered to be important. All these fine plans were being discussed on deck whilst old Don José, who could at last walk in comfort now that our floating home was still, was evidently enjoying the delights of being able to stroll up and down without fear of falling. He stopped only to roll his little cigarettes, and from time to time he smiled at our talk. I saw his smile, and wanting to know what lay behind it I asked him what he was going to do in town.

'Mademoiselle,' he replied with that Spanish composure which he possessed in the highest degree, 'I shall take care not to go there.'

'But are you not at all interested, Don José? You are quite happy to remain on board this ship where there is so little room to walk about?'

'I am just as interested as you are at the sight of land,

mademoiselle, but I have the advantage over you of my long experience, and I know what to expect from these coasts and others at which we might touch before we reach Lima. I think there is no point in leaving the ship in order to be much less comfortable on land; you'll discover that, but children must see everything with their own eyes. Well, go and see, and afterwards you can tell me whether I was right or wrong.'

We all protested against Don José's indifference; his nephew roguishly undertook to make him enthusiastic about La Praya; but the old Spaniard, who was typical of his race in every way, was unshakeable. He simply repeated: 'Go on, all of you, and when you come back, you will tell me whether I was right or wrong.' But youth is impatient of obstacles and will only believe what it wants to believe until disillusioned by personal experience: we were disdainful of Don José and his prejudices.

When we saw the longboat returning we burned with curiosity. As soon as the officers came on board we bombarded them with questions, but it was not the right moment for them to satisfy our curiosity. M. Chabrié and M. Briet were explaining what had to be done to the workers they had brought with them, and M. David, the perfect anglomaniac, was completely occupied in speaking the beautiful tongue of Lord Byron to the young and very elegant American consul whom he had just met, and whom he had brought to dine with us.

The next day after breakfast, the three young Spaniards, M. David, the captain and I went on shore. There is no mole at La Praya to facilitate landing: the approaches bristle with rocks of all sizes, against which the sea beats with a violence that would batter the strongest boat to pieces if precautions were not taken to avoid it. A sailor has to haul the boat, jumping from rock to rock as he does so, until he reaches a suitable opening, while the crew fend the boat off the rocks with their oars. It is very difficult to land without getting wet, especially in the morning when the sea is always rougher. However, thanks to the attentions of the gentlemen, I landed dryshod: a sailor picked me up in his strong arms and carried me to land. A narrow footpath leads over the rocks to the town, which is not without its dangers, for the black sand which covers the rock surface gives way under one's feet, and to trip might land one in the sea, falling from rock to rock. Leaving this path, we walked on the flat, smooth sand of the beach, on which the waves broke in silvery lines. It was refreshing to walk on this firm, continually sea-washed sand; but after only two or three hundred yards we had to take a most difficult stony way, up steps hewn out of the mass of rocks on which the town is built. It takes at least a quarter of an hour to climb. I was so weak that I had to rest three times. I could hardly walk, and good M. Chabrié was almost carrying me. M. Miota shaded me with his umbrella as my sunshade was inadequate, whilst M. David, bounding ahead like a deer, acted as scout and pointed out the route. A burning tropical sun stood right above our heads, and there was not a breath of wind to dry the perspiration which stood on our brows. We were tortured by thirst. At last we arrived on the plateau. M. David went ahead to warn the American consul of our approach, so that refreshments could be prepared for us, and we passed through the town, which we found almost entirely deserted. It was midday, and from then until three o'clock the heat is most intense – the inhabitants stay at home and sleep. The reverberation of the sunlight was so strong that we were blinded. M. Chabrié was conscience-stricken at having brought me into this furnace, which put him into a vile temper; the three young men were already beginning to miss their cabins, and I was very upset at feeling so poorly, fearing that I should be unable to visit whatever the town had to offer. Such were our various moods when we arrived at the consulate, where we found the consul sitting with M. David at a little table, drinking grog and smoking excellent Havana cigars.

The consul had brought to this dreary place all the comforts which are so dear to his nation. Some thirty years old, he had lived there for four years. His house was vast, well arranged and kept in perfect order. He had ordered an excellent cold collation for us, of hams, butter, cheese, pastries and many other things, all from New York. There was also fresh fish and a great abundance of locally grown fruit of many kinds. The drawing-room in which the repast was served was furnished entirely in the English style; a pretty carpet covered the floor; the window-blinds were decorated with paintings representing various harbours; fine engravings adorned the walls, some of hunting scenes, others of the departure of stage-coaches or children playing with dogs; there were also those vaporous female heads which the English engravers render so admirably.

The service was also according to English and American usage. We ate from large blue patterned plates, drinking our ale from large stem glasses and our port from small ones. Our large steel knives and forks were polished like new and, as there were no napkins, we all used the pieces of tablecloth nearest to us. The consul was clearly in his seventh heaven at having found in M. David an anglomaniac who spoke so well the language of his beloved country, and so he never ceased conversing with him. He also spoke English to the two negroes who served us, and, so strong is the effect of surroundings on the imagination, that I, a silent observer, felt at times that I was in a country house not far from New York. After the meal, Captain Brandisco came to fetch us to visit a lady who claimed to be almost French, because she had been married to a Frenchman, a M. Watrin of Bordeaux. M. David remained behind to speak English and to drink tea.

Mme Watrin was the wealthiest lady in town. Some fifty to fifty-four years old, she was tall, very fat, with a complexion the colour of dark café-au-lait, slightly curly hair and regular features. She had a sweet expression and well-educated manners; she spoke some French, and could read and write it quite well: all this she had learnt from her husband. He had been dead for four years, and she mourned him deeply.

She received us in a large dark room, unevenly flagged and of gloomy aspect: it was what she called her *salon*. The oddness of the furnishing struck us as soon as we entered. It was easy to see that a Frenchman had lived there. The walls were covered with inferior engravings of Napoleon in a number of varying situations; all the generals of the empire and the principal battles were depicted there, symmetrically arranged. At the far end was a grill-fronted bookcase, on top of which was a bust of the emperor, draped with a black veil. On the shelves were works by Voltaire and Rousseau, the *Fables* of La Fontaine, *Télémaque, Robinson Crusoe,* arranged without any order. On a piece of furniture stood two globes and a glass jar containing two foetuses in spirits of wine. Scattered around were objects which had been brought from France: a little work-table in mahogany, a lamp, two armchairs upholstered in horsehair, cages with birds in them, a beautiful cloth which covered the large table in the middle of the room, and a number of other smaller things. When we entered, Mme Watrin came forward to greet us, took my hand and led me to one of the armchairs. In my honour she had dressed in her best, and had invited a number of friends anxious to meet a young foreigner. Parisian ladies may perhaps be interested to know what the full dress of the ladies of La Praya looked like. Mme Watrin's costume contrasted strikingly with the rest of her appearance. Her dress was of cherry-coloured taffeta; it was short, with short sleeves and a very low neck. An enormous sky-blue crêpe-de-chine scarf, richly embroidered with white roses, was a combined shawl and head-dress, absurdly draped over the back of her head. Her fat arms were adorned with bracelets of all colours, her fingers were laden with rings of all kinds and large pendants hung from her ears; she wore a necklace of seven or eight rows of coral, white silk stockings and blue satin shoes. The other ladies were far less richly garbed than Mme Watrin; they were clothed merely in blue, red or white cotton; but their dresses and scarves were otherwise similar.

Mme Watrin asked me many questions about Bordeaux, which her husband had described to her many times, and then showed herself willing, with a readiness rare in people of that country, to satisfy my curiosity about anything I wanted to know. She showed me round her house, which consisted of three rooms on the ground floor and three under a mansard roof. Her house was on the edge of the plateau on the side facing away from the sea: the view was magnificent. Under the plateau were half a dozen very well cultivated gardens. The largest of these belonged to Mme Watrin, and a path hewn out of the rock led down to it. Beyond the gardens was an area of sandy desert, and beyond that again shady groves of trees.

Mme Watrin invited me to stay with her for as long as our ship remained in port. I was grateful for this courteous offer, but I admit I was not tempted to accept it. Land, the first sight of which at sea makes the heart beat faster, soon loses its charm when one finds one's self friendless amongst a people whose level of civilisation is still a long way from one's own. When Mme Watrin made her offer, M. Chabrié coloured and fixed his eyes on me with an expression of painful anxiety. I refused, and we took our leave of this amiable lady, promising to return two days later.

We toured the town. It was now six o'clock, and as the sun went down a light breeze made the fading heat more tolerable. The whole population was in the streets, breathing the cool air by their front doors. We were then assailed by the *negro smell*: there is nothing like it, it nauseates, it pursues one everywhere. If one enters any house, the foetid odour is there. If one goes up to a group of children to watch them play, one soon turns tail, so revolting is the smell. I, so sensitive that the faintest odour affects me either in the head or the stomach, suffered so unbearably that we were forced to hurry until we were out of reach of these African effluvia.

When we arrived at the bottom of the rocky path, I sat down to rest. M. Chabrié sat beside me, whilst the three young men wandered on the beach looking for shells. He took my hand, pressed it affectionately against him, and said in a tone of voice quite new to me: 'Oh, Mlle Flora, how grateful I am that you did not accept that lady's offer! How upset I should have been! To be separated from you, now that you are in my care, now that you are so unwell, to leave you alone on this foul rock, amongst these horrible negroes whom you find so revolting! I would never have permitted it, and then, who would look after you if I were not there?'

The passionate tone in which M. Chabrié spoke these words produced on me an effect difficult to describe. My feelings combined gratitude, affection and panic. Since we had left Bordeaux, I had completely lost sight of what effect my extraordinary situation might have on him. My state of health had prevented me from thinking of it. I put the kindness he had shown me and the care he had taken of me down to his good nature; it had never occurred to me that he could feel any emotion other than that of a friendly sympathy, such as my situation usually evoked.

For people with loving natures, who combine sensitivity with personal magnetism, one glance is enough to allow them to guess the secret of the person to whom they are speaking. M. Chabrié's expression clearly revealed his thoughts, and he also read mine. I took his hand. He then said, in a tone of the deepest sorrow: 'Mlle Flora, I do not hope to win your love. I only ask to be allowed to help you bear your troubles.' I gave him a smile of gratitude, and, pointing at the sea, said: 'My heart is like the ocean; sorrow has hollowed out great depths, and it is in the power of no human being to fill them.'

'Do you then attribute greater power to sorrow than to love?'

This reply startled me: at that time I could not hear the word 'love' without tears coming to my eyes. M. Chabrié hid his head in his hands. For the first time I looked at him: I was as yet unfamiliar with his features. He was weeping. I watched him closely and let myself sink deliciously into a deep melancholy.

Someone called: the boat was ready. I leant on M. Chabrié's arm. We were absorbed in our own thoughts and neither broke the silence. On board we found M. David with his consul friend and two musicians he had brought along to show me what the local music was like. We all gathered on deck; I lay on a double rug. The gentlemen all grouped themselves round me, and we listened, with more or less attention according to the nature of our thoughts, to the monotonous music of the two Africans. The concert would have gone on long into the night, if one of the musicians had not become seasick, despite the fact that the ship was motionless. As a result the consul was obliged to go on shore. I was thus relieved of the boredom which his English and his musicians had brought on. We stayed on deck until very late: tropical nights are so beautiful!

On the following morning M. David and M. Miota went on shore in order to make a trip into the interior of the island. They were going to visit a Frenchman who had a plantation eighteen leagues from the town, their object being as much to buy provisions from him as to see the scenery.

Two days passed during which M. Chabrié seemed embarrassed in his relations with me. His constrained behaviour, so unlike his normal self, I found upsetting; it increased the worry and the sad thoughts that the conversation on the rock had given rise to. At this period I had all the illusions of a girl without knowledge of the world, although I had already suffered cruelly; but, brought up in the countryside, completely isolated from society, and living later apart from the world, I had passed through ten years of sorrows and disappointments without my eyes being opened. I still believed in kindness and goodwill; I thought that ill-nature and false-heartedness were exceptions to the rule. The complete solitude into which I had withdrawn had left me ignorant of the world and what went on there. I had retired into myself and was unable to suspect in others the existence of vices of which I found no trace in myself or which, in the generosity of my heart, filled me with indignation. In 1833, love was for me a religion; my enthusiasm had deified it since the age of fourteen. Love, I thought, was the *breath of God*, his life-giving force, which created the great and the beautiful. In love alone had I faith, and I considered that anyone who could pass his life without experiencing a great love, pure, devoted and eternal, was hardly better than the beasts. I was fond of my country, I wanted to do good to my fellow men, I admired the marvels of nature, but none of these things was enough. The only attachment that could then have made me happy would have been a passionate, all-embracing love for one of those men who, through their devotion to a cause, call down misfortune on their heads, and whose sufferings enrich and ennoble them.

I had loved twice. First, when I was still a child. The young man who was the object of my love deserved it in every respect, but, lacking strength of character, died rather than disobey his father, who, through cruel pride, rejected me. The second time, the man with whom I was deeply in love, although completely correct and honourable towards me, was a cold, calculating character for whom a grand passion was a kind of madness: he was *afraid* of my love, he feared that I loved him *too much*. This second disappointment nearly broke my heart, and I suffered terribly. But I was far from defeated: sorrow gave my soul strength, I became even more devoted and firm in my faith. Every passionate nature needs a God to worship, a temple in which to shed joyful tears and to dream of the destiny so ardently believed in.

My sufferings had taught me the extent to which God had endowed me with the power of loving; and after my two disappointments I realised that this could only be understood by a man who was himself capable of acts of devotion, the sort of self-sacrifice which the common herd considers to be madness, because there is no personal advantage in it. These acts are remembered in after time as gracing with nobility the human beings who committed them: they are humanity's greatest claim to honour and evidence of progress.

At all times and in all countries there have been men and women who have undertaken the most onerous tasks, who have not counted the cost, who have shrunk from no sacrifice however great, in order to attain their objective. They are so far above the rest of mankind that they have always been misunderstood, and often the greatness of their acts has not been appreciated until centuries later. Both in ancient and no less in modern times have there been examples in the causes of religion and of politics. The sceptic and the egoist view the sacrifices of Joan of Arc, of Charlotte Corday, of the martyrs of all revolutions and religious sects as acts of folly; but those heroic souls were following an impulse which they had received from God; and although their objective was to succeed, they expected no reward on this earth.

I knew from experience how terrible it is to love a person who cannot understand one, whose love is not in proportion to the strength of the emotion experienced by the other partner. For this reason I was determined to do all I could not to be the cause of this in others, to try so far as I was able not to provoke an affection I could not return. I have never understood how anyone can enjoy exciting love in someone when they themselves feel none. Such enjoyment is pure vanity, and no sensitive soul could share it. I was not sure if M. Chabrié loved me or not, but I felt that in case this might happen, it was only proper to do what I could to prevent the development of a love to which I could not respond. Since M. David and M. Miota were away, this was made rather easier: the three other passengers understood no French, so that I could talk to M. Chabrié without risk of being overheard.

That evening I went up on deck, and after arranging a couch for myself on top of the chicken cages, I began to converse with M. Chabrié.

'How fortunate you are, Mlle Flora,' he said, 'to be so interested in everything! I admire your childlike curiosity. How enviable to have illusions! Life is indeed dull when one has lost them all.'

'But I hope, M. Chabrié, that you are not in such a plight as that? Such a noble nature as yours is forever young.'

'Mademoiselle, one is young so long as one is in love and loved; but even at twenty a man with an empty heart is old.'

'So you think that one needs to love in order to live?'

'I am sure of it, unless you call eating, drinking and sleeping like beasts living. I am sure, mademoiselle, that you know love too well to give existence without it the name of "Life". Yet that is how the majority of men pass their lives. When you think of it, do you not feel, as I do, ashamed of belonging to the human race?'

'No. The human race suffers and is not contemptible; I pity it for the sorrow it brings on itself and I love it because it is unhappy.'

'And you feel no spite against it?'

'Never.'

'But perhaps you have never had cause. You have probably only known people who love you, and have never suffered the terrible bitterness of infidelity.'

'That is true; but I know something worse than infidelity: insensitivity. The cold-hearted man, who responds with reason to outpourings of the heart, measures passion with a yardstick, a mere automaton untouched by God's breath who, incapable of appreciating the sublime beauty of devotion, looks with disdain on the love he has inspired – he is worse than the unfaithful man. Yes, he who, fearing to be loved too much, looks with complete indifference on the sufferings of the woman who loves him – he is worse than the unfaithful man. The latter, M. Chabrié, at least has love as his motive. The former, the prey of a disgusting egoism, concentrates all his affections on himself.'

In speaking these words, which escaped me almost unconsciously, I abandoned the reserve which I had scrupulously kept until then: my features and my tone of voice must have expressed a grief of superhuman proportions, for the sorrow whose memory inspired my words had been beyond a mere earthly experience. M. Chabrié was struck by my expression and said, looking at me anxiously, 'Great God! Could it be that you loved a man of so vile a character? Tell me, did you suffer a grief such as this?'

I could not speak, but nodded assent. I looked up to heaven as if to entreat for help; then, holding out my hand to M. Chabrié, I could only say: 'How I suffer! Oh, my God! How I suffer!' After this cry of pain which I had been unable to suppress, I let my head fall on my pillow. The outside world fatigued me and my eyes closed. As I sank into a welter of memories, I experienced an enjoyable sensation, a charm which came from the very excesses of my distress. I remained some hours without moving, my brain seething in a way I could not control. M. Chabrié had fetched my cloak and covered me with it, and with a silk scarf had protected my head against the dews of the night. I could sense that he sat beside me; sometimes he sighed convulsively, and from time to time he stood up, paced the deck for a while, then came back and sat down again.

When I emerged from this dreamlike state, the moon shone over the bay of La Praya, casting a dim light which threw a mantle of gloom over everything. Not a sound came from the town; the high masses of rock in shadow resembled the descriptions of hell left us by the ancients. The sea was calm; the three ships anchored off shore were motionless; and M. Chabrié, sitting on the end of the chicken-cage on which I was lying, his head resting on one hand in an attitude of melancholy which fitted the scene, contemplated the heavens with a sorrowful expression. I watched this scene for a long time in silence. On such a night, all created things, in their stillness, seem to be serenely happy; sorrow no longer exists. For a soul in torment, this silence is the most powerful of consolations. Little by little I felt the soothing influence which the moon has on all nature; calm entered my soul and I was able once more to admire the majestic beauty of the sky.

I dared not speak to M. Chabrié for fear of interrupting his musing; however I made a slight movement. He immediately turned round and, seeing that my eyes were open, stood up quickly; then, coming closer, he asked if I needed anything.

'I should like to know the time,' I said.

'Past midnight.'

'So late? Why are you not in bed? You planned to catch up on sleep, as soon as you had no watch to keep.'

'Like you, Mlle Flora, I enjoy these beautiful tropical nights. And now I am your *friend*, your old friend, who loves you too much to let you sleep on a chicken-cage without keeping watch beside you.'

I took his hand, which I pressed in mine. 'Thank you,' I said, 'oh, thank you. How grateful I am for your friendship, and how much good it does me; how I need it! You too have suffered; I will help to console you for the betrayals you have undergone, and your sorrows will appear light when you compare them with mine.'

'You accept me as a friend?'

'Oh, so willingly.' And I kissed his forehead with a gratitude which brought tears to my eyes.

It was nearly two o'clock when I went down to my cabin. I slept until ten next morning. I was awakened by the musical sound of M. Chabrié's voice, singing an old ballad about friendship. I got up; everyone had breakfasted and I was served by the cabin-boy. M. Chabrié came and sat with me, peeled my oranges and my bananas and chatted so freely and frankly that I liked him more and more.

At about three o'clock M. David and M. Miota returned, bringing with them the Frenchman at whose house they had been staying. M. Miota was exhausted and went to bed. M. David did not complain of tiredness, but was very angry because he had not shaved for three days and was dirty and dishevelled. We had to give up the whole saloon to him, so that he could have a thorough wash and change. This was no sacrifice for any of us, because the deck had been converted into a very agreeable sitting-room, by means of an awning which kept off the sun.

The little that M. David had said about the French landowner made me want to talk to him. He was a short, stocky man, sharp-featured, sun-tanned, with thick, black, straight hair, long at the sides. His dress resembled that of a peasant in his Sunday best. I addressed him in a friendly manner, as one tends to speak to a compatriot encountered in a far country. M. Tappe (for such was his name) responded to my show of interest, and although he was not very talkative by nature, I could see that he would be quite willing to tell me his story.

He had come to the Cape Verde Islands fourteen years before. I asked him why he had chosen such an arid spot. 'Mademoiselle,' he said, 'the choice was not mine; God, in his mysterious ways, has decreed that I should remain in this land of barrenness and poverty. From childhood, my parents destined me for the holy ministry of the church; I was sent to the seminary of La Passe, near Bayonne. The religious zeal which burned within me brought me to the notice of my masters. When the usurper had been defeated and the monarchy restored, our holy religion regained its all-powerful position, and in 1819 it was decided to choose, from all the seminaries of France, those who showed most dedication to the propagation of the faith, to be sent as missionaries out into the world to convert the savage races still sunk in idolatry. I was one of these, and we each set off for our allotted missionary field. Our ship, like yours, being in need of repairs, put in at the port of La Praya.

'Whilst we were lying at anchor, I went on shore and became friendly with an old Portuguese, who told me about the various resources which the islands had to offer. I realised that with very little capital it was possible to make a fortune in a very short time. Consequently I decided to change my destination and to remain where I was. But, alas! God, whose decrees I respect, has not allowed my hopes to be realised, and for fourteen years I have vegetated here on "the coast", in the most difficult circumstances.'

I was anxious to discover what sort of business it was that had decided M. Tappe to give up his missionary work for the opportunity of becoming rich, and asked him to explain by what means he had hoped to make a fortune.

'Dear lady,' he said, 'there is only one kind of trade on this coast, and that is the slave trade. When I arrived on this island, ah! then times were good. There was money to be made, and without too much work involved. For two years trade boomed, and prohibition itself meant that one could ask anything for one's negroes. But since then those damned English have insisted on the strict application of treaties to such an extent that the dangers and expenses involved in transport have utterly ruined the most lucrative trade that ever existed. And, moreover, there are now too many people in the game, and there's no more profit in it than in selling bales of wool or cotton.'

M. Tappe spoke with such artlessness and frankness that I was dumbfounded. I looked at the man, trying to guess from his expression what could be in his mind; but not once did he show the slightest emotion: he remained calm and impassive. I could find no words to answer him, and feeling an instinctive repugnance, I did the only thing possible to get rid of him: I went below. There I found M. David in his finest négligé, at table with his consul, who clearly could not be apart from him. When I entered, he threw away his cigar and said: 'Well, mademoiselle, what do you think of the nice compatriot I brought you? I hope you'll agree that there are superior Frenchmen in the Cape Verde Islands. There's a man who talks better Latin than Cicero. He can quote Horace, Juvenal or Virgil whilst talking of unripe lemons or stunted cabbages, to say nothing of his quotations from the Bible. And he knows Hebrew too. I am sure, mademoiselle, that you are pleased to find, here off the African coast, that our dear France is so well represented.'

'Enough of that, sir: that man is no Frenchman. He is a cannibal in sheep's clothing.'

'Oh, that's good, that's beautifully true! I must translate that to the consul.' And from that moment on, M. Tappe was nicknamed 'the cannibal sheep'. 'I cannot think', I continued, 'why you have brought that man on board. I would have given a lot never to have met him.'

'But how ungrateful you are, mademoiselle, to your friends and well-wishers! It was for your sake and only yours that I brought M. Tappe here.'

'And why, sir, I should like to know? What right have you to expose me to the sight of such a disgusting creature as that?'

'So that you can see with your own eyes that there are such disgusting creatures in this world.'

'But are there many men as bad as the one I have been talking to?'

'Unfortunately yes, mademoiselle. And since we are talking frankly, I would go so far as to say that the majority of the human race is just as bad as the honourable M. Tappe.'

'If that were true, sir, I should go this very moment and jump in the sea: but fortunately I can read in M. Chabrié's eyes the lie direct to what you, in your misanthropic way, more than frivolously assert.'

'Now what is M. David telling you?' said M. Chabrié, coming in at that moment. 'That men are evil, I warrant? It's his continual refrain, he never leaves it.'

'This time, I am doing more than say it, I am proving it, and it was in order to convince our dear passenger that I brought from St Martin the very holy and virtuous M. Tappe, who will dine with us, if you will kindly allow.' M. David then came up to me and said: 'Now, mademoiselle, I am no longer joking. I urge you to study that man. I am going to seat him beside you. Try to master your distaste. I think that for a traveller such an encounter is a piece of good fortune.'

During the first course, the ex-seminarist ate and drank; his greed was such that he had no time to speak a word: all the forces of his being were absorbed by his plate and his glass. I never ate the first course, so I had plenty of time to watch the man, a remarkable example of his type, as M. David said. I could tell from his expression what was the dominant passion of his nature, namely gluttony. How his little eyes shone at the enormous leg of mutton and other meats which were being served! His nostrils flared, he ran his tongue over his thin, pale lips. The sweat ran down his forehead. He seemed to be experiencing one of those moments when an uncontrollable enjoyment oozes out through every pore. To me, he was no better than a wild beast. When he had gorged himself, his features gradually returned to normal, that is, expressionless, and he began to address me in the same tone as before dinner.

'Your captain, mademoiselle, has given us a very good dinner. Eating is living, and in this miserable island I am deprived of it.'

'So you have nothing to eat on this island?'

'We have only mutton, poultry, vegetables, fresh fish and fruit.'

'But I should have thought that with all those things you could make up a very reasonable diet.'

'Yes, if one could have a cook and all the necessary things for preparing the food. But we have none of that.'

'Why do you not train one of your negresses to cook?'

'Ah, mademoiselle, I see that you know nothing about blacks. Those miserable creatures are so vicious that I cannot trust any of them without risk of being poisoned.'

'You must treat them very hard to feel so much hatred and animosity against their masters.'

'I treat them as negroes have to be treated if one wants to be obeyed – with the whip. I assure you, mademoiselle, that these scoundrels are more difficult to manage than animals.'

'How many have you at the moment?'

'I have eighteen negroes, twenty-eight negresses and thirty-seven children. For the last two years, the children have been selling very well, but it's been hard to get rid of the grown men.'

'What work do you set them all to do?'

'They work my farm and look after my house. It's all very well kept, ask these gentlemen.'

'M. David tells me that you are married. Are you happy at home?'

'I had to marry one of the negresses, as a life insurance. I had been poisoned three times. Fearing that I'd die of it, I thought that if I married one of these women, she might be interested in my survival, especially if I made her think that all my property also belonged to her. I make her do the cooking, and she has to taste in front of me whatever she serves me. I consider that this makes me very secure. I have three children from this young woman: she loves them very much.'

'So you are so tied to this country that you must give up the idea of ever returning to France?'

'Why do you think that? Because of that woman? Oh, that won't bother me. As soon as I've made my little pile, I shall bring my negress here one day when the sea is very rough, and I shall say: "I am going back to my country. Will you come with me?" As all these women are terrified of the sea, I am sure that she will refuse. Then I shall say to her: "My dear, you see that I do my duty, I offer to take you with me. You refuse to obey your husband; I am too kind to force you. I wish you all the luck in the world, and I'm off."'

'And what will happen to the poor woman?'

'Oh, don't worry, she'll be all right. She will sell her children and get a good price for them, and then she'll be able to find another husband whom she'll serve for her keep. She's a superb creature and only twenty-six.'

'But, M. Tappe, that girl is your wife in the sight of God; she is the mother of your children; and you are willing to leave them all to the mercy of whoever wants to buy them in the market place? This is quite dreadful of you!'

'Mademoiselle, it is the way people behave every day in our society.'

I had turned crimson and was choking with rage. M. Tappe noticed it. He looked at me in astonishment, muttered a few phrases in Latin, and said, with a nasty smile: 'Mademoiselle, you are still very young. I can see that you have seen little of the world, and suggest that you should endeavour to see more, for it is a good thing to know what people are like, otherwise one is everybody's dupe.'

INHABITANTS OF THE CAPE VERDE ISLANDS

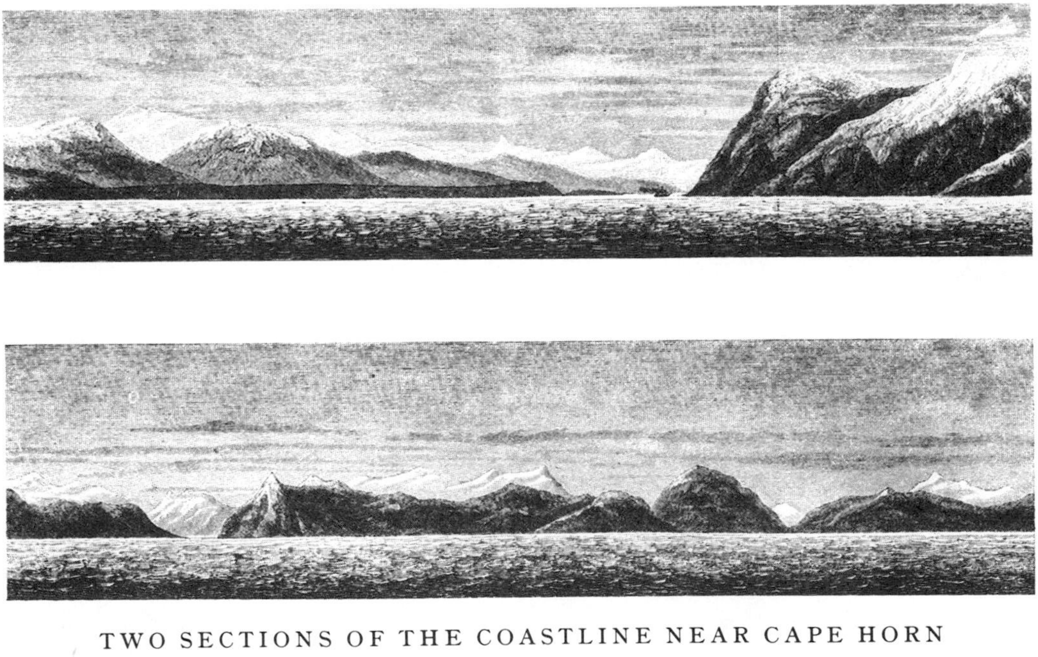

TWO SECTIONS OF THE COASTLINE NEAR CAPE HORN

After dinner, M. Tappe went on shore. When M. David and I were alone, he said: 'Well, what do you think of the pupil of the celebrated seminary of La Passe?'

'M. David, I repeat that I would rather not have met him.'

'Mademoiselle, I hope you will pardon me if, intent on doing you a service, I have caused you some disagreeable moments. You are, however, too reasonable not to realise that, sooner or later, you must make up your mind to get to know the people you are destined to live amongst. Society, I agree, is not a pretty sight when seen close to, but it is important to recognise it for what it is.'

A week went by without my going on shore, owing to my aversion to the negro smell. Politeness, however, made me overcome my reluctance and I decided to pay goodbye visits to Mme Watrin and the consul.

At the consul's house I was greeted by a revolting scene, the sort of atrocity which is so frequent in the countries where slavery, that monstrous outrage against humanity, still survives. The young consul, representative of a republic, elegant American that he was, so courteous to me, so friendly to M. David, was, it seemed, no better than a barbarous slave master. We found him in the lower room, whipping a big negro lying at his feet with a stick: the man's face was bathed in blood. I made a gesture as if to come to the defence of this negro, who was paralysed by his condition of slave. The consul asked M. David to explain why he was beating him: the man was a thief, a liar and so on – as if the greatest theft of all were not the one of which the slave is victim! As if a man deprived of his free will is in a position to be virtuous! As if a slave owed anything to his master and was not, on the contrary, justified in any sort of action against him! No, I cannot describe the painful impression that this hideous sight made on me. I thought of that beastly Tappe in the midst of his negroes. Good heaven, I thought, could M. David be right? Could men all be bad? These thoughts upset my moral convictions and I was plunged into the deepest melancholy. Mistrust, which is born of the evil we have suffered or witnessed, and which is the bitter fruit of experience, was born in me, and I began to fear that goodness was not as common as I had hitherto believed. As I went in the direction of Mme Watrin's house I looked carefully at all the black- and dusky-skinned people I saw. All of them, in their near nudity, were repulsive to behold. The men looked hard, even ferocious; the women insolent and stupid. The children, quite naked, were horribly ugly, thin and puny; they were like little monkeys. As we passed the town hall, we saw soldiers beating negroes at the behest of their owners. The sight of this cruelty, quite normal to these people, deepened the mood of gloom which the scene in the consulate had provoked in me. When we reached Mme Watrin's, I complained to her – apparently so kind – about all the barbarous acts I had seen committed in the town. She smiled, and answered in her gentle voice: 'I realise that for you who have been brought up differently, these customs must seem strange. But after a week here you would think no more about it.' This dismissiveness and hardness I found repellent and longed to be far away from all these people.

La Praya has about four thousand inhabitants in the wet season; in June, July and August the population is less, owing to the unhealthiness of the climate. The only commerce is the slave trade; there are no exports. The inhabitants exchange negroes for flour, wine, oil, rice, sugar and other produce, and for any manufactured goods that they need. They are poor and eat badly; mortality is high due to the many diseases to which they are exposed.

After spending ten days at La Praya for repairs to our ship, we put to sea once more.

III

LIFE ON BOARD

For the first week, I was as sick as I had been when we sailed out of the mouth of the river from Bordeaux. After that, my sickness followed a regular pattern: I vomited every morning; I felt better about midday; from two to four I felt queasy; from four until the following morning I was perfectly well. This daily routine continued until our arrival in Valparaiso. But when the sea was rough, I was sick night and day without ceasing.

A fortnight after we left La Praya we crossed the equator, and there our troubles really began. Our ship had been well repaired, and therefore took on no water; but a serious disadvantage arose from this. From the hold came a strong stench, caused, we thought, by the stagnation of the water which had remained there, and which the sea no longer renewed. This odour was so corrosive that it turned the table silver black. The whole ship was infected; we had to leave our cabins, because one could not remain below without running the risk of being asphyxiated. For twelve days we had a most disagreeable time. As we could not go below, we had to stay on deck night and day. Every quarter of an hour there were thunderstorms; then the equatorial sun would blaze down on our heads. The heat was intolerable and we could not put up the awning to protect ourselves against it because of the frequent changes of wind. We each of us tried to huddle in a corner of the deck where there was a little shade, but there was no way of avoiding either the sun or the rain. We were a pathetic sight, as wet as if we had been drenched by a wave, limp with heat, exhaustion and drowsiness. We suffered a raging thirst; there was no fresh fruit with which to quench it; our stock of water was in casks, all of which stood on the deck and were heated by the sun so that the water became quite warm. Our mouths were dry and scorched: we felt slightly crazed.

Despite the care and attention which the officers of the *Mexicain* showed me at this period and throughout the voyage, I thought I should not survive the exhaustion I experienced during this crossing of the equator. M. Chabrié had had the bottom knocked out of an empty barrel for me to use as a shelter: by using this movable residence, I was protected, unlike the other passengers, against both sun and rain. M. David had lent me his boots; M. Briet went without his great fishskin cape in order to lend it to me. This garment, which had been made in China of exquisite workmanship, was waterproof and extremely light. M. Chabrié had given me a large oilcloth hat, also waterproof. Dressed up in all this, I sat like Diogenes in my tub, reflecting sadly on the plight of humanity. M. David had some *personal secret* which enabled him to support both heat and cold with equanimity, and was always brisk, cheerful and well dressed. While the others wore only shirt and trousers, M. David wore a tie, stockings and a white linen jacket. He and the cook, in their different spheres, were the life and soul of our ship.* M. David was attentive to us all in a thousand different ways: he cooled water for us in bottles which were dragged in the sea, he made lemonade for us with the bitter lemons that the pious Tappe had passed off on us for good ones; he ordered soup for one, bananas for another, tea for a third and punch for a fourth; he was nurse to us all.

We were about seventeen days in equatorial waters. Gradually the stench disappeared. The saloon was scrubbed down, vetiver and vanilla were burnt, and the combined odours sweetened the room which was the capital of our little empire.

As the crew of the *Mexicain* were all progressives, there

* *Author's note:* When the cook was interviewed prior to being taken on for the voyage, M. Chabrié pointed out that a cook's life on board was very hard, to which he answered: 'Don't worry, Captain, I know my job, and in any case, the sea's my element': *'Pour moi, la mer est un élément.'*

was no baptismal ceremony when we crossed the line. This was our ship's first voyage, and as she had been launched without baptism she had no godfather or godmother. In addition we had first reached the open sea on a Friday and now the captain wanted no crossing-the-line ceremony: three facts which made Leborgne, the self-styled 'True Sailor', declare that his sisters would be likely to see their cherry-trees blossom twice before we saw land again. The crew did not dare to flout the captain's order, but a plot was hatched in the fo'c'sle, led by the cook. He penned a letter to the captain, in the name of Neptune, whose secretary he claimed to be. Leborgne delivered it: wrapped in sailcloth dipped in seawater, he passably resembled a messenger from the ocean god. Unfortunately I have no copy of this letter: the style, spelling and subject-matter were very characteristic. The wily cook spoke of the wrath of the god at seeing his empire crossed by captains who were non-believers. He threatened to sink them, unless they willingly agreed to pay the tribute they owed him. Our captain understood the meaning behind this ingenious fable, and to appease Neptune's wrath he sent his worthy representatives wine, brandy, white bread, a ham and a purse into which all of us who were crossing the line for the first time had placed a coin. The god seemed to be receptive to these gifts, for we could hear, as songs reverberated below, the shrill voices of the cook and Leborgne in piercing discord.

Between the equator and Cape Horn we had some fine weather. I could then with delight admire the sunrise in all its magnificence. What a sight it is in that part of the world! But I found the sunsets even more beautiful. There is no sight more sublime on earth, nothing grander or more divine, nothing more dazzling in its beauty than the sunset in the tropics. I shall not try to describe the magic light-effects produced by the last rays of the sun on the clouds and the water. Words are too colourless to depict them, and the paintbrush is powerless to bring them to life. Such sights enrapture, carry the soul upwards towards the Creator; but it is not in man's power to reproduce them or evoke the emotions they inspire.

After a beautiful sunset, I liked to stay on deck for part

of the night. I sat in the stern where I could delight in watching, as I chatted with M. Chabrié, the play of phosphorescence on the waves. The wake of the ship was like the tail of a brilliant comet. In their play, the dancing waves tossed up a wealth of diamonds. I also loved to see the shoals of great porpoises, swimming beside the ship and leaving behind them long trails of phosphorescence which lit up great stretches of the sea. Then the moon would rise, and gradually dispel the darkness of the night; the diamonds would disappear and the waves, now absorbing and reflecting the brilliant moonlight, shone like the stars in the sky.

How many delightful evenings did I spend in this manner, happily musing. M. Chabrié talked of the troubles that had darkened his life, especially the last disappointment that had left him cruelly heartbroken. He suffered, and the similarity of our heartaches, without our realising it, brought us sympathetically together into an intimate relationship. Day by day, M. Chabrié loved me more and more, and day by day I felt blissfully happy in the knowledge that he loved me.

We reached Cape Horn, with all its horrors. It has so often been described that I need not say more than that the temperature varies from seven to twenty degrees of frost according to the season and the latitude at which one goes round it. We rounded it at fifty-eight degrees of latitude in July and August and we had between eight and twelve degrees of frost. We had a good deal of snow, hail and ice.

At this point we underwent another series of mishaps. The sea round Cape Horn is constantly stormy. We almost always had to reckon with contrary winds. The cold sapped the strength of the crew, even of the strongest men. Our sailors were all young and strong; yet a number suffered from boils, others injured themselves seriously falling out of the rigging. One fell from the topmast on to the capstan and dislocated his shoulder. Those whose health stood the strain were exhausted through having to do the work of the casualties. In addition to all this these poor sailors had not a quarter of the clothes they needed. Due to the thoughtlessness engendered by their adventurous way of life, sailors fail to bring the necessary clothing with them to protect them against heat and cold when they embark on a long voyage. On the equator they often have no light garments, and at the Horn only their two woollen shirts to wear turn and turn about – the rest of their clothes are no better. I witnessed to the full the worst that can befall mankind: I saw sailors whose woollen shirts and trousers had *frozen on them,* every movement they made bruising the flesh of their numbed limbs. The cabins where the poor fellows slept were full of water (as is normal in the fo'c'sle of small ships in rough seas) and they had no other place to rest in. It was truly pitiful to see men reduced to such a degree of suffering.

The minister of the Navy could prevent the hardships which result from the lack of sailors' clothing, by laying down that the naval superintendent in the ports must, jointly with the captains, inspect the sailors' kit. Regulations will always be useless unless a means is provided of ensuring that they are carried out to the letter. On naval ships, the sailors' kit is frequently inspected: they are issued with regulation clothing, which they must not replace, and the value is deducted from their pay. Why should the same system of inspection not be introduced in the merchant marine?

The improvidence of sailors, their fecklessness, even about the risks they will have to run, are childish traits. We must think for them, not only for humanitarian reasons but in our own interests. Physical suffering, carried to extremity, demoralises a man to such an extent that he becomes useless. The officers gave me a number of examples of this. More than one captain has been forced, when rounding Cape Horn, to give his orders holding a loaded pistol in each hand when the sailors refused to go aloft. Excessive cold makes the sailor so demoralised that he becomes quite inert: it is useless to urge him and no amount of beating will make him move. At times the poor fellows' hands become numb, extremely painful and swollen, and if they are then in the rigging they fall, sometimes to their death. If these men were properly clad, if they had oilskins to keep their woollen clothing dry, they could, provided they were properly fed, survive any degree of cold. What happened on board our ship will prove my point. Five of our crew were well equipped and four very inadequately so. The five stood the cold without ill effects, whilst the four all went off duty sick. They had continuous fever, their bodies were covered in boils, they were unable to eat and became so weak that we feared for their lives.

It was during this terrible crisis of suffering and fatigue that our good captain's indomitable courage showed itself to the full. He was continually on deck, encouraging his crew by his example and gentle words. He would lend the man at the wheel oilskins and gloves, a hat to one man, a pair of trousers to another – boots, stockings, shirts, everything he could spare. He would visit the sick in the fo'c'sle, dress their wounds, comfort them, cheer them up. 'Well boys,' he would say, 'how are we today? Are those boils any better? Leborgne, they tell me that you do nothing but drink water: are you too hot, my boy?'

'Too hot, captain? I should think not: I'm shivering.'

'But you silly fellow, you're shivering because you have a fever.'

'Yes, and some fever! But captain, I'd always heard that a fever made one hot, and I'm frozen.'

'Of course you're frozen in that pink shirt of yours. You must have been mad to set sail to go round the Horn with one linen shirt and one miserable pair of trousers.'

'What could I do, captain? I hate luggage, it's in the way on board. And then a True Sailor ought to be like the snail that carries his house on his back.'

'You poor devil! Here you are, with ideas like that, thirty-eight years old, and all you have in the world is a pink shirt and a pair of linen trousers.'

'But captain, that's all a True Sailor needs, a sailor who does the job because he likes it, because he wants to see places, and I've seen some places, I can tell you!'

'And that's made you rich?'

'Captain, does a True Sailor want to get rich?'

'Well, boys, now that you've had your dressings done and you're tidied up a bit, I'll send along some soup and a dish from the table. Here's some chocolate and some chewing tobacco that Mlle Flora asked me to give you.

She tells you to be patient, and to let her know if there's anything you want that she can send you.'

'Thank you, captain, thank you! Tell the good lady that we are very grateful for the tobacco. Tobacco is life's blood to a sailor. Don't worry, captain, we'll be on deck in a week.'

Whenever M. Chabrié returned from visiting the sick he described to me the conversations he had had with these men, whose characters are so different from all others. One must live amongst sailors and take the trouble to study them to realise that their heads are full of the strangest ideas. The True Sailor, to use Leborgne's phrase, has neither country nor family. The language he speaks is international, it is an amalgam of words taken from all languages, from the negroes and the American Indians as much as from the tongues of Cervantes and Shakespeare. With no clothes other than those on his back, he lives a haphazard existence, taking no thought for the morrow; he ranges over the vast oceans, or treks through the forests with the savage tribes; on arrival in port he spends on prostitutes all the money he has earned during a long crossing. The True Sailor jumps ship as often as he can, serves on ships of all nationalities one after another and visits every country; he is satisfied with just seeing, without trying to understand what he sees. He is like a migrating bird which perches a while to rest on the trees it finds on its journey but never settles in the forest. The True Sailor has no attachments or affections, loves no one, not even himself. He is a passive being, useful for navigation, but as indifferent to where he lands as is the anchor to where it drops. When he reaches port, he abandons his ship and the pay he has earned, and, once ashore, will sell even his pipe to take a prostitute out to dinner. The next day he signs on again with the first English, Swedish or American ship that will take him. If the sea spares him in that dangerous career of his; if his health survives all the excesses and all the hardships to which he is exposed and he reaches an age when he is no longer strong enough to unfurl a sail, he resigns himself to remaining on shore. There he begs his bread in the port where his last voyage has left him; he takes the bread to eat on the beach, in the sun, and gazes at the sea lovingly; for the sea is the companion of his youth, and brings back many memories; he sighs at his weakness, and dies in the poorhouse.

Such is the life of the True Sailor – Leborgne was my model; but since everything degenerates in our society, his type becomes rarer and rarer. Now we have sailors who marry, carry round a well-filled trunk, seldom jump ship because they do not wish to lose their belongings and the money due to them, pride themselves on mastering their profession, and are ambitious to succeed. When they fail to make their pile, they end their working life in lighters or other boats used in ports.

The cold of Cape Horn, apart from its ill effects on the sailors' health, was fatal to the morale of even those who took good care to protect themselves. The officers had good, dry cabins, and everything that man has invented to keep out the cold and wet; so, unlike the sailors, they did not suffer to the point of falling sick, but the biting cold made them sullen-tempered. They had great difficulty in getting their orders carried out; they had to see their men suffer; they had to expend great energy to get through their work and were tired out as a result. All this caused a constant irritation which made them cantankerous, and the gentlest characters after a month in that region became unbearable. The only man who was always the same was the cook: not once did he fail to be his jolly, courageous self. He somehow managed to cook, despite the terrible weather which upset the stoves; he nursed the sick sailors, he assisted our cabin-boy to serve in the saloon, and in addition helped in the handling of the ship when needed and often even went on night-watch. During the whole voyage, he was never once under the weather, though he looked feeble enough, being so short, thin and pale. He came from Bordeaux, but as he had done his cook's apprenticeship in Paris, he had absorbed all the characteristics of a typical Parisian. He was a fine talker and a great reader of novels. He had served on board a naval frigate and had been round the Cape of Good Hope.

Sailing in July and August at the southern tip of the American continent, we had only four hours of daylight and, when the moon was obscured, we were for twenty hours a day in total darkness. These long nights increased the difficulties and dangers of navigation and resulted in a number of mishaps. The violent movement of the ship and the terrible shrill sound of the waves made it impossible to do anything. One could neither read, nor walk, nor even sleep. I cannot think what would have become of me during the six weeks of cruel hardships that we had to endure in these latitudes if I had been left to my own resources, without the comfort of M. Chabrié's gentle, pure, affection. Before going on deck for his watch, he would come to my bedside and ask me, softening his voice: 'Mlle Flora, please let me have a few words of friendship, so that I can bear four hours of cold, snow and ice.'

'Am I so fortunate, dear friend, that my friendship really can be of comfort to you? Ah, you can certainly count on it. But do you realise that when you say that I can mitigate your sufferings, you are turning me into a God?'

'Well, Mlle Flora, you *are* God, at least for me. So great is your power over me, that a word from you, a look or a smile from you, can give me strength and keep up my spirits. I go on deck, and for four hours I think of you and do not feel the cold.'

'How many women would be flattered to hear such words! They fill my heart with joy. I thank you, Chabrié, I shall remember them all my life. Go up on deck, dear friend, and since thinking of me can make you happy, you can feel that my friendship is greater, though of a different kind, than the love that other women have felt for you.' As I spoke these words, I pressed his hand whilst putting on his gloves for him; and often, as I tied his lined neckerchief to protect him from the cold, I would kiss him on the brow. I liked to care for him and caress him like a brother or a son.

I fully realise at this point the difficulty of my self-imposed task – though nothing that I have to say gives me any cause for regret; but I fear that the portrayal of one person's true love and another's pure friendship may, in this materialistic age, be taxed with improbability; I fear that few only, whose souls are in harmony with mine, will believe me. Moreover, before beginning this book, I examined all the possible consequences of my narrative, and, however taxing the duties imposed on me by my conscience, my zeal did not waver: I was determined to carry them out.

M. Chabrié, a man of sensitivity, could not see me suffering without being deeply moved: from friendship he progressed to love, as would have happened to almost any man of his age who found himself sharing with a young woman the intimacies of ship-board life for five months. On board, loving natures become more loving, religious natures more religious: isolated from the rest of human society, and with eternity all round them, they feel the need to love and to believe, and these two emotions remain pure from all worldly alloy. M. Chabrié was such a being; he had made a resolve to love me only as a friend, but love entered his heart despite his resolution. It must be said that the strangeness of our respective positions, the mystery with which I seemed to be surrounded and the strong friendship which I showed him all concurred to arouse emotions in him which in other circumstances might have remained dormant.

In accordance with the plan that I had decided on, I had had to lie to M. Chabrié: in giving him a short account of my life I had said nothing of my marriage. But I had had to admit to having had a daughter. He who lies to get out of a difficulty, little realises that he has entered a dead end. He must continue to lie, and the only way he can extricate himself from the tangle of the dark labyrinth is to go back to the beginning, to return to truth. I felt that I had to tell M. Chabrié that I had a child, although I was unmarried; I told him that this was the secret reason why I felt such repugnance towards marriage. This admission made M. Chabrié love me even more. He was too generous, too sensitive a soul not to understand to the full the painful situation of a girl deceived and abandoned by the coward who had seduced her. He began by feeling sympathy, and by respecting me as one who suffers a grief that is without remedy. But the sympathy he felt developed into the sublime idea of committing an act of devotion, of the sort which is not understood these days and which our stupid society even laughs at because it can understand nothing which does not relate to material gain, and because it is so selfish that it finds it easier to mock than to emulate such acts.

M. Chabrié planned to bring me back into the society from which I was excluded by offering me the protection of his name. This proposal, generous beyond all praise, filled me with the deepest gratitude, and at the same time with apprehension at the possible consequences of the lie which I had been forced to tell. So, when he asked me to marry him I hid my face in my hands, not daring to reply and fearing that he would read my innermost thoughts from my expression. It was a long time before I could utter a word. I felt humble before this great love of his, and realising that I could never respond to it at this celestial level, I wept tears of despair.

True love has a language, a tone of voice, a look, an expression of its own which cannot be feigned. I looked at M. Chabrié and saw that I was truly loved. This discovery gave me a thrill of delight, for love as I understand it is God's presence: we mortals, earthbound as we are, must worship this divine manifestation. But my feelings of gratitude were followed by others of deep despair at my situation. I could never be united to one who loved me. I could hear a hellish voice saying with a mocking laugh: 'You are married! – to a contemptible man, it is true: but you are chained to him for the rest of your life, there is no way you can cast off this yoke. Feel the weight of the chain that makes you his slave, and see if you can break it here, any more than in Paris.' I thought my head would burst. I was sitting on my bed, M. Chabrié close beside me. I drew his head on to my lap, intending to speak to him. I was about to tell him the whole truth, but my tears choked me: they fell freely and wetted his face. M. Chabrié could not understand me: he saw that I was overwhelmed by grief and yet felt that I was sincerely fond of him. I asked him to leave me: I was unable to contain my sobs and was afraid of being overheard by my neighbours. I begged him to love me always, but asked him to give me two days to recover from the state of agitation produced by this conversation.

Now that M. Chabrié had made his proposal, I could no longer doubt the sincerity and strength of his love for me – such a love as I had longed for all my life; but alas! this love, so pure, so devoted, a love that yet could have given me happiness – filled my heart with bitterness and despair, by bringing home to me all the horror and baseness of the marriage that I had been forced into. For two days I lived in the most painful uncertainty. At times I almost decided to follow my inclination and tell M. Chabrié the whole truth about my situation; but on reflection I soon repressed my tendency to over-frankness, as I thought of the possible consequences. I imagined how M. Chabrié would reject me, as all the others had done; I saw myself alone, abandoned, desperate. I admit that I recoiled at this prospect of increased misery which such an indiscretion might bring in its train, and which I feared would be insupportable. I was afraid of finding myself abandoned: my life might depend on the protection of others, and I clung to M. Chabrié's love as a castaway clings to a floating plank. Again, I hoped that I could make M. Chabrié understand that my friendship would be as precious to him as the love of other women. This was not presumption on my part: I was in good faith, but was completely mistaken.

When I was again alone with M. Chabrié, he asked me what I had decided about his fate. 'I have decided,' I said, 'that you will be my friend all my life, my very good friend, whom I shall love tenderly.'

'And nothing more?' he asked in a voice full of emotion. 'Unhappy man that I am!' and he hid his face in his hands. I watched him for a long time. The veins stood out on his forehead, he trembled convulsively, he was clearly a prey to profound grief. Then with a sudden movement he emerged from his thoughts. His expression was haughty, his smile sardonic, his voice hard.

'So, mademoiselle,' he said, 'you do not love me? Indeed, I realise that the love of an old sea-dog like me must seem quite ridiculous to you, used as you are to the smart manners of handsome young Parisians who know how to speak fine phrases but who feel nothing or, rather, my mistake, they feel *fear*, for did you not tell me one evening, when we were anchored off La Praya, that one of them was *afraid of your love*?'

'Chabrié, you call up memories which are extremely painful to me.'

'I beg your pardon, mademoiselle, but I rather thought, in my innocence, that when a woman is indifferent to the deep suffering that she has caused in another, she is unlikely to be much moved by a memory.'

'Chabrié, you are hurting me. You are unjust to me and do not love me as much as you say you do.'

'I do not love you as much as I say I do! But don't you realise that I love you more than I wish to?'

'If so, give me a proof.'

'What proof? Ask away. I am ready to give any proof.'

'Then love me as a friend.'

'No need to ask: you know that I am your friend and your daughter's friend for life.'

'And this affection cannot make you happy, as I so ardently desire you to be?'

'No.'

'Ah, Chabrié! What a difference between us! My friendship for you makes me happy, and my happiness would be complete if you felt a similar feeling towards me; but I see, with great regret, that you will never experience any joy from it.'

'Listen, Flora! If I loved you less, I might perhaps try to lie to you, as, in spite of my truthful nature, I have done on more than one occasion with other women. Tell me, do you think that a man of my age can sit near you for hours at a time, as I have done every day for the last three months, and not fall in love? You must realise that that is impossible. You can find such things in books, but they lie; and you, dear friend, are innocent enough still to believe in books.'

Next day and the days following, M. Chabrié returned to my cabin, and our conversation continued in the same strain. He still showed his genuine, pure love: but I saw that I must abandon any hope that he would be content to remain a friend only.

I do not know if our travelling companions noticed the way in which Chabrié paid me affectionate attentions; he acted with such dignity, that despite his long and frequent visits to my cabin, the other gentlemen showed me ever-increased friendship and respect, for such is the effect of pure love and its influence on those who witness it.

During the rough passage of the cape, I had often to act as peacemaker between my travelling companions, eight men whose rough, harsh tempers envenomed the slightest dispute. M. David had the coarse and ludicrous habit of uttering four or five swear-words or epithets whenever he gave an opinion or spoke to the servants. Nor did he ever speak of the Peruvians without a string of insulting expressions. M. Miota, who found this irritating, got his own back by translating, and no doubt amplifying, M. David's words, for the benefit of the Spaniards, who became indignant in their turn. Life on board is repugnant to our nature. Not only is there the perpetual torment of the ship's movement, whether gentle or violent, the lack of exercise and fresh food, all continuing so long as to sour the temper of the mildest of mortals, but also the misery of living together in a small room ten or twelve feet long, face to face with seven or eight other human beings, morning, noon and night, unceasingly. Such a torture must be experienced to be believed.

M. David rose very early, so as to have the whole table to himself for shaving, doing his hair and dressing. These operations were not performed in silence. He swore black and blue at the poor cabin-boy who was, indeed, both dirty and lazy; but as he was only sixteen and was almost always sick, some allowance should have been made. I had taken him under my personal protection; M. David did not dare strike him since the day when he had nearly knocked him out and I had intervened and had persuaded M. Chabrié to issue an order forbidding anyone to touch the boy. When he had finished his toilet, he would go into the storeroom and continue his swearing, this time at the purser's mate, Emmanuel, whose untidiness left everything in disorder. The ship's dog Cora then took the brunt of his abuse, after which he would curse everything in general – the sea, the wind, trade and the human race. He would rail especially, with the obligatory accompaniment of oaths, against Peru and its inhabitants. His voice, the cabin-boy's snivelling, Emmanuel's protests, the yelping of the dog all made such a din that anyone trying to sleep found it impossible. The officers who had been on night watch complained bitterly. M. Briet said that he had never been on such a noisy ship. M. Chabrié would then protest to M. David with some acrimony; the latter would reply in similar terms. An argument would develop which would increase the hubbub which had caused it.

At nine o'clock breakfast was served. Plaintiffs and defendants being seated together, the dispute would continue. From the outset of the voyage I had refrained from attending this repast, and this had become my set rule. Being a small eater, and almost always feeling ill in the morning, I preferred to rise only when breakfast was over and everyone was on deck. I was then freer to wash and dress and generally get myself ready. As my cabin door was merely a Venetian shutter I could hear and see everything that went on in the saloon without being seen myself. When these eight men sat down together to breakfast, their mutual recriminations started up again louder and with more bitterness than ever. M. Briet's voice was hard and dry, and his complaints provoked M. Chabrié's anger against M. David, who faced up to all of them with complete calm.

No sooner was I up than M. Miota would come and complain to me: he tried to make me share his indignation by insisting that I was included in M. David's insults against the Peruvian people. I calmed him as best I could and made him promise that he would not say one word in reply to M. David. Cesario, who was proud and violent by nature, was furious. He worked on his uncle and on Fernando, made plans of vengeance against M. David, and I had to use all my influence to prevent the boy from creating a scene.

I talked less often with M. Briet, but when I did, he told me frankly that he would never go into partnership again, nor would he set foot on a ship whose captain failed to carry out his prime duty, namely to win respect.

At three, M. David would visit me in my cabin to ask what two dishes of preserves I would choose for dinner. Not once, during the whole voyage, did he omit to defer to me in this manner, but the clever fellow knew exactly how to make me choose the dishes that he liked, regardless of whether they suited the others. I used this visit to scold him on his behaviour in the morning.

'Dear lady, forgive me for today. I promise that from now on I will swear much less. 'Pon my word, I thought you were asleep. You know that I never swear in front of you.'

'But, my dear David, so many accumulated swear-words? One is as good as a thousand. And that long string of adjectives you use? If the cabin-boy deserved them all, he would be a most remarkable being, don't you see? In heaven's name, for all our sakes, only one oath and one adjective! Don't shout interminably, for nothing that you say will make him cleaner, and it wakes us up and is a great nuisance.'

'Mademoiselle, I must say frankly that you are spoiling that boy. The rascal feels that you and Chabrié (who does everything you ask him) are on his side, and so you see how things are on this ship.'

'I think, sir, that everything is as good as it can be on board a small uncomfortable ship like ours. You are hard on a boy who is always sick, who has a weak constitution and who has to serve nine people; who is not very intelligent, it is true, but who certainly does his best.'

'You are so indulgent that you find excuses for everything; however, that's not my method. Without fear, there's no obedience, and that rascally cabin-boy . . .'

'And the names you call Peruvians? Do you think that M. Miota and I are pleased to hear our nation abused in that manner?'

'But, mademoiselle, you are French.'

'I was born in France, but I belong to my father's country. It is by chance that we are born in one country rather than another. Look at me and tell me what country I belong to!'

'Ah, you coquette! You ask me that so that I shall compliment you on your fine eyes and your beautiful Andalusian hair.'

'M. David, you must know better than anyone that I am proof against flattery; you are simply trying to evade my just reproofs. I repeat for the twentieth time, M. Miota is terribly hurt at the way you speak of the Peruvians in front of him.'

'You surely can't think, mademoiselle, that I ever intended to insult M. Miota, or, even less, you yourself. When you and he get to know the Peruvians, you will say: "David was right." Dear lady, you know how I respect you. I have many times heard your family praised; your uncle Pio is a highly respected man, but I assure you that in the mass the Peruvians are the vilest rascals that you can imagine.'

'If it is so, sir, why did you stay ten years in the country, and why are you going back there?'

'Because there's money to be made.'

'But it's ungrateful to speak ill of the people to whom you owe your fortune.'

'But they have no merit in that. I sold them my merchandise at the current rate; they bought it because they needed it. I cannot see any reason at all to be grateful to them.' Since M. David considered that self-interest was man's only motive, he was proof against gratitude. I feel nevertheless that one owes an obligation to a country which has protected one's person, one's belongings and one's work. If M. David had been consistent with his principles, he would not have accused the Peruvians of dishonesty, and if he had had any benevolence, he would have pitied their ignorance.

Then dinner time would come. We had all smartened ourselves up, and the conversation during the meal was quite different from at breakfast. We were gay or sad according to the way the wind blew, and when the going was good and the sea not too rough, the conversation became amusing and full of character. At dessert, the conversation turned to politics, travel or the places the gentlemen preferred. M. Chabrié was republican, M. David a Carlist,* and M. Briet a Bonapartist. The discussions inevitably led to the defeat of M. David, in spite of his imperturbable aplomb, since he had both sailors as his

* *Translator's note:* A supporter of King Charles X, who had been ousted in the 1830 revolution.

opponents. Chabrié's warm eloquence and Briet's cold logic together routed the 'Lord of the Store-cupboard', with his clever phrases, his Latin, his pedantries and his sophisms. When he found himself in a desperate situation, he showed great skill in changing the subject, switching Briet on to travel and Chabrié on to the town of Lorient. Briet alone could talk about China. He had resided for some time in that vast empire, and as no one else on board had been there, there was no one to contradict him. They listened, and calm descended. The subject of Lorient was more contentious. M. Chabrié had the defect of being a man of one place. His life of travel had in no way diminished his exclusive love of his native town. In his eyes, nothing was good anywhere but in Lorient, which was quoted as an example whatever was being discussed.

For my part, I seldom took part in general conversations. My situation imposed continual reserve, and I had not realised when I set off what a burden I was shouldering when I called myself 'Mademoiselle'. As a result, I had to repress all my past, my eight years of marriage, the existence of my children and the role of a married woman which is quite different from that of a spinster. Being very open by nature, finding myself often drawn into animated conversation by the wealth of my imagination and then speaking so fast that I expressed my thoughts as they formed in my mind and did not realise the implications until afterwards, I was scared to let myself go in this way and dared not speak. I feared that, forgetful of the situation, I would let slip a mention of my daughter; that, at some turn a conversation might take on any subject, I might not be able to contain my indignation against French marriage laws. I was in fact afraid of giving myself away; and this put me in a perpetual state of fear, kept my thoughts from taking wing, preserved my silence, and made me respond only briefly to appeals for my opinion.

I have a sanguine constitution, and this added to the embarrassments of my situation. I have often regretted that we cannot keep our ears closed in the same way as we can keep our mouths closed. At the slightest word, at an inflexion given to a phrase, at a look even, I blushed so much that the gentlemen noticed. It was torture to me to feel that my intimate thoughts might be revealed or misinterpreted. Only M. Chabrié could sometimes understand these sudden blushes. He did all he could to spare me them, but M. David's mischievousness and teasing, M. Briet's unbridled frankness and M. Miota's rather indiscreet questions all tormented me painfully.

Such was the life we led on the *Mexicain*; life on board, normally tiresomely monotonous, was varied by the diversity of our characters and our social positions, and by our efforts to cheat our boredom. We celebrated Sundays by eating pastries and preserved fruits at dinner, and by drinking champagne or claret. After dinner, M. Chabrié sang operatic airs or ballads. All the gentlemen were most attentive to me, and often read aloud to me. When M. Miota was well he would come into my cabin and read the authors he favoured, Voltaire and Byron; M. David read the *Voyage du Jeune Anacharsis*,* Chateaubriand or the *Fables* of La Fontaine. M. Chabrié and I read Lamartine, Victor Hugo and especially Bernardin de Saint-Pierre.

When we left Bordeaux I was told: 'In eighty or ninety days we shall be in Valparaiso.' And yet M. Briet was now writing in the log: 'The one hundred and twentieth day, and going badly.' It was then that we began to get really discouraged. A water shortage was feared and we were all rationed. A small padlock was put on the barrel in use, so that it could only be tapped in the presence of the officer of the watch. This provoked numerous contretemps: the sailors stole water whenever they could; the cook drank the water given to him for cooking and served soup so thick that we could not eat it. Don José became less philosophical as his store of little cigars diminished. M. Miota had no books left to read: his impatience and boredom knew no bounds. In short, everyone suffered from his own special weakness. The True Sailor, Leborgne, repeated endlessly that, whilst there was still a pig on board, we should have contrary winds.

M. Chabrié and M. Briet were, as sailors, horribly tired by the length of the voyage; but their mental anguish was

* *Translator's note:* A reconstruction of life in Ancient Greece by Abbé Barthélemy, 1779.

even worse. The three partners could not reasonably hope that the two ships sailing for the same port, in whose company we had left the Bordeaux river, had been delayed to the same extent as we had. They were extremely worried about the sale of their merchandise, since they were bound to arrive at Valparaiso only after the two competitors had glutted the market with similar goods. They were honourable men, and foreseeing that their trip would be a financial failure, they were tormented by the fear of being unable to fulfil their commitments. Their anxiety continued until our arrival: only fellow merchants will be able to appreciate what it meant to them. M. David swore at the wind in desperation; M. Briet said sadly: 'I can't think what made me risk the uncertainties of the sea once again, as I am not an ambitious man. But when I last returned to France, I found not one friend, and so there was no one to say to me: "Why leave again?" and having no definite plans, for want of something to do, out of habit, I went to sea again.' M. Chabrié was the only one of the three to face the disastrous prospect with courage. He always assumed the worst, paid the manufacturers with everything he possessed, and if this was not enough, in order to pay off his debts he relied on his energy, which was indefatigable, on his skill as a mariner and on his understanding of trade. I was upset by the thought that my friend, who had been so unsuccessful both in his business ventures and in his affections, might yet be ruined as a result of this voyage. I was always asking how the wind blew, and the helmsman's reply, or M. Briet's or M. David's answering look was enough to pierce my heart.

M. Chabrié's scrupulousness of behaviour came home to me in this context. I have already described how I had accepted his love, as much for his sake as for my own protection. From then on he produced endless optimistic schemes for our future, convinced as he was that he would find happiness in our union. At first I listened to these plans for a life of bliss without any intention of participating in them; but gradually his love so filled me with admiration that I got used to the idea of marrying him and settling down in California. I can see people who enjoy a settled family life, who are happy and respected, moralising about bigamy and holding up those guilty of it to shame and dishonour. But what causes the crime, if not the absurd law which decrees the indissolubility of marriage? Are we all so similar in our affections and inclinations – though so different in other respects – that when promises have been made, whether voluntary or enforced, they must be tied up with contracts dealing with questions of property? God gave us our sympathies and our antipathies: did he ever intend us to live slavish, sterile lives? Is a runaway slave a criminal in his own eyes? Is he a criminal when he follows the promptings of his heart, which are the law of nature?

The affection I felt for M. Chabrié was not the passionate love I had experienced before I met him; it was based on admiration and gratitude. Once married to him I should have loved him more, and felt that if I would not find in him the supreme unattainable happiness of my dreams, I should at least find rest, that longed-for calm, that true, secure affection so welcome after the bitter disappointments of an unquiet life. We confided our plans to M. David. He was fond of M. Chabrié, who was so used to his friend's original and amusing character that he had become necessary to him.

M. David was also very fond of me and – either because he suspected M. Chabrié's secret intention or with the object of dropping a hint – he had often said to him: 'Mlle Flora is such a dear. If we could only persuade her to settle in Central America, how happy we should be. I don't know why she is biased against marriage, but she obviously likes you very much, and I think that one day she'll decide to marry you. I, of course, have a sworn hatred of marriage, but I would live with you, and help to rock the cradle, as I am mad about children under seven or eight years old.' I for my part was getting used to M. David: he behaved obligingly towards me, was an educated man, I would not have minded having him in my household. He had no intention of returning to live in Europe, he much preferred the American climate, and if he could have found people of his liking to live with, would willingly have settled there. Such was my situation as the voyage drew to its close.

One evening, I think it was on the one hundred and twenty-eighth day, M. Chabrié said: 'Dear Flora, give me some comfort, for it upsets me to see David so desperate. Briet is sick, and I regret having involved him in this speculation.'

'What can you do, my dear? We can't alter the wind. The *Charles Adolphe* and the *Flétès* have probably arrived long ago at Valparaiso. The voyage is a dead loss: but, dear, you still have me.'

'Oh yes, my dear, I regret the voyage only for David's and Briet's sakes. For me it is an era of gladness: happiness has dawned for me during this voyage.'

'Neither of us, dear, has given a thought in our plans of life together to what financial fortunes await us. Allow me to broach the subject for the first time. You know that I am going to stay with my family, in the hope of being able to claim if not all, at least a part, of my father's inheritance. If I got it all, I would have a million; but as my legitimacy may be contested, I am not counting on so much; let us hope that, as an illegitimate child, I shall receive a fifth of that sum, plus a gift from my grandmother. Well then, my dear, all I possess is yours. With that money you can pay your bills and still supply David with enough to make a fresh start.'

'Such generosity is typical of you. But, dear Flora, I am going to open my heart to you. The fortune that you hope for, and that you so richly deserve, is something that I dread. I tremble at the thought of your having it.'

'But for heaven's sake, why, my dear?'

'My darling, I must remind you once again that you do not realise people's baseness, their spitefulness and the absurd prejudices that rule the world.'

'But Chabrié, I do not understand you.'

'Listen, Flora. You are now poor. If I marry you, people will no doubt say that I've done something silly on impulse. But the better, more generous people will approve, and say: "He did right to marry the woman he loved." If on the other hand I marry you when you have become rich, oh! then they'll all vie with each other in saying that I married you solely in my own interests, and that I did not hesitate to lay aside my honour; for, in this word "honour", people include their own silly prejudices. Flora, the thought torments me. The nearer we get to Valparaiso, the more it haunts me.'

'Ah! Chabrié, this is terrible! Like you, I tremble at the possible consequences of our marriage. In my ignorance I had not thought of it.' I hid my face in my hands, with dread at the thought of what might come from the lie I had told.

'My dear,' said Chabrié, 'do not grieve. Our position is no doubt difficult; for my character being what it is, I know that as your husband, I should challenge the first scoundrel (and there are plenty in America) who dared to say a word or cock a malicious eye in your direction, and I'd have his life or he mine. But, my dear, let us not think of such things until they happen. In any case, maybe you will not have a piastre of all that money. Good God, I hope not with all my heart!'

I was shattered. A pariah in my own country, I had believed that in putting the great ocean between me and France I could recover a shadow of my liberty. Impossible! In the New World, I was as much a pariah as in the Old. From that moment I gave up any thought of the tranquillity and the quiet happiness that M. Chabrié's love had led me to believe in. I had accepted his love out of my fear of loneliness and need for protection, but could not, once we arrived at our destination, continue to compromise the fortune, happiness and even the life of the honourable man to whom I owed the most sincere gratitude for five months of devotion.

At last, on the one hundred and thirty-third day of our voyage, we sighted the White Rock, and six hours later we anchored off Valparaiso.

IV

VALPARAISO

The large number of ships which anchor in Valparaiso Bay give an immediate indication of the great commercial importance of that port. On the day of our arrival, twelve foreign ships came in, a fact which did little to raise the commercial expectations of our officers. As they were well known locally, we had hardly cast anchor when they were greeted by a large number of people.

As soon as the arrival of the *Mexicain* was known, the French came to the quayside to wait for us to disembark. The two ships which had left Bordeaux at the same time as we had, had reached Valparaiso a month before and had set sail again for their various ports of call up the coast. The two captains had gossiped in the town about my expected arrival, and, unwilling to give the true reasons why I had not travelled with them, they impudently suggested that I had preferred M. Chabrié because of the handsome young men he had aboard, and that the prospects of such pleasant society had outweighed the inconvenience of travelling in so small a ship. The amiable French inhabitants of Valparaiso were expecting the arrival of a 'very pretty young miss', for these two spiteful captains had vengefully embroidered their description of me with malevolent insinuation. The handsome young men of the *Mexicain* were expected to be on the point of fighting duels over me, and this would have amused them hugely.

They were all standing on the quay when we landed. I was surprised at the sight which greeted me; I might have been in a French town. Everyone I met spoke French and everyone was dressed in the latest French fashion. I noticed that I was the cynosure of all eyes, but was at a loss to know why. M. David took me to the house of a Mme Aubrit, a Frenchwoman who kept a boarding-house in Valparaiso. He thought it more prudent not to lodge M. Miota at the same establishment, and took him to another hotel also kept by a Frenchwoman. Mme Aubrit's was by the sea, and my room looked out on to the beach. It was very well furnished, partly in the French and partly in the English style. On land after one hundred and thirty-three days at sea, I had forgotten how to walk. I still lurched to the roll of the ship; I felt giddy, and the soles of my feet were so tender that it hurt me to stand.

That evening M. Miota came to see me, and I asked him to find out about my uncle Pio and the situation in Arequipa, and especially if my grandmother were still alive. That night I was unable to sleep. A vague presentiment, like a mysterious voice, seemed to be warning me that a new calamity was about to befall me. I have had such presentiments at all the major crises of my life. I believe that when disasters are about to strike, Providence prepares us for them by secret warnings which we would take more seriously if we were not always led astray by our reason, our foolish reason which invariably misleads us. After going through all the possibilities, I settled for the worst: I imagined my grandmother to be dead, my uncle disowning me, and myself alone, four thousand leagues from home, without support, funds or hope. This was such a terrible prospect that its very horror restored my courage and self-confidence, and I awaited events resignedly.

Next day at about midday M. Miota returned. I immediately read in his face that he had bad news for me. 'My grandmother is dead!' I said. He tried to break it gently, but the blow had to be struck: she had died the very day I left Bordeaux. I admit that for a moment I felt drained of strength. By her death I lost my only refuge, my only protection, my last hope. M. Miota left me, realising the need for solitude at such moments; but as he went he said: 'I'll ask M. Chabrié to come and see you.' The good young man had no idea that, to me, M. Chabrié was also *dead*!

There is a kind of grief which is on a higher plane than

the common, which burns so deeply that there are no words in any language to describe it. Such were my feelings at the news of this death which was the death of all my hopes. I did not shed a single tear. I sat for two hours without moving, my eyes dry, burning and sunken, the veins of my neck and forehead tense, my hands cold and clenched, watching the sea which appeared to me like a horrible blank screen on which my life story was retold in letters of fire. They brought me dinner, which I ate. During this crisis of inextinguishable pain, my soul was quite separate from my body. Two creatures lived within me, one physical, which answered the questions put to it and saw the objects around it, the other entirely spiritual, living its life of visions, memories and presentiments. That evening, M. Chabrié came into my room, sat beside me, took my hand which he pressed affectionately, and wept. He had one of those fortunate natures which are able to find relief in tears. After a long silence, he said: 'Oh God, my dear, what can I say to comfort you? I am deeply distressed. Ever since this morning I have been unable to think straight. I dared not come to you, my poor Flora; your grief is there, weighing on my old heart like an anchor which has settled into the mud. What will be the outcome? For my love's sake, tell me what I can do for you!' I looked at the sea and made a gesture – I wanted Chabrié to fling me into it.

'Do you want me to take you back home?'

'Back home? Where's home?'

'Dear Flora, are you ill? Heavens, how cold your hands are, and how your forehead burns! My dear, calm down, I beg you, I cannot bear your suffering.' He too was looking at the sea, and great tears rolled down his cheeks. Suddenly he broke the silence with: 'Well, Flora, the more I think of it the more I feel that what has happened is a blessing for us both. If you had found your grandmother at Arequipa, all your financial affairs would have worked out as you wished: you would have been rich. Oh, my dear, does the thought not make you tremble? You rich, and I poor! You realise, Flora, that in that case I would have had to give you up! Give you up! It would have been the death of me. But now, as things turn out, you are mine!

Do you understand what that means, darling? Mine! Oh, I can't believe in such happiness, for my whole life has been so unhappy. Happiness has always seemed to me to be within reach, and at the moment I stretched out my hand to grasp it, it vanished. Dearest Flora, have pity on my joy, on my sorrow, on the cruel pangs that I suffer! So many things have happened within me since I learned of this death, that I truly do not know how to regain my reason.'

Chabrié was more agitated than I had ever seen him: he strode up and down the room, stopped at the window, came back to where I sat, covered me with my shawl, warmed my icy hands in his, talked of our marriage, of his happiness, of the arrangements he intended to make to hasten our union, consulted me about his business affairs and asked me to make the decisions according to my wishes. He was happy, and I, at the sight of his happiness, felt as if serpents were gnawing at my heart.

He withdrew. I flung myself on my bed; I was physically exhausted; my body slept but my soul remained awake. Those who have passed such nights feel that they have lived through centuries and travelled through different worlds. The soul leaves its sheath and darts forth eager for knowledge, into the vast universe of thought; it soars, like a comet, through a host of worlds, absorbing waves of light which it then reflects and sheds on to those whom it loves. Free of the body and its needs, the soul follows unhindered the impulses of God, who is love itself and in whom the soul itself originates and – being free – is conscious of itself and has forebodings of its destiny.

Two days after our arrival in Valparaiso, the fine three-masted ship *Elizabeth* set sail for France. Seeing her preparations for departure, I had a longing to leave with her, so haunted was I by the thought of what welcome my uncle might give me. I was prevented by the fear of upsetting Chabrié. If I had yielded to the temptation, I would generally have been thought to be mad; but this was not my reason for refraining. Already at this stage of my life I usually followed the dictates of my conscience: my affections could divert me from it but not the opinions of society. Chabrié's friendship was now more necessary to me, and his devoted love once again exerted its power over me. At times, I was on the point of flinging my arms round his neck, of admitting the whole extent of my suffering, and asking for his help and protection; I felt I could bear it no longer; but the fear of the sorrow it would cause him held me back; his conduct towards me during the entire voyage, those five months of love and kindness, filled me with such gratitude that I had not the courage to cause him grief. I do not know what would have happened and whether I should have been strong enough to follow the call of duty, had not something providentially occurred which made up my mind.

M. David came to my room each evening: all the gentlemen of the ship made it their meeting place. Their business prospects were not brilliant. The market was glutted; no money was coming in and their liabilities, now falling due, were worrying them horribly. M. David arrived one evening looking pleased. 'Dear lady,' he said, 'I have good news for you: we need no longer worry about the prompt repayment of our debts. We have just received letters from M. Roux in Bordeaux, in which he states that he will stand surety for us, and will undertake to pay all our liabilities as they fall due. He says that he regards M. Chabrié as a member of his family, as a son. You know', M. David added, 'that before we left Bordeaux, there was some question of a marriage between Chabrié and Mlle Roux: our friend was not in favour of it, because he felt that the lady was too young. Whatever the case, it is most fortunate for us; our venture is safe. The unexpected delays in cash receipts would have put us out of pocket had it not been for M. Roux's kindness, which will give us the necessary time.'

What M. David said opened up a new perspective for M. Chabrié which had not occurred to me. This marriage with Mlle Roux would suit him admirably; he loved M. Roux's family as much as his own and their relations were intimate. The two men were born in the same town, had been brought up together and had sailed for a long period on the same ship. Chabrié was eighteen years older than Mlle Roux, but if the girl loved him, what did the difference in age matter? I don't know if my second sight came to my aid at this point, but I saw clearly that Chabrié could find happiness and the repose he so much needed in this union with his friend's daughter; therefore, from then on, I decided to make every effort to persuade him to do so. Like M. David, I rejoiced at the way M. Roux's generosity and confidence had got them out of trouble, and when Chabrié came, we had a long discussion about it.

Next day I told M. Chabrié that the delay was damaging to my interests, and that I could no longer wait for his departure. I had therefore decided to set off alone direct to Arequipa. He was so surprised at this sudden decision that he could not believe my words, he made me repeat them several times. I allayed his distress by pointing out that it was in 'our common interests'. He begged me to wait at least two days, so that I could think it over. I persuaded M. David that it was urgent for me to leave as soon as possible for Arequipa, and he helped me to reconcile Chabrié to a separation in the near future. As soon as I had made the decision, I felt strong and free from all worry; I experienced that inner satisfaction which is so comforting when one is conscious of having done a good deed. I was calm: I had conquered myself, the voice of conscience had prevailed.

Thus free from care, I could play my part as an observer. I explored the town thoroughly. To describe a town, even a small one, one must stay there some time; one must get to know all classes of the inhabitants, and visit the surrounding countryside on which it depends; merely to pass through is not enough for one to understand its customs and the life that lies below the surface. I stayed only a fortnight in Valparaiso, too short a time to allow me to give anything beyond a superficial sketch.

M. Chabrié told me that when he visited Valparaiso in 1825, the town consisted of about thirty to forty wooden huts. Now the hills round the town are all covered with houses. The population has reached about thirty thousand souls. There are three distinct parts. The Port or Customs House quarter consists of a single street running along the seashore for about three miles. It has not yet been paved, and in rainy weather it is a sewer. The Customs House faces the harbour. It is a large commodious building devoid of architectural features. In this area are the big foreign commercial establishments, the warehouses and stores, and the fine shops selling luxury goods. This is the centre of activity, full of continual bustle and movement. Next to this is the district known as the Almendral, the town's only promenade. This is an area of *retiros,* villas with fine gardens. And finally, the third part is known as the *Quebradas,* which are canyons in the mountains which surround the town; there the Indians live.

The Chileans seemed to me cold, with stiff, haughty manners; the women were starchy and uncommunicative. In dress, they displayed great luxury but little taste. In what little conversation I had with them, I was not struck by their amiability and in this respect they seemed inferior to the Peruvian women. They are said to be excellent housekeepers, hardworking and home-loving. The proof of this would seem to be that all European men who come to Chile marry locally, while this is less true of Peru.

V

THE *LEONIDAS*

I had booked my passage on board the American three-master, *Leonidas*. The captain informed me that she would sail on Sunday the 1st of September 1833, at midday.

I got up very early that morning, having no servant to help me pack my trunks and make other necessary preparations. I had several letters to write: these various occupations kept my mind off the distress that I experienced. In the midst of these preparations I had a number of callers, whom, in the bustle of the moment, I could greet with apparent calm. In coming to say goodbye to me, some were moved by affection but the majority by curiosity. Poor Chabrié could not keep still. He came and went from the room to the balcony and back again, trying to hide his emotion from these importunate visitors; there were big tears in his eyes; his voice trembled so that he dared not say a word; his grief oppressed me.

Seeing that the *Leonidas* was preparing to weigh anchor, I said goodbye to all my callers. I had only known these people a short time; but we were in a foreign land, some had come from France with me, others were my compatriots who spoke my language, and it wrung my heart to see them leave. Then for a few moments I was alone with Chabrié. 'Oh, Flora,' he said, 'swear that you love me, that you will be mine, that I shall soon see you again; for if you do not, I shall not be able to bear to see you leave.'

'My dear, do I need to swear that I love you? Does not my conduct prove it? And as for the union that we plan, God alone knows what the future has in store.'

'But your wishes, Flora? Tell me again that, from this moment, I can look on you as my wife. Oh, say it again!'

I would much have preferred not to repeat a promise that I knew I could not keep; but his grief alarmed me. I was afraid that he could not control it, and that David or someone else would come in to find him in tears, so I promised that I would be his wife and that I would stay in America and share his fortune, good or bad. The poor man was drunk with joy, and too excited to notice that I was in the depths of misery. As he held me in his arms, he failed to notice that he embraced a corpse quite unable to return his caresses. He left me, as he could not summon up the courage to come with me, and I set off for the ship accompanied by M. David. I said goodbye to Mme Aubrit and the many French people I met on the way with a surprising composure, due no doubt to the dazed state I was in.

We were in the cutter: I was silent, doing my best to keep my painful emotions to myself, when M. David said: 'Mlle Flora, we are just going to pass close to the *Mexicain*. Won't you say goodbye to the poor old ship which you may never see again?' His words had an extraordinary effect on me. I suddenly began to tremble uncontrollably, and my teeth chattered. M. David noticed it, so I told him that I was cold; for a moment I thought that I would not be able to keep my head erect.

We boarded the *Leonidas,* where a crowd of English and Americans were saying goodbye to their friends. M. David, after recommending me highly to the captain, took me to my cabin, accompanied by the 'stuard' [*sic*], whom he enjoined to serve me well; together they helped me unpack and put away my things.

We had an excellent voyage: on the eighth day, at nine in the evening, we cast anchor in the Bay of Islay, on the coast of Peru.

VI

ISLAY

When we arrived off Islay, I could hardly see the coast of Peru. At that moment a fine rain was falling, like a fog, hiding the coastline. The sea was calm, and if an English ship had not sent a launch to tow us, I do not know how we should have made our way in. We were very disappointed at not being able to see what the country looked like.

The whole Peruvian coast is extremely arid; Islay and its surroundings have a generally desolate appearance. Nevertheless the port is extremely prosperous. According to Don Justo, the head of the Post Office, when it was established there were only three huts and a large shed for the Customs House; after six years there were at least a thousand to twelve hundred inhabitants. Most of the homes are made of bamboo and have no flooring; but some are well built in wood, with floorboards. The house of the English consul, which was being finished when I returned to Islay, is delightful. The Customs House is a very large wooden construction; the church is presentable and adequate in size. This port is better placed than Arica, and has attracted all the latter's business. If it continues to prosper as it has for the last six years, it may in ten years' time have four or five thousand inhabitants; but the infertility of the surrounding area will be a long-term obstacle to any greater growth, for there is no water and there are no trees or any other vegetation whatsoever. Artesian wells have not yet been heard of in this country, which is too backward for them to be practicable. There is only one small spring, which often dries up in the summer, and when this happens the inhabitants have to leave. The soil is a black stony sand, which would certainly be very fertile if irrigation could be introduced.

At about six in the morning the harbour-master came on board to carry out his inspection in the normal way. Passports had to be produced, and when mine was examined by the two or three customs officers, there was a cry of astonishment. They asked me if I was related to Don Pio de Tristan, and when I said I was a whispered conversation followed: they seemed to be discussing whether to offer me their services or whether to wait for orders from their chiefs. The result of this conversation was that I was to be treated with all the deference reserved for the most distinguished citizens of the republic. The harbour-master came and announced respectfully that he was an ex-employee of my uncle's, to whose generosity he owed his situation, since it was a gift of Don Pio's when he was prefect of Arequipa. He put himself entirely at my disposal. He told me that my uncle was not at Arequipa, but that for the last month he and his family had been staying at Camara, on a large sugar estate by the sea, forty leagues from Islay and the same distance from Arequipa. I accepted the harbour-master's offer to take ashore letters of introduction which I held for the Head of Customs, for Don Justo de Medina, the Head of the Post Office and for my uncle's agent. At eleven, after breakfasting and dressing, we landed with all our luggage.

Islay has as yet no harbour, and landing is at least as difficult as at La Praya. I was received, on arrival at this, my first Peruvian township, with all the honours due to the titles and rank of my uncle Pio. The Head of Customs,

Don Basilio de la Fuente, invited me to stay at his house; Don Justo de Medina, Head of the Post Office, made me the same offer. I chose the latter, as I felt more attracted to him.

We passed through the whole village, which consisted of an irregular main street, from which boulders and bumps had not been eliminated, the ground being covered with sand in which we sank half way to our knees. I was the cynosure of all eyes, much more even than at Valparaiso: I was an event. Don Justo put me in the best room in his house; his wife and daughter eagerly offered me whatever they thought might please me. Poor Dr Castellac hung on to my coat tails, as it were, and to reward me for all the treatment he had given me during the voyage, I appointed him 'my doctor', so that he could enjoy the advantages of the generous hospitality accorded to the niece of Don Pio de Tristan. The doctor was also given a room in Don Justo's house, and from then on he followed me everywhere.

I must now put the reader in the picture concerning the relations between my uncle and myself, and my uncle's standing amongst his countrymen. My mother's marriage had not been regularised in France, and as a result of this formal omission, I was considered to be illegitimate. Until I was fifteen, I had known nothing of this absurd social discrimination and its unnatural consequences; I worshipped the memory of my father and expected the protection of my uncle, about whom my mother spoke frequently and warmly although she knew him only through his correspondence with my father. I had read and re-read this correspondence which constituted an extraordinary memorial to the love of two brothers. I was fifteen when my mother revealed to me (I was anxious to get married at the time) the position in which the circumstance of my birth had placed me. My pride was so wounded that, in my first indignant reaction, I renounced my uncle Pio and the whole family. In 1829, after a long conversation about Peru with M. Chabrié, I wrote my uncle the following letter, in which – as the presiding judge in Arequipa has since told me – I had put my head into the noose:

THE PORT AND VILLAGE OF ISLAY

A CHACARERO, OR FARMER, FROM THE AREQUIPA VALLEY AND A CHOLO AND CHOLA, OR WASHERWOMAN, OF THE AREQUIPA AREA

To Monsieur Pio de Tristan

Sir,

As the daughter of your much-loved brother Mariano, I take the liberty of writing to you. I like to believe that you know nothing of my existence and that not one of the more than twenty letters which my mother has written has reached you. Were it not for a final disaster which has reduced me to the depths of misfortune, I should never have made any approach to you. I have found a reliable way of getting this letter to you and I hope that you will not reject it. I enclose my baptismal certificate: if you still have doubts, the famous Bolivar, a close friend of my parents, can dispel them: he witnessed the fact that my father brought me up, as he visited our home frequently. You could also consult his friend, known to us by the name of Robinson, and M. Bompland, whom you must have known before he was taken prisoner in Paraguay. I could cite others, but these suffice. I will set out the facts in a few words.

In order to escape the horrors of the revolution, my mother went to Spain with a female relative. The two ladies settled in Bilbao, where my father got to know them; this friendship grew into an irresistible love between my father and mother, so that they became necessary to each other. The ladies returned to France in 1802, and my father soon followed. As a soldier, your brother could not marry without the king's permission. Not wishing to ask for it (and I respect my father's memory too much to try and guess why this was so), he suggested to my mother a marriage by religious ceremony only, though such a marriage has no validity in France. My mother, who felt that she would not be able to live without him, agreed to this proposal. The wedding ceremony was conducted by a qualified priest, M. Roncelin, who had known my mother since her childhood. Once married, they moved to Paris.

You are aware that at the time my father's sole income came from the 6,000 francs which his uncle, the Archbishop of Granada, had left him as an eldest son of the Tristan family. He also received certain sums sent by you, but the largest of these were lost: 20,000 francs were seized by the English, and 10,000 went down in the *Minerva*.

However, thanks to my mother's economy, my father lived quite respectably. Thirteen months before his death, he bought a house at Vaugirard, near Paris. When he died, the ambassador, Prince Masserano, seized all his papers. You must have received them through the Spanish ambassador, and with them the contract of sale of the house.

My father had paid for the property in part. If my mother had inherited it, it would have helped to educate my brother and myself; but, ten months after my father's death, the state confiscated it as being the property of a Spaniard because of the war that then existed between the two countries. Since then, it has been sold, and the state holds the surplus of 10,000 francs which was still due on the purchase price. However my mother paid 554 francs transfer tax on behalf of the heirs, for which she has never been reimbursed.

You can imagine, sir, how much my poor mother had to suffer, left without funds and burdened with two children (my brother lived until he was ten). Well, despite her straitened circumstances, she was determined that the memory of the man she had loved should not be tarnished. Because of the war, my father had received no money for twenty months and as a result was very hard up; at my mother's request, my grandmother lent him 2,800 francs, without asking for any written acknowledgment, which meant that when he died she had no proof of debt. My mother paid the full interest on the money, for my grandmother needed this in order to live; when she died, my mother repaid a third of the sum to her sister, and the other third to her brother.

I do not wish to distress you by going into the details of the misfortunes to which I have alluded. With your tender memories of a brother who loved you 'like a son', you would suffer too deeply when you realised the gap between my lot and what should have been due to the daughter of your brother Mariano; that same brother who, when struck down by a sudden and premature death (a fatal apoplexy), was only able to utter these words: 'My daughter ... You only have Pio now ... Unhappy child!'

And yet, sir, please believe that whatever the results of

my letter to you, no slur will ever be cast by me on my father's memory, which will always be dear and sacred to me.

I am appealing to you for justice and for kindness. I put myself in your hands in the hope of a better future. I ask for your protection, and pray you to love me as the daughter of your brother Mariano has some right to expect.

Your very humble and obedient servant,

Flora de Tristan

The reader of this letter can see how sincere I was, displaying as I did my complete ignorance of the world, my belief in the honesty of others, my credulous confidence in their good faith, my conviction that others were as good and as just as I was myself: all the naive faith which my uncle, who had professed so great a love for my father, was to destroy. Here is the reply which he sent me:*

Mlle Flora de Tristan
Arequipa, 6th October 1830

Mademoiselle and esteemed niece,

It was with as much surprise as pleasure that I received your precious letter of the 2nd of June last. I have known since General Bolivar was here in 1823 that at his death my beloved brother Mariano de Tristan left a daughter; before that, M. Simon Rodriguez, known to you as Robinson, had told me of your existence; but as neither of them had given me any subsequent news of you or of your whereabouts, I was unable to take up with you certain matters of mutual interest. I was informed officially of your father's death by the Spanish government, who had received the information from Prince Masserano. I therefore gave power of attorney to General Goyeneche, now Count of Guaqui, to enable him to deal with all business connected with my brother's inheritance; but he was unable to act owing to the invasion of Spain by the French,

*Translated by the author from the Spanish into literal French.

which forced him to travel to the South American continent for matters of great importance. This invasion was also the reason why we were without communication for many years, after which the South American war took up our time to such an extent that it was impossible to deal with matters rendered so difficult by distance. However on the 9th of April 1824 I sent special powers to M. Changeur, a merchant of Bordeaux, to enable him to discover your whereabouts through his Paris agents, and to determine what funds had been left by the deceased. I gave him the address where my brother was living at the time of his death. Both before and after sending him this power of attorney I on several occasions urged him to spare no trouble to ascertain whether you and your mother were alive. The only result was a bill for the fruitless researches he had made, details of which I hold. How was I to know, twenty years after the death of my brother, without any news of you or your mother, that you were still alive? Yes, my dear niece, we must ascribe to fate the fact that none of the many letters written to me by your mother reached me, whereas the first addressed to me by you arrived punctually. I am very well known in this country and the communications between the coasts of our two countries have been frequent enough for the last eight years for at least one of these letters to have arrived. This clearly proves that you have acted with a certain carelessness in this respect.

I have examined the baptismal certificate that you sent me and accept it as genuine, although it is not, as it should be, authenticated and signed by three notaries certifying the signature of the priest who drew it up. As regards your mother and her status as the legitimate spouse of my late brother, you yourself admit and confess that the manner in which the marriage ceremony was conducted is null and void both in that country and throughout Christendom. In fact, it is extraordinary that a self-respecting cleric, such as M. Roncelin, should have allowed himself to proceed in this manner, without the proper accompanying acts for the benefit of the contracting parties. It is irrelevant that at the time of your baptism you were declared to be a legitimate daughter, as is the document that you say was sent from Bilbao through M. Adam, in which ten persons in that city declare that they have seen and known your mother as the legal spouse of Mariano; this document merely proves that she was given that status and title for reasons of propriety. I have, moreover, in my brother's own correspondence up to a short time before his death, a fact which, although negative, may serve as a striking proof of my contention, namely that my brother never mentioned this marriage to me, an extraordinary fact since there were no secrets between us. Moreover, if there had been a legitimate union between my brother and your mother, neither Prince Masserano nor any other authority would have been able to affix the seals on the property of a deceased person who had a legitimate heir who was known and born in the country. Let us agree then that you are only the illegitimate daughter of my brother, which is no reason why you should be any the less worthy of my respect and my tender affection. I am most willing to regard you as my beloved niece, even, I add, as my daughter; for anyone loved by my brother must interest me deeply; neither time nor death can ever efface the tender attachment I felt for him and shall retain all my life.

Our honoured mother is still with us, and is now eighty-nine years old. She is in possession of all her mental and physical faculties and is beloved of all her family, amongst whom she has had the goodness to divide her property at the present time, in order to have the pleasure of watching them enjoy it before her death. We were in fact in the process of arranging this partition, when your letter reached me. I read it to her and having learned of your existence and your situation, at the request of the family she has made you a legacy of 3,000 silver piastres, which I beg you to regard as a proof of my particular concern for you, and of our mother's unfailing love for her son Mariano, and the whole family's ineffaceable memory of him.

Meanwhile, in view of your questionable right to the property of my late brother, which I have administered by virtue of the power of attorney which he gave me on the 20th of November 1801, in the presence of the Notary

Royal of Our Lady of Begoña, in Biscay, J. Antonio Oleaga, I send herewith a copy of the current account as it stood between my brother and myself. It will convince you that no funds remain to his credit account, because the Ibañez affair has absorbed what remained at the time of his death. This affair would have been settled immediately if I had known of it, or if the creditors had not been so negligent as to allow eleven years to pass after my brother's death before they made any application for a payment, though they must have known of it; as a result, the interest on the debt, though only four per cent, doubled the sum to be repaid. His death was disastrous in every respect, the how and the when have been the reason for your misfortunes and have caused me no end of troubles. Let us forget all that and try to find a remedy so far as is possible.

My agent with power of attorney at Bordeaux is M. Bertera, and I send you a letter of credit for 2,500 francs for him to imburse. In order to receive this sum, you will have to send him your life certificate drawn up in the presence of a notary. Try to make do with this, until I find means of sending you the 3,000 piastres, the amount of your legacy, to be credited to you and dispatched at your risk; however, I shall take the necessary measures for its security. You would do well to invest these 3,000 silver piastres either in public funds or elsewhere if political events cause instability, so that you have a settled income, payable twice yearly. You will be able to recognise in my behaviour a demonstration, though modest in extent, of my attachment to you, and if I live and if we are able to meet each other, time will prove how much I love the daughter of my brother Mariano.

Write to me as often as you can, sending your letters through M. Bertera in Bordeaux, and I will also write through the same means. Tell me where you live, how you are faring, what plans you are making, what you may need, with the confidence born of my sincerity. I write in Spanish, because I have quite forgotten my French.

I am married to one of my nieces, Joaquina Florez; and we have a son named Florentino and three daughters aged eight, five and three. God grant that one day they may greet you with kisses, and that you can return their caresses in your own country.

Until that pleasure, please believe in my entire affection

(*signed*) *Pio de Tristan*

When I received this reply I understood, in spite of the good opinion I had of mankind, that I could expect nothing from my uncle; but my grandmother still remained, and all my hopes turned to her. It seems that my uncle had deceived me when he said that he had read my letter to my grandmother and the whole family; for hardly any of the members of the family had heard of my existence before I apppeared, and I am convinced that my grandmother also was unaware of it.* I had not informed my uncle of my departure for Peru, and as I had not had time to warn him, he still knew nothing of my arrival. Such were my relations with him; I shall now say something of the position he occupied in his country.

Don Pio de Tristan had returned from Europe in 1803 with the rank of colonel. He took part in the terrible war of independence in which the Peruvians fought so tenaciously for their freedom. My uncle was one of the most talented soldiers ever to be sent by Spain to her colonies. When the troops of King Ferdinand were forced to evacuate Buenos Aires and the territory of the Argentine Republic, it was he who was second in command under our cousin Mariano de Goyeneche, whom I have mentioned. My uncle was then a brigadier. They retreated towards the Peruvian highlands, and traversed the enormous distance which separates Buenos Aires from Lima,

* *Author's note:* Shortly before my grandmother's death, my uncle got her to make a will leaving 20,000 piastres to his wife, and 3,000 to me. This will is very long, and my grandmother, who had complete trust in her son Pio, signed it without knowing what it contained. I was not named in it as the daughter of Mariano, but simply as 'Florita', without any reason being given for the legacy. When the property was divided amongst the heirs, my existence was revealed to the parties affected by the deduction of the amount of the legacy. The question was asked, 'But why give 15,000 francs to a stranger?' 'Because there is a presumption that she is my brother's daughter.'

fighting frequent battles as they went, crossing rivers and travelling through trackless territories. These gaudily-dressed soldiers of the king, warriors covered in gold braid and accustomed to the easy life of Spanish American cities, suffered much hardship in these wildernesses. During this remarkable trek they lived off food obtained at the point of their bayonets, off wild animals they hunted and provender they managed to buy. My uncle has often described to me how, when army funds were exhausted, he made the cavalrymen – whose spurs were of *solid gold* – draw lots as to which would sell a spur to purchase rations for all. One single soldier of those days had more gold on him than would be needed now to equip two hundred republicans. This arrogant display of wealth of the Spanish army in South America gave them a high idea of themselves and their superiority over the peoples they were keeping in submission. But the efficacy of such methods is soon exhausted. With what it cost to maintain one Spanish soldier, the King could have kept twenty Germans. The native population is not outstanding in the martial arts, and scattered as it is over a wide area would easily have been controllable if the troops had been more numerous, and this Spain could have achieved without increased expenditure. In the opinion of those who knew South America, its independence was still a long way off and Spain was strong enough to repress the revolts which had been set off by Bonaparte's invasion of the Peninsula. But events, as so often, confounded all predictions. The Riego insurrection paralysed the Spanish monarchy by turning the armed forces, whose role was to keep the colonies in submission, against the crown, and Latin America gained its independence. General Goyeneche and my uncle had five thousand men under their command when they left the River Plate; and when, after two years of marches, they reached Peru, only a third of that number answered the rollcall. The war in Peru between the royal troops and the republicans lasted fifteen years; my uncle took part in all the battles between the two sides including the final one which gave victory to the republican cause, the famous battle of Ayacucho, won by the Peruvian patriots. My uncle was appointed interim viceroy, having the courage to accept this high office at a moment when it had more dangers than advantages to offer. After losing the battle, the royalist party was completely wiped out, and the viceroy and all the officers were forced to leave the country. My uncle then announced that he would return to Spain with his family and his fortune. But the republican leaders, who valued his gallantry and military talents and who realised that their new government had need of such men, offered him a command with a change of rank from royalist brigadier to republican general. He refused the command and preferred to be appointed governor of Cuzco, which he administered for six years. In this he followed the dictates of prudence, moved entirely by personal interest and the desire to avoid making enemies. Things turned out differently: in revolutionary times, confidence can only be built up by acts of devotion: administrative skill could not cover up faults of political conscience and lack of principle. My uncle permanently alienated the royalists, who considered him a traitor, and inspired the republicans with deep distrust. He vainly used every endeavour of which he was capable to reconcile the two parties, preferring the old party but serving the new for reasons of personal advancement: but he could make no headway. The royalists feared him because he was in a position of power, but rejected him for his treachery, whilst the republicans kept so tight a control over his actions that it became difficult for him to carry out his functions. My uncle fought for a long time against the opposition which he encountered from all sides and with a determination which I might almost be tempted to call admirable. Eventually the animosity became so violent that he considered it prudent to leave the area, fearing for his life. He returned to Arequipa, where he could have lived as well and as luxuriously as a man who has an income of 200,000 francs a year can live anywhere in the world; but he had become used to authority, and the enjoyment of his fortune by itself did not attract him. He had to be surrounded by a brilliant staff or a large crowd of employees. For him to feel alive, his mind had to be occupied with great projects. In an attempt to satisfy this need, he made a tour of all his sugar mills and built a country residence; yet none of this was enough to deflect him from his ambition. He indulged in secret intrigues, and these clandestine manoeuvres were so successful that he missed the presidency of Peru by only five votes. *As a consolation* his supporters appointed him prefect of Arequipa. My uncle carried out his new duties with intelligence and zeal, embellishing the city in a number of ways and exploring all means of developing the prosperity of the community. But as his public esteem increased, so did all the ancient hatreds revive. The royalists repeated their recriminations and the republicans once again showed their mistrust. The newspapers, which are more abusive in Peru than anywhere else, attacked my uncle so violently that after two years he was again forced to resign; and once again, his life was in danger. A cousin of ours, a military man of very violent temper, was so angry at the attacks and outrages which continually appeared in the newspaper *The Republic*, that he called on the chief editor, quarrelled with him and then settled the matter by hitting him so hard that he nearly blinded him in one eye. The enraged editor swore that he would take his revenge on my uncle who, realising the extent of the enmity of the political parties towards him, thought it better not to wait for the editor to recover enough from his injuries to carry out his threats, and left for Chile.

When I arrived in Peru, he had only been back ten months, and his aim was now to become president. His ambition was at least as great a cause of his return home as any desire to see his family again. Through his scheming, my uncle was quite capable of attachment to various political groups, but one may conclude from the foregoing sketch of his career that he had won the affection of no class of citizens. He was feared by all, particularly the government employees, because he was almost always in power, and in reality he was hated by all.

The Peruvians are political in all that they do; sycophantic, base, vindictive and cowardly. These characteristics combined with my uncle's powerful influence in the government, will easily explain their behaviour towards me.

Let us now return to the Post Office at Islay, and the

home of Don Justo de Medina. From my room, I could see everyone who visited Don Justo in his office or the ladies in the adjoining room. I was surprised to see how many people called at the house. I also noticed that they all looked worried and preoccupied. I spoke little Spanish, but understood it well, and a few phrases I caught here and there made me realise that all these visits had something to do with me. The doctor had gone to the Customs House to fetch our trunks; when he returned he came to see me full of a mysterious glee which I could not fathom.

'Ah, mademoiselle,' he whispered, 'you've no idea what a rascally country this is! These Peruvians are as base flatterers as the Mexicans. Oh, dear France, why is it that a small doctor like me cannot make a fortune in Paris?'

'What, doctor, are you already calling curses down on this country? What harm can these people have done you?'

'None yet; but judge by the sample I'm about to give you, what they must be capable of. I give the impression that I don't understand Spanish, so that they speak frankly in front of me. Well, do you know that the rascals were discussing whether they ought to make you welcome, or whether it might not be wiser to turn the cold shoulder for fear of offending Don Pio de Tristan! Luckily for you, one of your uncle's sworn enemies is here – a priest and a parliamentary deputy. He is considered the head of the republican party. He is on his way to Lima, and his name is Francisco Luna Pizarro. He is staying with the Customs Officer, Don Basilio, who consulted him about how to behave towards you. The priest replied at once that you must be treated with the greatest respect, and is coming to visit you himself. He will be here shortly.' And indeed a few minutes later, the famous priest Luna Pizarro, a small Peruvian version of La Menais,* called with Don Basilio de la Fuente and the local notables. After this official visit came, first, the ladies of Arequipa who were staying at Islay for the sea-bathing, and then other

* *Translator's note*: F. de Lamennais, 1782–1854, a French philosopher who, although in holy orders, preached a revolutionary doctrine.

persons of a lower social standing. Don Justo gave us a good dinner and, in my honour, engaged local musicians and dancers in order to give a Peruvian-style ball for my entertainment. The dancing continued until after midnight.

I waited impatiently for all the guests to leave, as I was tired out. At last, I could go to bed – but alas! no sooner was I in bed than I felt what seemed like an ants' nest – of fleas! I had been much bothered by fleas since my arrival, but not to this extent. I could not sleep a wink, and the bites so inflamed my blood that I became feverish. I got up as soon as day broke, and went out into the courtyard for some fresh air. There I found the doctor, who was washing his face, his neck and his arms, swearing at the fleas. My only reply was to show him my hands, all covered with bites. Good Don Justo was most upset that the fleas had prevented us from sleeping. His wife said with embarrassment: 'Mademoiselle, I did not dare tell you what to do to prevent them from bothering you: this evening I will teach you.'

That morning my uncle's agent called to tell me that he had sent a messenger to Camana to inform my family of my arrival. He was sure that my uncle would send for me as soon as he learned that I was at Islay. I thought it over rapidly and, knowing what I did about my uncle, I did not think it would be wise to go immediately to him in the country, thereby putting myself to some extent at his mercy. I thought it much better to go direct to Arequipa, so that I could make enquiries, find out how the land lay and wait there until my uncle himself brought up the question of money. I told the agent that I would leave for Arequipa on the following day, as I was too tired to go to Camana. I entrusted the preparations for the journey to the doctor, with the intention of leaving at dawn next day.

The rest of the day was spent in receiving farewell visits and in exploring the area. Then in the evening I went to the house of the Customs Officer, who had invited me to a tea-party. To enhance the grandeur of the occasion he had, like Don Justo, engaged the town musicians and dancers, and the dancing continued until one o'clock in the morning. In order not to drop off to sleep, I drank several cups of coffee: it was excellent, but made me very nervous. When I went to my room, Señora de Medina came and showed me how to avoid the fleas. She put four or five chairs next to each other in a row, so that the final one was close to the bed. On the first chair, she made me undress. I then got on to the second wearing only my chemise. The señora took all my clothes out of the room, telling me to rub myself all over with a towel, so that the fleas sticking to my body would fall off; then I went from chair to chair until I reached the bed, from which I picked up a white nightdress which had been liberally sprinkled with eau de cologne. This procedure gave me two hours' peace; but after that I was attacked by thousands of fleas which had reached the bed. One has to have lived in countries where such insects abound to have any idea of the torture that their bites can cause. The irritation grates on the nerves, inflames the blood and causes fever. Peru is infected with these insects. In the streets of Islay one sees them jumping about on the sand. It is impossible to avoid them entirely, but if the customs of the country were more cleanly, one would be much less bothered by them.

VII

THE DESERT: ISLAY TO AREQUIPA

At four o'clock in the morning the muleteer arrived to fetch the luggage. I dressed whilst he loaded the mules; I was worn out, utterly weary, but as usual I was able to revive by drinking large quantities of coffee.

As I prepared to mount my mule, I realised it was a very poor creature and singularly ill-saddled for so long a journey. I drew the doctor's attention to this – it was he who had been responsible for finding the beast – by congratulating him on being luckier than I, since his mule was in quite good condition and properly saddled. He assured me that he had combed the neighbourhood and could find nothing better. I believed him. I would never have thought that a man to whom one had done some service could so soon have forgotten, or been as ungrateful or indifferent as an industrialist, that exploiter of workers, to the result of their toil. Don Justo lent me a rug to spread on to the straw-filled cushion which had been put on the animal to do duty as a saddle: this cheap device is locally known as a *torche*. I made myself as comfortable as I could. Everybody around us said that I was most unwise to set off so badly mounted; since the journey was long and hard they felt it would be better to delay my departure. But youth is headstrong and brooks no delay. I relied on my moral strength, on my will-power which has never let me down, and ignored the entreaties of good Justo and his wife and daughter, who told me how they had nearly died of fatigue on their last journey to Arequipa. I set off: it was five o'clock in the morning on the 11th of September, 1833.

At first I was reasonably comfortable on my mule. The coffee I had drunk had given me an illusion of strength, I felt tireless and very pleased with the decision I had made. We had hardly left the neighbourhood of Islay and begun to penetrate into the mountains when we were joined by two gentlemen on horseback. They were cousins of the Administrator of Customs at Islay: one was called Don Balthazar de la Fuente and the other Don José de la Fuente. They came up to ask if I would be willing to accept them as travelling companions. I thanked them for their gallantry and was delighted at the fortunate encounter, because I had certain doubts about M. de Castellac's bravery. Used to travelling in Mexico, where the roads are infested with brigands, he had expected the same of Peru. He was bristling with weapons, although fighting was not his strong point; they were for frightening the brigands off, rather than for use; he hoped to function as a kind of scarecrow. His accoutrements made him look rather like Don Quixote, though he was not endowed with the prowess of that noble knight. At his waist he had a pair of pistols; higher up he wore a swordbelt from which hung a long lancer's sabre; from a shoulder belt hung a long hunting knife, and two more pistols were fixed to his saddlebow. This warlike appearance contrasted most comically with the puniness of his person and shabbiness of his clothing. He was wearing the same leather breeches that he had worn on his Mexican journey, top-boots with long spurs also from Mexico, a short green hunting jacket, so tight and so worn that it seemed likely to burst at any moment. On his head he wore a black silk skullcap, and over it a huge straw hat. Add to this a collection of baskets and bottles on the forepart of the mule, and behind, blankets, rugs, scarves and coats – in a word, the paraphernalia of a man who, used to travelling in the desert, carries everything with him in case of need. I on the other hand knew nothing about such journeys, and had dressed as I would to ride from Paris to Orleans. I wore grey twill ankle boots, a brown linen house-coat, a silk apron with my knife and handkerchief in the pocket, and a small hat in blue Indian silk. I had, however, brought my coat and two scarves.

A dangerous path down the mountains brought us into Guerrera, a league from Islay, where we saw springs of water, trees and a little vegetation. There were five or six huts inhabited by muleteers. The Señores de la Fuente engaged me in conversation, telling me of the astonishment which my arrival had produced: I was completely unexpected, as my uncle had never mentioned me. They then spoke of my grandmother, and not realising how painful the subject was, deplored my loss of so excellent a person, as generous as she was just. What Don Balthazar and his cousin said about my grandmother brought all my sorrows to mind, and upset me so much that I could not keep back my tears. When they saw the effect of their words, they tried to calm me by changing the subject; but my sensibility had been aroused and I felt an overwhelming need to weep. I let them ride ahead with the doctor, and, alone, I allowed my tears to flow freely.

I thought that tears would bring relief, but soon after I experienced a violent headache. The heat was beginning to be unbearable; the thick white dust kicked up by the hooves of our beasts added to my suffering. I needed all my courage to keep on my mule. Don Balthazar sustained my morale with assurances that once out of the mountain gorges we would be in open country where the air would be pure and fresh. I had a raging thirst, and took frequent doses of water mixed with the local wine; this mixture, which is usually so beneficial, made my headache worse, because the wine was so heady and strong. We emerged at last from the stifling ravines where there was not a breath of wind and the burning sun on the sand made it as hot as an oven. We climbed the last mountain, and from its summit we saw the vastness of the desert, the mountain chain of the Andes and the three gigantic volcanoes of Arequipa. At the sight of this magnificent spectacle, I forgot all my woes: I was lost in admiration. Were these the courts of Heaven? And was Paradise itself behind that ridge which stood between earth and sky, beyond the sea of undulating sand? I contemplated sand and sky, and in between them the endless chain of high mountains with its countless peaks covered in sparkling snow, marking the western limit of the desert in all the colours of the rainbow. I was overwhelmed by a sense of the infinite, and God became manifest to me in all his power and splendour, just as he manifested himself to the shepherd on Mount Horeb. I shifted my gaze to the three volcanoes of Arequipa which spring from the same base, a picture of chaos itself, with their three peaks covered in snow, which sometimes reflects the sun and sometimes the flames which turn the mountain into a huge three-branched torch, lit up for who knows what mysterious ritual, the symbol of a trinity which passes human understanding.

Whilst I was contemplating all these marvels, the doctor and Don José, instead of being lost in admiration for eternal snows and burning sand, had made up a bed for me on rugs and put up a small tent to shade me from the sun. I lay down, and we made an abundant repast. Kind Mme Justo had given the doctor a basket well-stocked with roast meats, vegetables, cakes and fruit. The two Spaniards had also provided well for themselves: they had brought sausages, cheese, chocolate, sugar and fruit, and to drink they had milk, wine and rum. We spent long over our meal: I was never tired of that view. When we had eaten, it was the doctor's turn to admire it. But we finally had to leave. There were thirty-four leagues to go, entirely without water; we had covered only six and it was already ten o'clock.

Don José let me ride his mare, because she was better than my mule, and we set off. My mind was for a time still fascinated by the effect of the magnificent panorama; my senses were numbed and we had been making painful progress for nearly half an hour before the ghastly desert we had begun to cross made any impression on me. But physical discomfort finally put an end to my ecstatic state; my eyes were suddenly open, and I found myself apparently in the middle of a sea, clear and blue like the sky reflected in it and with gently moving waves. But I thought that this must be a sea of fire, rather than of water, since it gave off heat like a furnace, and the air was stifling, full of a fine dust which settled on the face, invisible but stinging like the down on the leaf of a nettle. Raising my eyes to the Andes, I felt the tortures of a fallen angel, cast out of Heaven.

'Don Balthazar!' I asked him in startled tones, 'are we walking through molten metal? How long do we continue in this sea of fire?'

'You are right, mademoiselle, the sand is so hot that one could well take it for molten glass.'

'But, señor, is the sand liquid?'

'Mademoiselle, it is the *mirage* which gives you this illusion; look, our packmules are in it up to the hocks, yet they too think that a lake lies ahead of them. See how they push ahead to reach this ever-receding water, spurred on by thirst. The poor beasts could not long survive this tantalising torment.'

'Have we water to quench their thirst?'

'They are never watered on the march. The host at the *tambo* [inn] has provisions for passing travellers.'

'Don Balthazar, in spite of the explanation you have given me, I can still distinctly see what look like waves.'

'This *pampa* is covered with little ridges of sand made by the wind; as you see, they are shaped like waves, and the mirage makes them seem to move in the distance. In fact, they are not much more stable than the waves of the ocean; the winds shift them continually.'

'Then it must be dangerous in the *pampa* when the wind is strong?'

'Oh yes; a few years ago, some muleteers travelling from Islay to Arequipa were buried with their mules by a whirlwind; but such events are rare.'

By midday the heat was so great and my headache became so bad that I could no longer ride. The sun and the reflection from the sand burnt my face, and my throat was dry with thirst; a general weakness, that my willpower could no longer combat, made me fall as in a swoon. I was twice near to losing consciousness altogether. My three companions were at their wits' end. The doctor wanted to bleed me, but fortunately Don Balthazar would not allow it, for I should certainly not have survived a *sangrado*. They laid me flat on my horse, and surely an invisible hand must have held me there, for with God's help I did not once fall off. At last the sun disappeared behind the great volcanoes and gradually the cool of the evening revived me. Don Balthazar, to spur me on, used a trick often employed in such circumstances, which consists in deceiving the traveller over the distance which separates him from the *tambo* (this one was a half-way house). He maintained that were only three leagues from it. 'Cheer up, dear mademoiselle, you will soon see the light of the lantern hanging over the inn door.' The crafty fellow well knew that we had still over six leagues to go; he was relying on the first star to appear over the rim of the Andes to give credibility to his trickery; but the night grew pitch black and our anxiety increased considerably. No track crosses the desert, and without stars to guide us we risked losing our way and dying of hunger and thirst amidst these vast wildernesses.

In this *pampa* country the nights are as cold, due to the wind from the mountain snows, as the days are hot from the sun and sand. The cold wind revived me; I felt stronger and my headache subsided. I spurred on my horse with a vigour which surprised my companions. Two hours before I had been at death's door – now I was strong again! I had

THE ROUTE ACROSS THE *PAMPA* TO AREQUIPA

RUGGED HILLS NEAR AREQUIPA

not been fooled by the trick that Don Balthazar had tried to play when he pointed to a star and claimed it was the inn lantern, and I was the first to sight the real one. I shouted aloud and set off at a gallop. It was still a long distance off, but the sight of this little lantern kept my courage up. We arrived there at midnight. Don Balthazar had gone ahead with his servant to prepare a bed for me and some hot soup. When we arrived I went to bed and drank my soup, but could not sleep. Three things prevented me: the fleas, which were even more numerous than at Islay, the ceaseless noise in the inn, and my anxiety that my strength would fail and I would not be able to finish the journey.

I hastened our preparations for departure and we left the *tambo* at four o'clock in the morning. It was very cold: Don Balthazar lent me a great *poncho,* well lined with flannel, and a scarf was twisted round each of my hands. Thanks to these precautions I travelled without feeling the cold too keenly.

The character of the country changed completely at this point. The *pampa* ended and we were now in a mountainous country, but still one where there was no sign of vegetation. It was a dead nature of a most depressing kind. No bird flew in the air, not the smallest beast ran on the earth; nothing but black sand and stones. Man, in passing through, had increased the awfulness of the place: this desolate land was scattered with the skeletons of animals which had died of hunger and thirst in the wilderness – mules, horses, donkeys and oxen. Llamas are not exposed to journeys such as these, as they are too delicate; they need large quantities of water and cool temperatures. I found the sight of these skeletons profoundly depressing. These animals, living on the same planet and the same soil as ourselves – are they not our companions? Are they not also God's creatures?

The sun rose and the heat got stronger and stronger. The sand we travelled over got hot and clouds of dust as fine as ash burnt our faces and dried up our mouths. At about eight we entered the *Quebradas* (gorges), a mountain area renowned for its difficulty. Whilst we were climbing I lay along my mule's neck, letting Providence be my guide; but I could not do this whilst we descended. Although my mule was very sure-footed, the continual dangers of the way forced me to take the greatest care. We had to get the animals over crevasses which lay across our path, make them climb great rocks and sometimes follow narrow paths where the sand crumbled away under their hooves, putting us in great danger of falling over the precipices which yawned below. Don Balthazar took the lead, to show the way. His cousin, who was the kindest and most thoughtful man I have ever met, kept as close to me as he could, so as to be able to help me if necessary. The doctor, a cautious man if ever there was one, took up the rear, fearing that if one of us were to fall he would be dragged down as well. He cried out each time his mule stumbled, calling on the Almighty, cursing the track, the sun and the dust, and lamenting his unhappy fate.

I managed the descent of the first two mountains fairly well, but when I reached the top of the third I felt so weak and ill and the motion on muleback had given me such a pain in my side, that I could no longer hold the reins. We stopped there on the summit, where the air was pure and fresh. We were panting, running with sweat, and in need of relief. I was suffering the same symptoms as the day before: oppressive spasms in the chest, which caused the veins of my neck and forehead to swell; tears fell uncontrollably, I could no longer keep my head erect and had no sensation in my limbs. All I could feel was thirst, raging thirst.

Don Balthazar, realising that in my condition I could not ride my mule without risk of falling over a precipice, suggested that we should make the descent on foot. He and his cousin took me by the arms, almost carrying me, and so we reached the bottom, with M. de Castellac leading the animals by the halter. Having succeeded by this method, we repeated it on all the other peaks we had to traverse, and there were seven or eight of them.

If on the previous day I had been profoundly impressed by the sight of dead animals, how much more was I affected, now that my nerves were sensitive to an even greater extent, by the spectacle of creatures in the throes of death in the midst of the desert. We came across two unfortunate beasts, a mule and a donkey, which were in the agonies of death by hunger and thirst. I cannot describe the effect this had on me. Seeing two creatures dying in such anguish, and hearing their feeble cries, made me sob as bitterly as if I had been present at the death of two humans. Even the doctor, in spite of his self-centred nature, was moved: one realises how, in such dreadful places, all creatures are prey to the same dangers.

As we climbed the last peak, I had one more ordeal to undergo, one more encounter with Death, the reigning deity of the desert. A tomb had been placed beside the track in such a way that one could not avoid it. Don Balthazar wanted me to pass by quickly, but an uncontrollable curiosity led me to read the inscription: a young man of twenty-eight had died here on his way to Arequipa. He was ill when he left Islay, where he had been for the sea bathing, and was unable to survive the hardships of the journey; a mother's sorrow, the deepest sorrow of all, had been recorded here in the wilderness – a final tragic touch. The tomb had been erected at the very spot where the young man died, and his unhappy fate had been recorded on the stone. I could so well imagine what he suffered when he died, in this place far away from his loved ones. My imagination was so vivid that for a moment I thought that I too would die, in that very spot. A horrible moment! I thought of my poor daughter and begged her to pardon me for coming here, to die four thousand leagues from home. I prayed God to take her under his protection; I pardoned all those who had wronged me and resigned myself to departing from this life. I was prostrate, unable to leave the tomb. Don Balthazar again came to my rescue: he lifted me on to my mule, secured me to it with his *poncho* and held me with his strong arm. Urging the beasts on, he achieved the impossible and we reached the top of the last peak. They laid me on the ground, and my three companions all began to speak at once in joyous voices: 'Dear mademoiselle, open your eyes. Here is the green country! Look at Arequipa, and see how beautiful it is!'

'Look,' said the de la Fuente cousins, 'there is the Congata river, and see those great trees. Have you any more delightful countryside in France?'

Alas! I tried, but failed, to open my eyes. I was utterly exhausted, and felt nothing of the cool breeze which fanned my forehead; the voices of my companions reached me through a haze, my consciousness was slipping away, I was held to the earth only by a narrow thread which could have broken at any minute. We still had some water, with which they washed my face. They rubbed my hands and temples with rum, they gave me oranges to suck, and then, better than anything, the cool wind brought me back to life. I revived gradually and opened my eyes. I then saw the smiling valley and it filled me with such sweet emotion that I wept tears of joy. I rested a long time; hope revived as I looked at the view; my energy returned. However I was still physically exhausted. I tried to get up to descend the last mountain but was unable to stand. Don Balthazar this time decided to take me up behind him. The track was better, and we had only half an hour's journey to Congata. We reached there at two in the afternoon.

Congata was not a village, for it consisted of only three or four houses and a handsome farm which did duty as posting stage, inn and meeting place for travellers crossing the desert. The owner of the house also managed the establishment and was called Don Juan Najarra. When we entered the courtyard, Don Balthazar told him who I was and explained the urgency with which I needed succour. My uncle's name was a powerful recommendation; Señor Najarra, his wife and numerous servants busied themselves with such effect that within ten minutes I was served a very good soup. They took off my shoes and stockings and washed my feet with warm water and milk, and also my face and arms. Then they carried me into the farm's little chapel where a bed had been made up for me on the ground. Señora Najarra, helped by a negress, undressed me, put on a clean white cambric nightgown, carried me to the bed, tucked me in with the greatest care, put a cup of milk by the bedside and then withdrew, closing the door of the chapel.

According to what I had heard at Islay, my uncle was unlikely to return to Arequipa in under two months, and needing to seek hospitality from other relatives I had written on the eve of my departure to the bishop and his brother Señor de Goyeneche, who were my cousins. The doctor, who knew about this, told Don Balthazar, so that when he arrived at Arequipa he could warn the Goyeneches of my arrival at Congata and of the alarming state I was in.

As soon as Don Balthazar was thus informed he set off at speed, making up for the nuisance he had suffered through the slowness of the journey so far. The de la Fuente cousins had made the greatest sacrifice that a Peruvian can make, by travelling slowly for my sake. If they had been alone, they would have taken sixteen to eighteen hours, whereas we had been on the road for forty.

That kind lady, Señora de Najarra, looked after my health, whilst the doctor ignored it completely; she advised me to stay in bed and said that she would send my dinner to me.

I got up at about six o'clock. My body was aching and my feet were swollen. However, I went for a walk in Señor Najarra's little wood. After two days spent in the desert, what a pleasure to find one's self amongst cultivated fields, to hear the murmur of the broad stream which ran beside our path, and to see the beautiful tall trees! I was enchanted by the sight of that charming valley. I was discussing agriculture with Señor Najarra, when a negro came to announce the arrival of Don Juan de Goyeneche. He was the first relative whose hand I had shaken. I liked him: he was extremely polite and gentlemanly. He invited me, in the name of his brother, his sister and himself, to consider their house as my own; adding, that my cousin, my uncle Pio's niece, had said that she would not allow me to live anywhere but in my uncle's house, and that she would send for me on the following day with an invitation to take up my residence there. Señor de Goyeneche was accompanied by a Frenchman, a M. Durand, who came on the pretext of acting as interpreter, but was really a busybody who had come out of curiosity. After they had gone, I returned to my chapel and went to bed in high spirits.

Next morning when I woke up I was completely well again. Señora de Najarra was kind enough to arrange a bath for me, prepared under her direction. I stayed in it for half an hour, then went back to bed between my fine embroidered cambric sheets, and an excellent breakfast was brought in.

At about midday M. de Castellac came to tell me to hurry, for four gentlemen from Arequipa were asking to meet me. When I came out of the chapel, which was at the end of the covered walk which surrounded the house, I saw a young man of eighteen or nineteen coming towards me, who was so like me that he could have been my brother. He was my cousin, Emmanuel de Rivero. He spoke French as if he had been born in France. He had been sent there at seven years of age and had only been back a year. We felt immediate sympathy for each other. His first words were: 'Ah, cousin! How is it that I have been unaware of your existence until now? I was alone in Paris for four years, without a single friend. You were in the same city, and God did not allow us to meet. Cruel thought! No, I shall never get over it.' I was fond of this young man from the first moment I saw him. He was French in character, friendly, good-hearted; and he too had suffered.

Emmanuel gave me a letter from my cousin, Doña Carmen Pierola de Florez, who, in the name of my uncle Pio, invited me to stay at his house, the only one proper for me to live in. The whole letter was in this vein; I could see by the style that I was dealing with an intelligent woman, but a cautious and calculating one. For the ride to Arequipa she had sent me a very fine horse with a superb English saddle. In addition she had sent two riding habits, shoes, gloves and a number of other objects in case, not having my trunks with me, I was in need of clothes. The three gentlemen who had come with my cousin Emmanuel were Señor Arismendi, Señor Rendon and M. Durand, all close friends of my cousin Carmen. I chatted with them awhile, then left them with the doctor, to go for a short walk with my cousin. I learned from him that my arrival was the talk of the town, and that everyone assumed that I must have come to claim my father's inheritance. He told me all about the character and position of my uncle, who had done much to wrong him, having cruelly refused to pay him an allowance, for only three years, to allow him to finish his studies in France. Emmanuel's father had wasted a large fortune and plunged his family into poverty. My grandmother had come to the children's help: she had left them annuities which gave them just enough to live on. My cousin told me all his family troubles with affectionate openness, as if we had known each other for ten years. And I too felt that I loved him as if he were my brother.

We wanted to leave, because my cousin Carmen had made it clear that she expected us for dinner; but our kind hosts pressed me so warmly to share this last meal with them that I accepted happily, touched by their friendly interest. When dinner was over, at about six o'clock in the evening, I left Congata farm, dressed in a smart green woollen riding habit, a man's hat with a black veil, riding on a fine spirited horse. I rode at the head of the little troop, and that inseparable doctor took up the rear.

The road from Congata to Arequipa was good compared with the other roads of the country; however, it was not without hazards. The river Congata had to be forded, and this can be dangerous at certain seasons. There was little water when we crossed it, but the stony bottom makes the horses liable to slip, and a fall into that river might have serious consequences. My horse was so lively that I found it hard to control him. But dear Emmanuel was my squire and thanks to him I emerged safe and dry. After crossing the river, I saw well-cultivated fields and hamlets which appeared to be poor and thinly inhabited.

When we reached the high ground of Tiavalla we stopped to enjoy the enchanting view of the valley and city of Arequipa. The effect is magic; here was something, I felt, straight out of the *Arabian Nights*. This beautiful place deserves a detailed description, and I shall speak of it elsewhere.

At Tiavalla we encountered a great cavalcade coming to meet us, led by my 'saviour' Don Balthazar and his cousin. The others were friends of my cousin Carmen and seven or eight Frenchmen living in Arequipa.

At last we arrived. Congata is five leagues from Arequipa and it was dark when we entered the town. I was relieved in that I was hidden from public gaze; the noise of the cavalcade passing through the streets certainly brought the curious to their doors, but it was too dark for anyone to be recognised. When we reached the Calle de Santo Domingo I saw a house with an illuminated façade. 'That is your uncle's house,' said Emmanuel.

A crowd of slaves was at the door. As we approached they rushed inside to announce our arrival. My entrance was as spectacular as anything you could see at the theatre. The courtyard was lit by resin-burning torches fixed to the walls. The great drawing-room filled the whole length of the wall facing the entrance; in the middle was a great doorway preceded by a porch or hallway at the top of a flight of four or five steps. This hall was lit by lamps, and the drawing-room itself was brilliant with the light of a fine chandelier and innumerable branched candlesticks with candles of various colours. My cousin Carmen, who was in full evening dress in my honour, came forward to the steps and received me with all the ceremonial prescribed by etiquette and custom. I dismounted and went forward to meet her: I was deeply moved. I took her hand and thanked her most warmly for all that she had done for me already. She led me to a large sofa and sat beside me. I was hardly seated before a deputation of five or six monks of the order of St Dominic came forward. The grand-prior of the order made a long harangue in which he spoke of the virtues of my grandmother and her munificent gifts to the convent. While he made this speech I had time to examine the people who thronged the drawing-room. It was a mixed crowd. On the whole, the men rather than the women looked as if they belonged to the best society. They all greeted me in pompous terms, with offers of service which were so exaggerated that they could hardly be sincere. In fact in case of need I could not have counted on them for the slightest assistance, and their words were no more than a servile homage intended for Don Pio de Tristan, although addressed to his niece. My cousin Carmen told me that she had ordered a supper which would be served whenever I gave the word. I was tired, and in any case did not care to be the cynosure of all eyes any longer. I therefore asked my cousin to excuse me from attending the supper and asked her permission to retire to the apartment assigned to me. I saw that my request, which my cousin could hardly refuse, was not at all to the taste of the honourable company. I was conducted to a part of the house where there were two large, very scantily furnished rooms. A number of people including the monks accompanied me as far as my bedroom; the latter even laughingly offered to help me undress. I asked Emmanuel to tell my cousin Carmen that I wanted to be left to myself. Everyone departed, and by midnight I was at last alone in my room with a little negress who had been assigned to me as servant.

VIII

AREQUIPA

Here I was at last in the house where my father was born – the house I had so often visited in my childish daydreams, and which I had been deeply convinced all along I would one day visit. This conviction originated in my admiration of my father, whose loving image I preserve to this day.

When the little negress had gone to sleep, I yielded to a desire to examine the two vaulted rooms which I had been allotted. I wondered if they had been my father's, and this idea made them feel like home, in spite of the fact that the immediate impression on entering had been of coldness and gloom. The furniture of the first room consisted of a large oaken chest of drawers, which must have been shipped over soon after Pizarro's expedition, and which evidently dated from the reign of Ferdinand and Isabella. There were a modern table and chairs, in the style introduced into Spain by Philip IV, Duke of Anjou,* and

* *Translator's note:* Flora means Philip V, grandson of Louis XIV, Duke of Anjou and King of Spain from 1700 to 1746.

a large English carpet covering almost the whole floor. The walls were whitewashed and hung with maps. This room was at least twenty-five feet long by twenty wide, and was lit only by a small window of four panes set high up in the wall. The second room took its light from the first, and was divided from it by a partition which stopped short of the ceiling; it was much smaller, and was furnished with a small iron bedstead, hung with muslin curtains, an oak table, four old chairs and an old Gobelins carpet on the floor. The sunlight never reached this vast apartment, which in its shape, atmosphere and gloom resembled an underground vault. My inspection of the lodging that my family had chosen for me filled me with depression. I thought of my uncle's meanness and of all that I had dreaded. It is easy to judge the master of the house by the behaviour of those who act on his behalf. If Doña Carmen had given me such rooms in my uncle's absence, it was because she knew that he would have done the same. As if to underline the fact, she had said as she led me to them that though the rooms were unsuitable, they were the only ones in the house available for the use of relatives and friends. This was typical of my uncle. Not only was he head of a large family, he was personally acquainted, by virtue of his high office and his own merit, with all the top people in the country, and enjoyed enormous personal wealth, yet all he could offer to his friends and relatives was a cold cavernous room, so dark that even at midday one needed a lamp to read by. The thought made me blush with shame. Was I destined, I wondered with an involuntary exclamation, to be associated with people whose hard hearts made them proof against noble sentiments? Then I remembered my grandmother, so noble, so charitable; and my poor father, so warm-hearted, and Emmanuel, so good, and his excellent mother; and I was comforted by the fact that there were some individual members of the family whom I could accept as relatives. My thoughts were so disturbing that it was almost dawn before I went off to sleep.

Next morning my cousin told me that the town notables would be paying me visits, as was the custom, and that I should appear early in the drawing-room. I felt ill and depressed, and not at all willing to greet these people. To be frank, my refusal was first and foremost due to vanity: during the journey across the desert the sun, the dust and the scorching sea wind had burnt my face and my hands. The ointment which Señora Najarra had kindly provided had begun to make my skin less red and was gradually restoring it to its natural state, and I was anxious to wait a few days longer before appearing in public. My excuse that I was indisposed was accepted for two days, but on the third complaints began to be heard, and M. Durand, who understood the mentality of the inhabitants, advised me to put in an appearance if I did not wish to lose the goodwill which they were prepared to show me. This is typical of immature societies: their hospitality has its tyrannical side. At Islay, although exhausted, I had to stay at the ball until midnight. At Arequipa, in spite of what I had suffered on the journey and the fact that I was in mourning for my grandmother, I had to be visited by the whole town on the third day after my arrival. A black dress was hastily made for me. I made my appearance in my uncle's large drawing-room dressed entirely in black like the rest of the family, and feeling even gloomier than my garments.

It was customary in Peru for upper-class women, when they arrived at a town or if they were foreigners, to stay at home for a whole month to receive visitors. After that, they would return the visits. My cousin Carmen, who was a strict observer of the rules of etiquette, gave me careful instructions in the belief that I shared her respect for them; I had every intention of carrying them out to the letter, but I found them in the end too burdensome and decided to ignore them. My cousin disliked visitors as much as I did, and applauded the unceremonious way in which I avoided them, though she was incapable of such behaviour herself. Before continuing my story, I must introduce my cousin Doña Carmen to the reader.

Unfortunately, truth compels me to state that poor Carmen Pierola de Florez was ugly to the point of deformity. Smallpox, that terrible scourge, had done its worst. She was about thirty-eight or forty years of age. However, God provided a compensation, in that she had the prettiest feet, not only in Arequipa, but perhaps in all Peru. They were miniatures, the most darling feet, dream feet that I can still conjure up before my eyes. Just imagine a foot only six inches long, proportionately narrow, perfectly formed, with a high instep, shapely leg and slim ankle; but what was extraordinary was that though Carmen herself was very thin, her legs and feet were rounded and dimpled. These pretty little feet, full of grace and character, were always stockinged in pink, grey or white silk of fine quality, and shod with elegant satin shoes in various colours. She wore her dresses very short, and rightly so, as her feet were small masterpieces of nature, too pretty to hide. She was flirtatious and dressed with taste, but in a style too young for her.

She was a most unusual woman. She was self-educated, and very intelligent. Sadly, she had lost her mother in childhood and here her misfortunes began. She was brought up by a strict and overbearing aunt, and her life became so miserable that, the alternatives being marriage or the cloister, she decided to marry the son of one of my father's sisters, who, attracted by the size of her dowry, had asked for her hand. He was a fine-looking man, and amiable enough; but he was a gambler and libertine, and he spent his own fortune and his wife's in debauchery of every sort. Doña Carmen, who had a proud nature, suffered horribly during the ten years that the marriage lasted. She loved her husband, and he, a complete sensualist, brutally rejected her love, humiliated her by his behaviour and insulted her by the excuses he gave for it. He several times left her to live publicly with mistresses, who would walk by her window, stare at her impertinently, sneer, and insult her. When, during the early days of her marriage, she ventured some complaints, either to members of her husband's family or to mutual friends, she was told that she should consider herself lucky to have a handsome husband and that she ought to put up with his behaviour without complaint. In the opinion of these people, the wife's ugliness and the husband's beauty were sufficient excuses for his robbing her of her fortune and for his outrageous behaviour. Such is the moral code which comes from the principle of the indissolubility of marriage.

Moreover, there are some men so twisted as to be more cruel than nature itself, who think that they can behave as they like, with mockery and insults, towards those who have any deformity. Such behaviour is not only cruel and stupid, but blasphemous. Only those defects which can be corrected may be ridiculed. There are no monsters in the eyes of God: the straight tree and the twisted tree both have their function. Both Aesop and Alcibiades were endowed by Providence with the shapes which fitted their destinies. To criticise the work of the Creator is to put our intelligence above His. The madman who laughs hysterically at the sight of people is less abnormal than the sane man who mocks and insults any of God's creatures, be it a plant or a human being. After this fruitless attempt, Doña Carmen never complained again, kept her counsel, and going to the other extreme, she cast out all human affection from her heart, leaving only feelings of scorn and hatred. To deaden the pain, she went into society; and although she had neither wealth nor beauty, her wit won for her a circle of admirers. She was too intelligent not to see through the flattery she received, and her various flirtations taught her much about the human heart; the more she learned, the more she despised the human race. If my cousin had had the slightest religious feeling, she would, instead of spying out men's vices in order to feed her hatred, have tried to discover their good qualities, so as to bring them out; but God had no part in her thoughts; she needed the society of the very men she despised, and flattered them so as to be flattered in return.

After ten years of marriage, her husband, now aged thirty, returned home. He had squandered both their fortunes, was deeply in debt and was suffering from a horrible disease which no doctor could treat. So long as the money lasted, the courtesans, and even the society ladies, had competed for the favours of the handsome fellow; but when not a penny was left, the shameless creatures rejected him, with mockery and loud reproaches for his conduct. Poor man, he now discovered the truth about the unworthy creatures on whom he had wasted his money. Ruined, friendless, he instinctively returned to his wife, whom he had humiliated and abandoned, and sought refuge with her. She received him, not with affection – since that emotion had withered in her heart – but with the secret pleasure which people of her type experience when they see the opportunity of revenge, a justified revenge which leaves them in a position of superiority. The wretch paid a high price for his disorderly life; for sixteen months he lay in bed, a prey to the most cruel tortures. During these sixteen months his wife never left him for a moment: she was his nurse, his doctor and his priest. She slept on a sofa at the foot of his bed, and ministered to him night and day. What an experience for her, and how it fed her aversion and contempt for the human race! She watched this young man die, the man whom she had once loved, who was still in the flower of his youth, but in a state of decrepitude brought on by debauchery, and she saw him die the death of a coward. Never once weakening, Carmen bore patiently the dying man's whims, rebuffs and fits of despair. This long illness exhausted my poor cousin's last financial resources. After her husband's death, she was forced to return to her aunt's house with her only child, a girl.

Since then, her life had been a continuous ordeal. She was without funds, yet longed to appear in society and keep up appearances; she had to depend on her hard-hearted and stingy aunt, and although she had hardly enough for her basic needs, she endeavoured to give the impression of living in luxury. When I arrived in Arequipa, she had been a widow for twelve years, and for twelve years she had vegetated in this way, hiding her penury under an appearance of opulence. She passed six months of every year at the sugar plantation at Camana, near my uncle's. She disliked living in the country, but necessity drove her to it; however, when I arrived, unexpected circumstances had, for the first time, kept her in town. We both felt that Providence had had a hand in this, for if chance had not prolonged her stay in Arequipa, there would have been no one to receive me at my uncle's house.

The coldness and ugliness of my poor relative made a disagreeable first impression on me, but I soon realised that underneath lay a noble nature and a superior intelligence, and these attracted me. She was warmly affectionate from the start, was extremely kind in all sorts of ways, and offered to be my language teacher. Thanks to her, I rapidly mastered Spanish. She had remarkable patience in teaching and in correcting my mistakes. Her house was opposite my uncle's, so that we were continually together in one house or the other. In the morning, she sent breakfast over to me, and at about three o'clock, I went over to dine with her. She always intended to invite friends to join us, so that I could have company to amuse me; but I preferred to be alone with her, for her conversation was an endless source of information on the people and the customs of the country.

The day after my arrival in Arequipa, I wrote to my uncle to tell him that I was at his house, that my health did not permit me to travel to Camana, and that I awaited his return with the greatest impatience. There was no reply from Don Pio for a fortnight. I was worried, and my cousin no less so. She was afraid of my uncle, and feared that his silence was a sign of disapproval of the way she had conducted herself towards me. My uncle's behaviour revived the interest that my arrival had produced among both his enemies and his friends; the former said that he was afraid of me, the latter that he had some trick up his sleeve, some trap to catch me; the alarmists among them went so far as to suggest that he might have me arrested. My room was thronged, from morning till night, with these busybodies, who came to tell me their fears, and to offer their advice and their extravagant ideas. I wrote again and again; my cousin M. de Goyeneche and others also wrote. Don Pio made no reply. It was a period when he was totally discredited, and this fact worked in my favour, for everyone was on my side. At last, on the twenty-first day after my arrival, we each had a letter, and each of these letters was so artfully written that Talleyrand himself would not have denied the authorship of such little masterpieces of diplomacy. My uncle should have been the prime minister of an absolute monarchy. In different times, he would have left renowned statesmen like Nesselrode and Metternich far behind him. Indeed he later often complained to me that fate had limited him to secret intrigues for the control of a miserable little republic, when he felt that he had the necessary talents to direct the affairs of a great monarchy. He would say: 'If I were only forty or fifty years old, I would leave immediately for Madrid. It would only take me a couple of months to dethrone the mandarins of San Ildefonso, and I would have all the strings of government in my hands.'

This first letter from my uncle had the effect that he probably expected. He expressed so much goodwill towards me, and recalled the service that my father had done him with so much gratitude, that I believed he was ready to respond to my affection and that I could count on his good faith. One had to be as ignorant of the world as I was to be taken in by Don Pio's fine words. Alas, I needed affection, I believed in honesty and gratitude; and if from time to time I had doubts about my uncle, I smothered them, determined not to believe the ill spoken of him. His whole correspondence, during the three months that I awaited his arrival, was equally warm, good-natured and straightforward. In the end I discovered that I had been duped; his actions bore no relation to what he wrote in his letters, and this contradiction revealed what he took so much trouble to hide from me. The correspondence I received from other members of my family was very friendly and, I believe, more sincere.

There was no time to be bored whilst I lived alone in my uncle's house. I was so busy receiving callers or returning their calls, in writing and in exploring the area, that time passed very quickly.

I had arrived at Arequipa on the 13th of September. On the 18th I experienced an earthquake for the first time in my life. It was the one still remembered for its disastrous consequences, completely destroying Tacna and Arica. The first shock came at about six o'clock in the morning, and lasted two minutes. I woke with a start and was almost thrown out of bed. I thought I was back on board ship, and was being tossed by the waves, so I was not frightened; but my negress had leapt up shouting: *'Señora, temblor! Temblor!'* She opened the door and went out into the courtyard, where I hastily followed her, throwing a dressing-gown over my shoulders. The quaking was so violent that we had to lie prone to avoid falling. The bravest would have been seized with fright at feeling the heaving earth and seeing the houses shake. All the slaves were in the courtyard, on their knees and praying, petrified and seemingly giving themselves up for dead. I went back to bed. My cousin arrived, her features contorted with terror. 'Ah, Florita,' she said, 'what a horrible *terremoto*! I am sure that part of the town has been destroyed. One day I shall be buried in the ruins of my own hovel. My dear, you are not used to such convulsions: what sensations did you have?'

'Cousin, I thought I was still on board my ship, for that is how it feels to be tossed by the waves, and I was only frightened when I was in the courtyard and I saw the houses leaning, the paving stones heaving and the skyline tilting as it does at sea. Then I understood all the terror that man can feel when faced with a scourge of nature which makes him feel so powerless. Are earthquakes common in this area?'

'There are sometimes three or four in the same day, and a week seldom passes without a fairly strong one. We owe this to the proximity of the volcano.' Doña Carmen stayed to talk to me. Sitting on my bed smoking her *cigaritos* she told me about the innumerable disasters caused by earthquakes in the country. At about seven o'clock, we heard a muffled sound which seemed to come from the bowels of the earth: it was the voice of the earthquake! My cousin uttered a cry of terror and ran out of the room. At that moment I happened to be looking at a slight crack in the middle of the ceiling; I saw it widen suddenly and the great stones of the vault were dislodged. I thought that the whole mass of masonry was going to come down on my head, and fled in terror. This shock was less severe than the first; we came in, and I went back to bed, numb with fear. I admit that I was very upset. My cousin sat down beside me again; her distress was alarming. 'Vile country!' she exclaimed in a tone of concentrated fury. 'And to think that I am condemned to live here for ever!'

'But cousin, if you hate it so much, why do you stay here?'

'Why, Florita? I am forced by the hardest law of all, the law of necessity. Those without means depend on others, they are slaves who must live where their masters chain them.' And she ground her teeth in a gesture of revolt that showed that she was not made for slavery. I looked at her and said, unable to hide my feeling of superiority:

'Cousin, I am poorer than you are; I wanted to come to Arequipa, and here I am!'

'And what do you conclude from that?' she asked, with a look of jealousy.

'That freedom depends on the *will*. Those who have received from God a will that overcomes all obstacles are free, whilst those whose will tires or yields when thwarted are slaves, and would be slaves even if by strange chance they found themselves on a throne.' My cousin had no answer to this: she knew instinctively that I was right, yet could not understand what gave me the strength to speak in this manner. She gazed at me for a long time in silence, blowing rings and strange figures with the smoke of her cigar, which I watched mechanically. Suddenly she stood up and said petulantly: 'God help me, Florita, you frighten me. Where can I go to hide? I daren't return home, for fear that my house tumbles about my ears, and by the Holy Virgin I daren't stay here, listening to you calmly say things that would make a monk tremble and brand you as a madwoman!'

'Really, my dear? Don't be afraid of me: come and sit here so that I can wrap your mantilla round me, and tell me why you think that I am mad.'

'But dear Florita, you say that to be free all that one needs is a strong will; and yet you, who dare advance such a paradoxical idea, are yourself a mere woman, a slave to laws and prejudices, subject to countless infirmities, too weak physically to overcome the slightest obstacle. How easy it is to see that you have never been subjected to the yoke of a hard tyrannical husband and been forced to give in to his every whim, to endure his injustice, his scorn and his insults; also, that you have never been under the domination of a proud and powerful family, nor exposed to the black wickedness of mankind. You are unmarried, without any family, you have been free in all your actions, you are absolute mistress of yourself; no duty binds you,

you owe nothing to the world and no slander can touch you. Florita, there are very few women in your happy position; almost all have been married very young, their faculties have been stunted and impaired by the oppression, be it light or heavy, of their masters. You have no experience of how such long suffering, which must remain hidden from the eyes of the world, which one must hide even from one's self, will weaken and paralyse the morale of the most gifted person. At least, such is the effect that suffering has on us women who are not part of an advanced civilisation. Is it different with your European women?'

'Cousin, there is suffering wherever there is oppression, and oppression wherever the power to exercise it exists. In Europe women are subjected to men as they are here, and are still forced to suffer their tyranny. But in Europe, to a greater extent than here, there are women whom God has endowed with the moral strength to throw off the yoke.' As I spoke, I was carried away by the strength of my feelings, and my cousin was surprised by the expression of my voice and my eyes.

'Now this time, Florita, I admire you, you look superb! I have never met anyone who spoke with such warmth. It is very generous of you to feel so strongly about the lot of women; it is indeed very unhappy, but you can only know part of the story. To realise the depth of sorrow which a woman is condemned to suffer, she must have been married. Oh, Florita! Marriage is the only hell that I believe in!'

Feeling the blushes come to my cheeks at the indignation that this conversation awoke in me, I had hidden my face in a corner of Doña Carmen's mantilla; and as she spoke, my only care was to regain my composure. It was this first conversation which revealed to me how much she must have suffered when her husband was alive. Women here, I thought, are made as unhappy by marriage as they are in France; they are equally oppressed in that state, and the intelligence that God has given them remains inert and sterile.

On the day after the earthquake I had a crowd of callers. All the good people of Arequipa were most anxious to know how it had impressed me. Many of them seemed to imply by their manner: 'You have none of these nice things in France.' This earthquake entirely destroyed the town of Tacna, on the coast, demolishing all the houses; the church, which had just been finished and had only opened to the public a fortnight before, collapsed; eighteen people died there and many others were seriously wounded. The town of Arica was nearly as seriously affected. The Sama area and the provinces of Moquegua and Torata were laid waste. At Locumba, the earth opened and whole houses were engulfed. In all these places many perished or were injured. Arequipa suffered little; the houses are so solidly built that any earthquake that could demolish them would devastate the whole of Peru. The shocks were also felt in Valparaiso and Lima, but to a much lesser extent, and no damage was caused. One has to have lived in earthquake country to have any idea of the terror they inspire and the calamities they cause, when they first start their horrible convulsions, and the earth moves this way and that or up and down in waves, or opens up under one's feet.

On the 24th of September, to celebrate Lady's Day, a great procession moved through the town, in which the clergy displayed the maximum of ostentation. Such processions are the only amusements of the people. The feast days of the Peruvian church give an idea of what the pagan Bacchanals and Saturnalia must have been like. Never, in the times of the greatest ignorance, has the Catholic religion brought into public view such indecent clowning, such scandalously profane exhibitions. The procession was headed by bands of musicians, all disguised. Negroes and *sambos** earn a *real* for taking part in this religious farce. The church dresses them up in the most fantastic garments, as Pierrots, Harlequins or Dunces and other similar characters, and provides them with unprepossessing masks in various colours to cover their faces. The forty or fifty dancers gesticulated in a rude and brazen manner, provoking the negresses and coloured girls who lined the streets and shouting obscenities at them. The girls joined in, trying to find out the identity of the mas-

* *Author's note:* A *sambo* is a half-breed of Indian and negro.

querader. It was a grotesque riot, with shouts and convulsive laughter; I turned my face away in disgust. After the dancers came the Virgin, magnificently dressed; her velvet robe was sewn with pearls; there were diamonds on her head, her neck and her hands. She was carried by twenty or thirty negroes, and behind her walked the bishop and all the clergy. Then came the monks of all the monasteries, who gather together on that day to walk in the holy procession. Last came the officials, followed by the mass of the people, laughing and shouting and anything but praying. These feast days and all the magnificence which accompanies them are the delight of the Peruvian people. It would take a very long time for their religion to become spiritualised.

That evening a mystery play was performed on the Plaza de la Merced, in the open air. I am sorry not to have been able to get hold of the text of this religious drama; to judge from the little I saw and what I was told, it must have been a good example of its kind. Doña Carmen loved any sort of spectacle, and I let her take me along with her. But it was impossible to get close to the stage. The front seats had been occupied by women of the people, who had been there since the morning. There was a struggle for any place with some sort of view. I have never witnessed such enthusiasm. With the help of the gentlemen who accompanied us, I managed to climb on to a boundary stone, and from there I could enjoy a magnificent view of the square. A sort of stage had been built under the church porch, consisting of planks resting on barrels. The scenery had been borrowed from the theatre, and was supposed to be illuminated by four or five lanterns; but the silver beams of the moon made up for the economy of the management: in Arequipa's beautiful sky, it casts a brilliant light. It was a new experience for me, a child of the nineteenth century, straight from Paris, to see a mystery play acted under a church porch, watched by a vast crowd of people; but what was interesting about the spectacle was the crowd itself, its brutality, its rough clothing, its rags, its extreme ignorance, its stupid superstitiousness, all of which made me feel that I was back in the Middle Ages. All their faces, white, black or bronze, expressed a savage ferocity, an exalted fanaticism. The mystery play was basically similar (I can say nothing of the beauties of the dialogue, since I could make out few of the words) to those of the fifteenth century that were played with much pomp in the hall of the Palais de Justice, for the edification of the good people of Paris, as described by Victor Hugo in *Notre-Dame de Paris*. With the help of a word or two which I caught, some explanations given me by local experts, and by watching the play of the actors, I got the gist of the story.

The Christians were fighting the Turks and the Saracens in the land of Islam, to bring them to the *true faith*. The Moslems defended themselves stoutly: they had the advantage of numbers. The Christians crossed themselves, but were on the point of defeat when the *Lady Virgin*, arm in arm with St Joseph and followed by a long line of Heavenly Maidens, arrived among the Christian host. This celestial vision revived the enthusiasm of the Christians: they immediately rushed towards the Moslems, shouting 'Miracle! Miracle!' The moment was well chosen, for the latter were petrified, apparently having forgotten to use their weapons. Their amazement was chiefly caused by the sight of the crowd of pretty girls of every shade, their heads girt with crowns of yellow paper, who mingled with the soldiers. The Moslems were afraid to harm this bevy of houris from paradise, and it seemed to me that the Christians rather unfairly took advantage of this to make mincemeat of them. In short, the sultan and the Saracen emperor were beaten and dishonourably stripped of their insignia of office. In this state of destitution, they opted to be Christian kings rather than dethroned monarchs, implored the mercy of the *Lady Virgin*, and were baptised along with their soldiers. I felt that the credit for this large number of conversions belonged rather to the ladies who accompanied the Virgin than to the soldiers of her Son. Anyway, the Virgin seemed delighted with this mass conversion; she spoke with great politeness to the sultan and the emperor, appointing the former Patriarch of Constantinople and the latter Archpriest of Mauretania, both retaining their temporal powers. They both swore on the crucifix, which was brought to them on a silver salver, to pay their annual tithe to the Catholic clergy throughout their vast realms, and St Peter's pence to the Pope in Rome. At a signal given by the Holy Virgin, the choir of girls sang hymns, to which the soldiers, Turks, Christians and Saracens alike, responded at the top of their voices. Then they all began to abuse the Jews, many of whom had mingled with the Moslem army with the objective of buying the spoils of the Christians. As they refused to be converted, the Christians and the new converts attacked them, stripped them of their clothes and gave them rags in exchange. These absurd scenes were warmly applauded. The singing of psalms began again, during which the emperor and the sultan were divested of their pagan robes, and the Virgin ceremoniously reclothed them in the vestments of their new offices. Then Jesus Christ entered, accompanied by St Matthew. He greeted His Mother and blessed the two mingled armies. A table was then laid, round which sat, in order of rank, Jesus Christ, the Holy Virgin, St Joseph, St Matthew, the Christian generals, the Saracen emperor and the sultan. There were thirteen places, and a Jew, who wanted a free dinner, slid furtively into the unoccupied thirteenth place. Jesus broke bread and passed the cup round to the guests, at which point the fraud was discovered. The Jew was immediately dragged from his seat and hanged (at least in effigy) by the soldiers. Meanwhile the dinner continued, and all eyes were on Jesus, who re-enacted his miracle at the wedding at Cana by changing the water into Canary wine. What really happened was that a little negro boy, hidden under the table, quite adroitly substituted a jug of wine for the jug of water. During the meal, the choir of virgins sang hymns, unaccompanied. The audience were wild with delight. They clapped, jumped with joy and shouted at the tops of their voices: 'Long live Jesus Christ! Long live the Holy Virgin! Long live our Lord Don José! Long live our master the Pope! Viva! Viva! Viva!'

It is by such methods that the superstitions of the peoples of Latin America are kept alive. The clergy may have helped the revolution along, but they have no intention of losing their power, and will preserve it for a long time to come.

Doña Carmen's love of spectacle was so great that she would have been quite ready to go that same evening to see Christ crucified (performed in Latin American countries in Holy Week), after that to the theatre to see tight-rope dancers, and then to a cock-fight. My dear cousin had looked disdainfully on the crowd in the Plaza de la Merced but had nevertheless shared the pleasure of the multitude in watching the antics of the Virgin and the soldiers, though she would never have admitted it. Aloud she called it 'stupid nonsense', and was really quite annoyed that I had witnessed it.

The Frenchmen who went with us to the show simply made fun of it, and were not otherwise affected. So far as I could see, I was the only one who came away saddened. I have always been most interested in the well-being of the societies in which I find myself, and I was really shocked at the way these people had been kept in degradation. Their happiness, I realised, had never counted in the calculations of any government. If the leaders had really wanted to create a republic, they would have sought to develop the civic virtues in even the lowest classes of the population, by educating them. But since power and not freedom is the objective of the crowd of schemers who take turns in ruling the country, they continue the methods of the despots and, to ensure the obedience of the exploited masses, are in league with the priests to keep the superstitions alive. That country had been torn by twenty years of civil war and was in a deplorable state, but it was useless to look to the ruling classes for any hope of a better future: there was only an overweening pride combined with profound ignorance, and a boastful rhetoric which would not hoodwink the simplest European sailor. There were no doubt exceptions among the Peruvians, but they did nothing but complain about the state of their country, and as soon as they could leave it they did so. True patriotism and devotion were non-existent and only some great calamity could bring about the political and moral education of the race. Maybe poverty, which increases daily, will eventually lead to the emergence of a taste for work and those social virtues which arise from it; or else perhaps Providence will provide a man of steel to lead this nation to freedom and finish the work begun by Bolivar.

Every Sunday, by ten o'clock in the morning, I had to be in full dress in the drawing-room to receive callers until three o'clock, when we dined, and then again from five until eleven o'clock at night. I have never done a more irksome task in my life. The ladies came to show off their clothes, the men because they had nothing better to do, and they all looked permanently bored. As nothing happens in the region worth talking about, conversation is always cold, stilted and monotonous. One is reduced to malicious gossip, or talk of one's health or the weather. Boredom makes people inquisitive: it was obvious that all my visitors were anxious to discover why I had come. But the fact that they themselves were careful and reserved made me keep a check on myself to an extent that I had hardly thought possible: no one found out anything about my affairs, not even my cousin, the person with whom I was most frank.

On the 28th of October, M. Viollier, a Frenchman employed in the firm of M. Le Bris, came and told me that the *Mexicain* had arrived at Islay. He was on his way there, and would be returning on the next day or the day following with M. Chabrié, who wished to come to Arequipa. Since leaving Valparaiso, I hardly dared to think about M. Chabrié. My heart was heavy with the thought of his love, which I could not return, and of the promise that he had dragged from me and that I knew I could not keep. I was too afraid to imagine the consequences; and the thought was so painful that, unable to admit to myself that Chabrié was still alive, I almost wished that he would die a tragic death so that I could weep sweet tears over him. How often at night, when sleep would not come, had I vainly tried to allay the memory! Against my will, my thoughts would return to the *Mexicain*; I saw Chabrié as he leant on the edge of my bed, talking of his hopes of happiness, describing the joys of our future life in beautiful California. I could see all these visions of love and repose in my mind's eye; they were conjured up before me by some invisible power, it seemed, to sharpen my regret, and then the conflict that had raged within me at Valparaiso began again. Personal advantage fought stubbornly against more noble considerations; a demon and an angel struggled in my soul, but the heavenly power always won.

When M. Viollier gave me the news, I blushed and trembled and then turned so pale that he could not help asking me if I was put out by it. 'Not at all,' I told him, 'I like the good captain very much. He is rather blunt in his manner, but he was so kind to me during my five months of suffering that I am sincerely attached to him.' In spite of the emotion that I could not hide, M. Viollier had no suspicion of the truth; no one, in fact, would have thought it possible that I could have had any intentions towards M. Chabrié, or that I could, on account of the goodness of his heart, have overlooked his very considerable faults of character.

I was extremely agitated during the following night and day. I prayed, because I felt my courage failing. M. Chabrié did not come next day, so I had another night and day to strengthen my resolution and prepare to receive him. On the Saturday, at about eight in the evening, as I was walking up and down my cousin's drawing-room, talking philosophy with her as was our custom, I saw Chabrié enter! He came to me, took my hands, which he pressed and kissed tenderly, while great tears rolled down his cheeks. It was fortunately so dark that my cousin, who was at the far end of the room, could see his gestures but not his tears. I took him to my own apartment, and there he was incapable of restraining his joy, and with him, joy, like sorrow, expressed itself in tears. He sat beside me, pressed my hands, hid his head in my lap, caressed my hair and said in loving tones which cut me to the quick:

'Oh, my Flora, my dear Flora! At last we meet again! Oh God! how I longed to see you! My darling, speak to me, I want to hear your voice. Tell me that you love me, that it is not all a dream. Oh! Tell me, let me hear it! I can bear it no longer . . .' I was unable to breathe. My bosom seemed to be bound by an iron chain. I pressed his head against me, but could find no words to say. We remained like this for a long time, bound in silent contemplation. Chabrié was the first to break the silence. He said: 'But Flora, you are not weeping.'

At this, I realised that Chabrié could never understand the depth of my feelings, for my expression proved my love more eloquently than any tears. He loved me as much as he was capable of love, but alas! how far was his soul from mine. I sighed sorrowfully and thought with bitterness that I had never been allowed to meet on earth one whose affection was in sympathy with what I felt I could give in exchange.

Our conversation was short, for M. Viollier arrived to fetch Chabrié, who stayed with M. Le Bris for the six days which he spent in Arequipa. They left me, for they were extremely weary, having made the journey at high speed. M. Miota and Fernando, who had been unable to keep up with them, were still at Congata. The next day was Sunday, and I had no chance of talking with Chabrié; there were people around me until midnight. On the Monday he called, and I let him tell me the plans he had made, which were the same as at Valparaiso. In addition, he wanted me to marry him immediately, so that it would be evident to all that he was marrying me *for love,* since it would be before any hopes materialised through my uncle. I had not foreseen this new requirement, which increased my embarrassment; I did not know what to say, and was driven mad with the worry of it.

That night, not wishing to be alone with him, I took him to a house where they were having a musical evening: he sang, to please me, but his ill humour was such that everyone noticed it. On Tuesday, he reproached me bitterly for having wasted an evening in this way, when we had hardly enough time to settle our own affairs. The *Mexicain* was running up costs of 110 to 120 francs a day, of which Chabrié had to pay a third. M. David wrote letter after letter, asking me to send Chabrié back immediately, but the latter told me point blank that he would not leave until we were married.

In all my life I had never found myself in such a painful position as Chabrié's obstinacy now put me in. I gave him all the reasons I could think of to make him see sense; he answered them all with the perpetual refrain: 'If you love me, prove it; if you are happy about our proposed union, why delay it? I must now leave you again; my profession exposes me to mortal danger at any time, and perhaps I shall never see you again. Why then not take this opportunity while we are still alive to enjoy it?'

Of course I exerted all the influence I had over Chabrié to persuade him that it was important for our own interests, for our happiness, that before the marriage took place, he should finish his business and I should finish mine. But some demon had taken possession of him, and my words, my prayers and my strongest arguments were without success. He had been cruelly betrayed on more than one occasion, and this had made him suspicious; in addition, jealousy deprived him of the faculty of reason.

I spent Wednesday night in the most painful perplexity. It was not that I hesitated as to whether to sacrifice my affection for him to his happiness, but I was embarrassed and anxious as to what reason I would give him for refusing to marry him. I was firmly convinced that if I told him the truth he would seize on it eagerly, and would see it as an extra reason for a hurried marriage, so as to protect me and give me the security I so much needed. I had thought differently on board ship: I had believed that if I had told him that I was married, he would leave me alone, and this might have been so at that time. Since then, his love had become an obsession which dominated his whole being. Chabrié respected convention, since in order to defy it, he had suggested that we should live out of France. He was a strict observer of the law in anything connected with property, but believed that whilst it was the province of laws to regulate possessions, they had no jurisdiction over matters of the heart. Far away from his own country, he would, I am convinced, have been willing to flout this tyranny. If on the other hand I was wrong about this, if my married state were an obstacle that he dared not overcome, then I could not admit it without compromising a secret that it was important for me should not be divulged: for his indignation against me for having made him believe that I was unmarried would have known no limits, and of this I later had proof.

I now realised that if I accepted Chabrié's love I would

be condemning him to misery and eternal regret at having abandoned his country and his family to bury himself with me on the coast of California, and this revived my courage and made me puzzle out a way to alienate him from me permanently. Knowing that he was a man of integrity and strict honesty, I decided to make this my point of attack. God must have helped me carry out a plan which was beyond human capabilities; in my efforts to make Chabrié abandon his love for me, I ran the risk of also losing his esteem, which – together with his love – had been for the last eight months my only, and much valued, consolation. Well, I had the courage to take this risk! God alone knew the extent of my sacrifice.

On Thursday evening, Chabrié arrived, full of eagerness. I had promised him the night before that I would give him a definite reply on the morrow. 'What is your decision?' he said as he came in, with the excitement of a man who impatiently waits to hear his fate.

'My decision, M. Chabrié, is as follows: if you love me as much as you say, prove it by doing something for me that I shall now explain to you. You know that my baptismal certificate is insufficient to establish my legitimacy; I need another document which certifies my mother and father's marriage. If I cannot produce it, I can expect not one penny, for my uncle will give me nothing. Well, you can give me a million. Find out some old missionary in California who will make out this marriage certificate, pre-dating it, and for a hundred piastres we shall have a million. That is the condition on which my love and my hand in marriage depend.'

The poor man was stunned; his elbows on the table, he stared at me without saying a word and with the look of an innocent man who has just heard himself condemned to death. I walked up and down the room, avoiding his eyes, considerably distressed at the deep suffering I was causing in someone of whom I was very fond. Then he said in a tone of profound indignation:

'So, when I want to marry you as a woman without fortune and in your present situation with a child; when I am prepared to sacrifice everything, *but everything*, you, you make conditions! And what conditions!'

'But M. Chabrié, do you hesitate?'

'Hesitate? Why no, mademoiselle; whilst this old heart beats in my breast, I shall never hesitate between honour and dishonour.'

'But how is my proposal dishonourable, since I am asking you to help me to get what belongs to me in all justice?'

'I cannot judge of your rights. But you want me to be your tool, you wish to use me for your ambition. This is how you respond to my love.'

'If you loved me, M. Chabrié, you would not hesitate a moment to do me the service that I ask of you, and yet you refuse.'

'But Flora, my dear Flora, are you in your right mind? Has a fever affected your brain? Has ambition turned your head? You want me to carry out a dishonourable act? Ah, Flora, I love you enough to sacrifice my life to you: with you, I would suffer poverty without complaining, but do not ask me to debase myself, for, by the love I bear you, that I will never do.'

His response was what I had expected. With such a man, I could have lived in a desert and enjoyed moments of great happiness. What delicacy! What love! I felt my resolution weaken once more, but made a final effort and, adopting an ironical, harsh tone of voice, I continued speaking in a way calculated to hurt his pride even further. He became so exasperated that he showered me with bitter reproaches and frightful curses, losing all restraint in the grief caused by this final disappointment to such an extent that at one moment I thought he would attack me physically. At last he left me, and I collapsed exhausted. That was the last time I ever saw him. His last words as he went were: 'I hate you now as much as I loved you before.'

It had become so urgent to stop Chabrié from pursuing me, to terminate his love for me, that, finding no alternative, I made him my strange proposal without realising that it was really too far-fetched for Chabrié to be likely to take it seriously. Since then I have wondered how he could believe me to have been so silly as really to think that I could regularise my mother's marriage by means of a document forged in California. If I had been capable of resorting to forgery, would I not have thought of it in Europe rather than at Arequipa? Would it have been feasible at all? How could one hope to find on the Californian coast a priest who had once officiated at a church in one of the towns near the Spanish frontier where my mother had lived before her marriage? How could one hope to legalise the document, stamp it and so forth? Only in Spain would there have been any chance of succeeding in such a project. If Chabrié had been cool-headed enough to give the matter ten minutes' thought, he would have easily realised that it was only a trick, a pretext for breaking with him. But he was so violently agitated that he had banished reason completely. My proposal hurt his pride very deeply, which was why he kept on repeating: 'You make conditions! To me, Chabrié! No one has ever made conditions to me. You want me to be a tool, to serve your ambition. When I want to marry you without a penny to your name, and after giving you so many proofs of my devotion, it turns out that you only love me for your own advantage.' The thought that I had made a fool of him, as several other women had done, maddened him; he was filled with jealousy and pride, and he was carried away by grief. Thus, when we are stirred by any passion, we can be made fools of, not only by others, but by ourselves.

He left next day for Islay. He had uprooted his love of me from his heart; he could now make a marriage of convenience, perhaps be happy, for, warm-hearted as he was, it might well be enough to have a home and children for his contentment. I felt great relief when I knew for certain that a man of whom I was really fond was no longer tied to my cruel fate. I had asked him to take an interest in my daughter, and was sure that he would look after her if I happened to die, and this conviction was a great comfort to me. Oh, it is not surprising that there are few virtuous people! I again felt how, in such circumstances, superhuman strength is needed for one to be virtuous!

The letters I wrote to Chabrié after our rupture were designed to keep him thinking along the same lines. Six weeks after leaving Arequipa, he left Lima for California, after which I had no news of him until he returned to France, three months after my arrival there.

The origin of the town of Arequipa is uncertain. However, there is in Cuzco a chronicle of Indian traditions, which states that in about the twelfth century of our era, Maita Capae, ruler of the City of the Sun, was overthrown. He escaped his enemies and wandered through forests and over the frozen tops of mountains with a small band of followers. On the fourth day, half dead of hunger and thirst, he stopped at the foot of the volcano. Suddenly, under divine inspiration, he planted his spear in the earth, and said: 'Arequipa!', which means in Quechua, 'Here I stop!'; then, turning round, he saw that only five of his companions had followed him there. But the Inca trusted in the voice of God and kept to his word. Round the planted spear, on the slopes of the volcano surrounded on all sides by desert, the men built their houses. Like all conquerors and founders of empires, Maita was only the blind instrument of the secret purposes of Providence. Some of the cities which have developed on this earth have, like the men who have lived in them, owed their greatness to their own merit; but others owe it to chance causes which seem to have little basis in reason.

Although Arequipa is on 16°13′2″ of southern latitude, its height above sea level and the fact that it is surrounded by mountains give it a temperate climate. The town stands in the middle of a diminutive valley of exquisite beauty; the valley is not more than three miles wide by six long. It is rimmed on all sides by high mountains and watered by the River Chile, whose source is at the foot of the volcano. As it runs the river makes a sound like a Pyrenean torrent; its bed is unusual, very wide in places and narrow in others; strewn with large boulders or pebbles, it is nevertheless composed of soft, level sand, pleasant to walk on. A torrent after the rainy season, it nearly always dries up in summer. The valley is cultivated, growing wheat, maize, barley, alfalfa (a kind of lucerne) and vegetables. There are few country houses. The Peruvians are too busy with all their intrigues to care for country life.

THE CITY AND VALLEY OF AREQUIPA

THE GREAT SQUARE AND CATHEDRAL AT AREQUIPA

The city occupies a large area of the valley. From the heights of Tiavalla, it looks even larger: seen from there, it seems that there is only a small strip of land between the town and the mountains. The great huddle of white houses, the multitude of domed roofs gleaming in the sunshine, surrounded by the valley with its various shades of green and the grey mountains, are a sight which impresses the spectator as quite unearthly. The traveller who looks on Arequipa for the first time is tempted to imagine that it must be inhabited by mysterious people of another kind, and that the volcano whose gigantic height amazes the senses must be protecting them, or at least means them no harm.

The volcano of Arequipa is one of the highest mountains of the Andean chain; it stands quite alone, shaped like a perfect cone. It is uniformly grey, which gives it a sombre look. The summit is almost always covered in snow, which varies in depth and decreases in extent during the daytime. Sometimes smoke rises from the crater, particularly towards evening; I often saw flames in the smoke. When no smoke rises for some time, an earthquake is expected. Almost always there are clouds on the summit, which seem to cut it off; layers of variegated clouds are clearly visible. This vaporous mass in many shades, crowning a cone-shaped mountain of one single colour, reminds one of a giant hiding his sinister head in the clouds, and is one of the most magnificent sights that the world has to offer.

My cousin Althaus had climbed this volcano and descended its crater as far down as the third chimney. He kept very interesting notes and drawings on the expedition, which I do not, alas, possess or I would pass them on to the reader. He took with him ten Indians armed with climbing irons. Only five were strong enough to go with him all the way: three gave up, and two were killed in falls. It took three days to reach the top, and they could only stay there a few hours owing to the intense cold. Coming down was much more difficult than going up. They were all badly injured, and Althaus narrowly escaped death. 'The volcano' (as it is always called, having apparently no other name) is twelve thousand feet above sea level. The two nearest mountains, visible one on its left and one on its right, are a long way off and even higher; their summits are covered in eternal snows which glisten in the sunshine. The first is called Pichaimpichu, the second Chachaur. The great height of these three isolated peaks, whose bases are themselves very high above the *pampa*, makes them look from this angle as if they were the triple peaks of one mountain.

At the time of the conquest, Francisco Pizarro established a bishopric and a centre of government at Arequipa. Earthquakes have repeatedly caused terrible disasters: in 1582 and 1600 the town was almost entirely destroyed by them, and those of 1687 and 1785 were hardly less severe. The streets are broad, set at right angles and quite well paved. A stream runs down the middle of each. The main streets have pavements of white slabs.* The streets are well lit, because each householder is obliged, on pain of a fine, to hang a lantern at his door. The main square is large; the cathedral takes up the north side, and the town hall and prison are opposite. Private houses occupy the other two sides. Except for the cathedral, all these buildings have arcades, under which there is an assortment of shops. This square is used for markets, feast days and military parades, etc. The bridge over the River Chile is roughly constructed, and hardly strong enough to resist the torrent that rages through it at certain seasons.

There are a large number of convents and monasteries, all of which have fine churches. The cathedral is enormous, but dark, gloomy and heavy in style. The churches of Santa Rosa, Santa Catalina and San Francisco have the most beautiful domes, of a great height. In all the churches there are grotesque statues in wood or plaster, representing the idols of Peruvian Catholicism; coarsely executed oil paintings give a comic image of the saints they portray. The Jesuits' church is an exception in this respect: the saints whose images are offered to the worshippers are more appropriate. Before independence, all

* *Author's note:* When Don Pio was prefect, he made a number of new pavements and repaired old ones. Under his administration the town was kept very clean. My uncle paid particular attention to matters of public health.

these churches were richly decorated with candlesticks, balustrades, altar columns in solid silver, and other ornaments in gold; both metals were displayed with more profusion than taste. But faith no longer provides security for all this wealth; already a number of presidents and party leaders, having exhausted the public treasury in their strife, have unscrupulously robbed the churches. The altar fronts, columns and chandeliers have been melted down to pay the soldiery and to enable the generals to pursue their vices. Those precious ornaments which have been respected are likely to go the same way in the end; during the latest war between Orbegoso and Bermudez, there was some question of removing the pearls, diamonds and other precious stones from the statues of the Virgin.

Arequipa has one hospital for the sick, one for lunatics and a third for foundlings. All three are rather badly run. I shall speak later about my visit to the first; I also went to the foundling hospital, and was no less dissatisfied with the treatment given to the children than I was with that given to the sick: it was pitiful to see those poor little creatures naked, thin, in a deplorable state. It is felt that charitable duty has been fulfilled if they are given enough food to support their wretched existence. Apart from that, they are given no education, nor are they taught any trade; so those who survive become vagabonds, an inevitable result of this culpable neglect. The contrivance used to bring those unfortunates into the institution seemed to me quite ingenious: the baby is placed in an opening in the outer wall so no one inside the hospital can see who puts it there; this allows the unfortunate mother to abandon her child without the obligation of revealing herself. It is this lack of responsibility which has been the cause of so many crimes.

The houses in Arequipa are very solidly built in fine white stone, and are of one storey only, with vaulted ceilings because of the earthquakes. Most of them are spacious and convenient. There is a large carriage gateway in the middle of the façade. All the windows are barred and unglazed. The houses are built round three courtyards: the drawing-room, the bedrooms and the study are round the first. The second is a garden, and round it are the dining-room, which is in an open gallery as the climate requires, the chapel, the laundry and various offices. The third courtyard, at the back, is occupied by the kitchen and the slave quarters. The walls are five to six feet thick; the rooms, although vaulted, are very high; sometimes they are papered half way up; mostly they are quite bare and whitewashed. Because of the vaulted ceilings the rooms resemble cellars, and the monotony of the white walls is tiresome and depressing. The furniture is massive; the beds and chests of drawers gigantic, the chairs and tables heavy; everything seems to have been made to stay put. The mirrors are made of metal; the curtains are tasteless. English carpets have for some years been available so cheaply that everyone has covered their floor tiles with them; floor boards are never used.

The Arequipans love eating, but are incapable of providing themselves with the delights of the table. Their cooking is vile; the materials are poor, and the culinary art is still in a barbarian state. The valley of Arequipa is very fertile; nevertheless the vegetables it produces are inferior: the potatoes are floury; cabbages, salads and peas are tough and tasteless; the red meat is dry, and even the poultry is so unyielding that it seems to be under volcanic influence. The butter and cheese come from a long distance away and never arrive fresh; neither do the fruit or the fish, which come from the coast. The oil used is rancid and unrefined, the sugar is coarse, the bread ill-baked – in short, nothing is good.

Their meals are as follows: breakfast is at nine, and consists of rice with onions (they serve onions, cooked or raw, with everything) and roast mutton, so bad that I could never eat any; then comes the hot chocolate. Dinner is at three o'clock. They first serve an *olla podrida* (called *puchero* in Peru), which is a hotch-potch of unrelated foods – beef, bacon, mutton, all boiled with rice, seven or eight different vegetables, together with any fruit they happen to have, such as apples, pears, peaches, plums, grapes, etc; no choir of voices singing out of tune or concert of discordant instruments is more revolting than the sight, smell and taste of this barbaric mixture. This is followed by crayfish, served with tomatoes, rice, raw onions and pimento; meat with grapes, peaches and sugar; fish with pimento; salad with raw onions, eggs and pimento: the latter ingredient is used in profusion in all their dishes, together with a number of other spices – it burns one's mouth; to be able to bear it, the palate must lose its sensitivity. Water is the normal drink. Supper is at eight, and the dishes are the same as those at dinner.

The service and the table-manners are as lacking in propriety as is the cooking in harmony. Even today, in many houses, there is only *one glass* for all the guests. The plates and cutlery are dirty; this cannot entirely be blamed on the dirtiness of the slaves, for the slaves of the English are perfectly clean. It is polite to pass round on the end of a fork a piece of food from one's plate, to any one of the guests whom one wishes to honour. The Europeans find this custom so shocking that it has now fallen into disuse; but it was only a few years ago that pieces of *olla*, fish, and chicken wings dripping gravy used to circulate round the table, carried by slaves on the end of forks.

As everything is very expensive, dinner parties are fairly rare, and *soirées* largely took their place as soon as the custom was introduced. Every Sunday at my uncle's house there was a family dinner to which intimate friends were also invited, and in the evening tea, chocolate and cakes were served. The only things that I found to be good in Arequipa were the cakes and sweetmeats made by the nuns. Thanks to my many acquaintances, I was never without them during my stay, and this allowed me to enjoy delicious little snacks between meals.

The Arequipans love all sorts of public performances; they flock with equal zeal to theatre or church. Their complete lack of education creates this need and makes them an audience easy to please. The theatre is built of wood, and so badly that it is not rainproof. It is too small for the population, and seats are often unavailable. The standard of acting is very low; there are some seven or eight actors, rejects from Spanish theatres, plus two or three locally recruited Indians. They put on all sorts of plays, comedy, tragedy and opera; Lope de Vega and Calderón are murdered, and the music is excruciating, yet the public applaud. I went four or five times, and saw tragedies performed. I noticed that instead of cloaks the actors draped old silk shawls round themselves. Cock-fights, tightrope walkers, Indian strong men – all attract crowds. A French acrobat in a double turn with his wife made thirty thousand piastres in Peru.

The Peruvian church exploits this love of show in the population in order to maintain its influence. Apart from the great processions of the main feast days, no month goes by without some parading through the streets of Arequipa. One day it will be the Greyfriars with a procession 'for the dead', during which they beg money 'for the dead'; another day, the Dominicans come out on the streets in honour of the Virgin Mary; or there'll be one in honour of the Child Jesus. Then there are all the saints – it's a never-ending list. I have already described a procession on a main feast day; I shall not weary the reader by describing those on the saints' days; there is less luxury and pomp, but basically they are just as farcical; the indecent fooling, which the people love so much, is just as scandalous. And all these processions have one thing in common: the monks ask for money and the people give. But it is in Holy Week that the Peruvian Catholics hold their greatest saturnalia. In all the churches of Arequipa, earth and stones are heaped up and branches of olive are planted in the heap to imitate Calvary with its rocks and trees. On this artificial mountain they act out the story of the Passion. Jesus is arrested, flagellated and crucified with the two robbers. The whole story is acted out, from beginning to end, accompanied by chants and responses. When Christ is dead, the candles are snuffed out and darkness reigns: the loose morals of the crowd packed into the churches suggest what may go on at this moment; but God is merciful and the friars, God's ministers, are able to grant absolution. The Descent from the Cross is the second tableau: a mixed crowd of men and women, whites, Indians and negroes, besiege the Calvary with wailing cries; they have soon uprooted the trees and picked up the rocks; they drive away the soldiers, seize the Cross and remove the body. Blood flows from this cardboard Christ, and the howls of the crowd rise to a new pitch. The crowd, the priests, the Cross, the olive branches, all tumbled together pell-mell, create a tumult, a frightful confusion that one would never expect to encounter in any temple of any religion; and, in the disorder, people are always injured, more or less seriously.

In the evening, people can be seen on their way to carry out their religious duties in all the churches: as they go, they pray aloud. The most zealous kneel down and kiss the earth; some beat their breasts; some walk barefoot carrying a cross on their backs; yet others put paving stones on their heads, and everywhere extravagant practices show what superstitious piety can suggest to fanatic minds. They never look to their consciences to tell them where their duty lies, but always to the magic element in their creed. Such is the result of isolating faith from charity.

On Easter day, visits are paid to all one's friends. The festivities of Holy Week are the only subject of conversation, and can be summarised as follows: 'Well, *mi señora,* did you have a good time? Was it not splendid at Santo Domingo and Santa Rosa? Oh, how I enjoyed it!' – 'In my opinion, señor, it was nowhere as good as in previous years; religion is losing its splendour. It wasn't fun at all in the cathedral. At Santa Catalina, they didn't do the Descent from the Cross; and I got bored watching all those *sambos* fighting for a piece; it really isn't worth the trouble attending all the services.' – '*Mi señora,* the good days are over, our churches are not as rich as they were. The ladies of Santa Catalina spend their money buying pianos imported from France, instead of putting on a Descent from the Cross.'

On Sunday at mass, the men all stand, chat and laugh together, or watch the pretty women kneeling in front of them, half hidden in their mantillas. The women themselves are very inattentive and never carry a prayerbook. They either examine their neighbours' clothes or chat with their negresses who sit behind them. One sometimes sees them lying listlessly on their rug, sleeping or chatting together.

The friars who say mass are always dirtily dressed, and the poor Indian servers are bare-footed and half dressed. In all the churches the music is quite awful. Two violins and a kind of bagpipe accompany the organ. All these instruments are so discordant, and the singing so out of tune and out of time, that it is impossible to listen for a quarter of an hour without one's nerves being on edge for the rest of the day. In Europe, the fine arts at least cover the insipid sterility of the church services with a brilliant gloss. But in any case, the Peruvian churches are really only used as meeting-places.

The degree of civilisation reached by a culture is everywhere revealed. Thus the celebrations of Carnival in Arequipa have no more decency than the farce and foolery of Holy Week. There are people who spend the whole year emptying egg-shells, which they fill with coloured liquid – pink, blue, green, red – and then close the hole with wax. These they sell. The ladies take a basketful of these eggs, and, dressed in white, sit on the domed roofs of their houses and amuse themselves by throwing the eggs at the passers-by. The latter, either on foot or on horseback, always have a provision of the same projectiles and reply in kind. But to improve the game even further, the eggs can also be filled with *ink, honey* or *oil*, and sometimes with the most disgusting things. A number of people have had an eye put out by this new form of combat: several were pointed out to me, yet in spite of it the Arequipans remain quite addicted to the game. The girls show off the stains on their dresses and seem quite proud of those strange marks of gallantry. The slaves also take part: they throw flour at each other, which is cheaper, so many other people do it too. The negresses with their woolly hair look quite hideous when daubed with flour. In the evenings there are balls at which some of the dances are quite indecent. Many of the guests wear extraordinary disguises; but there are no true fancy dresses. These amusements last a whole week.

There is a great contrast between these disgusting eggs and the Roman custom of throwing down sugared almonds on the passers-by. There is a similar contrast between the farces held in the churches in Arequipa during Holy Week – with their uncouth music, the pathetic daubs and barbaric ornaments with which they are decorated – and the majestic ceremonial, the exquisite music and the mag-

THE BATTLE OF THE EGGS DURING HOLY WEEK IN AREQUIPA

LADIES OF AREQUIPA, ONE IN FULL DRESS, THE OTHER DRESSED FOR CHURCH, ACCOMPANIED BY HER CARPET-BEARER

nificent artistic productions – all the brilliant and poetic marvels with which Rome still bolsters up its decrepit religion.

The population of Arequipa with its surrounding area is between thirty and forty thousand souls; about a quarter are white, a quarter black or half-breed, and half are Indian. As everywhere in America, European origin gives a title of nobility. In the upper classes, the word white is applied to those whose ancestors are not Indian or negro. I saw a number of ladies who passed for white, though their skin was gingerbread colour because their fathers were born in Andalusia or the kingdom of Valencia.* The non-slave population therefore consists of three classes, each from quite different races: European, Indian and negro. In the latter class are included, under the name of 'coloured people', all those of mixed race. As for the slaves, of whatever racial origin, their lack of liberty makes them all equal in misfortune.

During the last four or five years there have been great changes in the customs and habits of the Peruvians. Paris fashions now rule supreme: there are only a few rich and ancient families which remain rebellious, like old trees whose sap is drying up, but which still persist, like the dungeons of the Inquisition, as witnesses of how far things have changed. The dress of the upper classes is no different from that of Europe; both men and women dress like Parisians; the women follow the fashions with the most scrupulous care, except that they go hatless and that in church custom still demands that they dress in black, wearing the mantilla, with all the severity of Spanish costume. French dances are replacing the fandango, the bolero and those national dances which are now considered indecent. Arias from our operas are sung in Peruvian drawing-rooms – and they have even started reading novels; the time will come when they will only go to mass when there's good music to listen to. The well-to-do spend their time smoking, reading the newspapers and playing faro. The men ruin themselves by gambling and the women by spending all their money on clothes.

* *Translator's note:* Valencia was a kingdom under the Moors.

The Arequipans in general have plenty of natural wit, great facility of expression, good memories, much gaiety, and aristocratic manners; they are easy to get on with, but born intriguers. The women, both here and in Lima, seemed to me far superior to the men; but the women of Arequipa are not as pretty as those in Lima. Their customs and their characters are also different. Their proud, dignified bearing is imposing, and the first impression is that they are cold and contemptuous; but when one gets to know them, one learns to appreciate their subtlety of mind and delicacy of feeling, which are further enhanced by their grave exterior. They are sedentary, industrious, quite unlike the ladies of Lima, who are continually away from home seeking pleasure or intrigue. The ladies of Arequipa make their own clothes, with a perfection that would surprise our fashion houses. They dance with grace and decency, love music and play it well. I met four or five of them whose fresh, sweet voices would be admired in the salons of Paris.

The climate of Arequipa is not healthy. Dysentery, headaches, nervous complaints and especially colds are very frequent. The inhabitants also have the habit of always believing themselves to be unwell, and they give this as a pretext for continual travel. The requirements of their imagination, combined with their lack of education, explain this passion for change. It is only by moving around that they can renew their thoughts, find new ideas, experience new emotions. The ladies especially go to and from the coastal townships such as Islay, Camara and Arica, where they take sea baths and partake of the mineral waters. There are several such springs near Arequipa, whose properties are renowned: at Ura, the waters are miraculously effective; they are green and burning hot. The resorts both on the coast and inland where the upper classes go for bathing are quite extraordinarily dirty and inconvenient, yet are much patronised: people will spend a great deal of money on a stay of three weeks or a month.

The ladies of Arequipa keenly embrace any opportunity for travel in any direction, to Bolivia, Cuzco, Lima, Chile; they are deterred neither by expense nor the great hardships involved. I imagine it is this love of travel that makes girls prefer foreigners. By marrying a foreigner, they have a chance of visiting his country of origin, be it France, England or Italy. They hope to fulfil a long-cherished dream, and this lends a charm to marriages which they would otherwise often conspicuously lack. The thought of travel has made the French language fashionable amongst these ladies; many learn it in the hope of being able to use it one day; meanwhile they enjoy reading some of our good books, and thus by developing their lively minds they are able to support the monotonous life of their country with less boredom. All the educated men also speak French.

The Pantheon, a fine newly constructed cemetery, is some six miles from the town, on the side of a hill, facing the volcano; it covers a very large area. From a distance, its high, white, crenellated walls give the strangest and most mournful impression. In the upper part of these walls, there are three rows of niches into which the coffins are placed and sealed with a stone. On these, the relatives of the deceased affix inscriptions in which vanity rubs shoulders with death: on marble or bronze plaques and in letters of gold, one may read: 'Here lies the distinguished Field Marshal, the famous General, the Venerable Priest . . .' Other, simpler, epitaphs enumerate the virtues of the defunct. In all the cemeteries of the world there are only good fathers, beloved husbands, loving mothers, etc., for in the grief of the moment we exaggerate the virtues that we have failed to appreciate during the lifetime of the deceased. For the poor there is a common grave, sealed in the same manner when it is full. The bodies of Protestants are not allowed to lie in the churches; some people object to this, and buy from the convents, for considerable sums, a place in their churches. This was how my grandmother had her grave in Santo Domingo. With money, it is fairly easy to get round the civil and religious laws in this country; and the latter are the cheaper of the two.

At Arequipa, death of the well-to-do benefits not only the heirs; in addition, the friars are able to sell for a high price their grey, black, white or carmelite brown habits. It is the custom, and considered proper, to be buried in a monk's habit; this is why these holy men almost always wear new ones, which contrast with the dirtiness of the rest of their costume. As soon as anyone dies, he or she is clothed in one of these male religious garments; the corpse lies on its bed, so garbed and with face uncovered, for three days, whilst the visits of condolence are made. The relatives, including the most distant ones, 'keep the mourning', that is, they remain in the room to receive the visitors. The latter, both men and women, are also dressed in mourning; as they enter, they make a solemn salutation to the relatives, who are on a dais, then go and sit in a corner or kneel in prayer. The body is carried to the church, and also after the ceremony it is carried out of the town; it is then taken by tip-cart to the cemetery.

There are no carriages in Arequipa. Previously, important people were carried in sedan chairs. There was one at my uncle's, which was used by my grandmother, and which he used himself when he was ill. It was like the ones used in France before the revolution. Everyone travels by horse or by mule. Donkeys are only used to carry loads in the mountains. The Indians use llamas for this purpose.

The llama is the beast of burden of the Andes; all transport is by means of this animal, and the Indian uses it to trade with the valleys. This graceful animal is a most interesting study. It is the only domestic animal that man has not succeeded in debasing. The llama does not accept beating or ill-usage; it is willing to be useful, but only if it is *asked* and not *ordered*. These animals are always in herds, of varying sizes and led by Indians who walk well ahead of them. If the herd feels tired, it stops, and the Indian stops also. If the stop is too long, and the Indian, seeing the sun near setting, becomes anxious, he decides, after taking all sorts of precautions, to request his beasts to set off again. He stands some fifty or sixty yards off, adopts a humble posture, makes an affectionate gesture with his hand, looks at them tenderly, calling out to them at the same time in a gentle voice and with a patience that I always admired: 'ic-ic-ic-ic-ic-ic.' If the llamas feel inclined to resume their journey, they follow the Indian in an orderly manner, steadily and fast, since they have very long legs; but when they are ill-humoured, they do not even turn their heads towards the man who is calling them so lovingly and patiently. They remain still, huddled close to one another, some standing and some lying, gazing at the sky so tenderly, so mournfully, that one wonders if these beasts have a knowledge of the afterlife, a better world. Their long necks, which they carry with such grace and majesty, the long silky wool of their coats, always so clean and glossy, their supple shy movements, all combine to give them an appearance of nobility and sensitivity which commands respect. Respect they certainly deserve, for the llama is the only beast in man's service that he dares not strike. If it happens (and it very rarely does) that an Indian loses his temper and tries by force or threats to get the llama to do what it does not want to do, then as soon as the animal hears the rough words or sees the rough gestures, it raises its head with dignity, and without attempting to escape from the rough treatment (the llama is never tied up or hobbled), it lies down, and looks up towards the sky; great tears run down from its beautiful eyes, it sighs deeply, and in half to three quarters of an hour it is dead. Fortunate creatures, who can escape so easily from suffering by dying! Fortunate creatures, who seem to have accepted life only on condition that it is pleasant! These animals are of great commercial importance, since they are the only means of communication with the mountain Indians; but it is evident that the almost superstitious reverence in which they are held is not due only to their utility. I have often seen thirty or forty of them blocking the way in one of the busiest streets of the town: the pedestrians would look at them cautiously and turn back. One day a score of them came into the courtyard of our house, and stayed there for *six hours*; the Indian was in despair; our slaves could not do their work; no matter, they put up with the inconvenience without giving as much as an angry glance. Even children, who respect nothing, *dare not touch llamas*. When the Indians wish to load them, two together come close to the animal and hide its head, so that it cannot see that a burden is being placed on its back; if it saw it, it would fall dead; the same procedure has to be followed for unloading. If the weight of the load were to exceed a certain amount, the animal would immediately lie down and die. These beasts are very abstemious: a handful of maize lasts them for three or four days. Yet they are very strong, climb mountains with great agility, withstand the cold and snow and all sorts of hardship. They live a long time; an Indian told me that he had had one that lived thirty-four years. No one in the world but the Andean Indian would have enough patience or enough gentleness to make use of the llama. It is undoubtedly from that extraordinary companion that Providence has given to the Peruvian Indian, that he has learned to die whenever more is demanded of him than he is willing to give. The moral courage which allows us to escape from oppression by death, so rare in our species, is very common amongst the Peruvian Indians, as I shall often have the opportunity to point out.

As you must have realised by now, life in Arequipa is boring in the extreme. It was especially so for me, as I am a constantly active person; I could not get used to this monotony. It was only at M. Le Bris's house that I found some amusement. All the gentlemen of his firm showed an affectionate interest in me and did their best to please. Whenever a foreigner arrived at Arequipa, M. Viollier would come and tell me, describe the man and ask me if I wanted to meet him. I would accept or refuse, according to whether he sounded interesting or not.

One of my cousins by marriage arrived from Lima: the most unusual man I have met in my life, and whose name I have already mentioned, M. d'Althaus. We were friends from the moment we met. Althaus is a German, but speaks perfect French, having spent much of his life in France, and from the moment he arrived my life was full. He had fought in wars from the age of seventeen; he had served as an officer of engineers in both the French army and the armies of the allies. In his eyes, the profession of arms was the most important, the one to which all others should be subordinated. He was a soldier because he enjoyed it, and was interested in the science of war, though indifferent to the cause for which he fought.

After 1815, he remained in the German service; he had a very high rank, and good pay, and could have led a gay life in all the garrison towns. But his love of war would not let him enjoy a life of ease; he needed the opportunity to practise his profession, he needed the reality of battle, the thrill of suspense between success and failure, the joy of victory or the salutary lessons of defeat. He resigned his commission, left his family by whom he was much loved, and like a true adventurer came to Peru to try his luck in the wars. He had now been in Peru fourteen years. He had fought in all the battles without ever having been wounded. In 1825 he came to Arequipa with Bolivar, and went to stay with my uncle Pio, whom he already knew well. He there met my cousin Manuela de Florez, the daughter of a sister of my father's, fell in love with her, was loved in return by the girl, and, after some slight opposition from my uncle, who was her guardian (she being an orphan), finally obtained her hand. Althaus married my cousin in 1826. By the time I came to Peru, they had three children, two sons and a daughter. Althaus had all the honourable qualities that a man can have; these stemmed from his nature and from his education. He also had defects which seemed to be irreconcilable with his virtues, and which were no doubt due to the long exercise of his profession.

From Camana, my uncle had gone to Islay for the sea bathing. I realised that he was deliberately putting off his return to Arequipa under various pretexts, in order to make it obvious that he was not afraid of me. I had been in his house for three months waiting for him. Finally he announced his departure from Islay, and invited me to come and meet him at his country house, where he intended to stop en route. So I was at last going to see the uncle on whom all my hopes now rested, the man who owed everything to my father, his education, his promotion and finally his worldly success! What welcome would he give me? How should I feel when I saw him? At this thought my heart would beat violently: in my youth I had so loved this uncle, that I saw him in my imagination as a second father. I had suffered so much when my mother had said: 'Your uncle Pio has deserted you,' that I could never think of him without great emotion.

On the 3rd of January, at about four in the afternoon, I rode out accompanied by my dear cousin Emmanuel, Althaus and good M. Viollier, my three best friends, and followed by a crowd of other people who came rather to satisfy their curiosity than through any interest in me or respect for Don Pio de Tristan. We headed towards the beautiful country house that my uncle always referred to as his *chacra** which is situated some four and a half miles from the town. As we approached the buildings, Emmanuel and Althaus went ahead to announce my arrival. A little later, I saw a horseman galloping towards me. I exclaimed: 'Here is my uncle!' I urged my horse forward and in a moment I was beside him. What I felt at that moment I find difficult to express in words. I took his hand, pressed it lovingly and said: 'Oh, uncle, how much I need your affection!'

'My daughter, it is entirely yours. I love you like my own child. You are also a sister to me, because your father was like a father to me. Ah, my dear niece, how happy I am to see you, and to look on a face which recalls so faithfully that of my poor brother. It is my brother himself, my dear Mariano, in the person of Florita.' He drew me to him, and I leant my head against his breast, at the risk of falling off my horse, and remained there for some time. When I raised my head, tears were rolling down my cheeks. Were they tears of joy, of sorrow or of memories? I know not. My emotions were too strong and too confused for me to be sure of the cause. I wiped my eyes, tried to calm myself and went forward with my uncle in silence. When I entered the courtyard, my aunt – who is also my cousin, being the sister of Manuela – came to greet me, and gave me a very gracious welcome, but I sensed a great coldness underneath it. I kissed her children, the three girls and the boy, and they all seemed to me very cold. My cousin Manuela was quite different; she flung herself in my arms, kissed me tenderly, and with tears in her eyes and a voice full of emotion, she said: 'Ah, cousin, how I have longed to meet you! Ever since I heard about you, I have loved you; I admire your courage and deplore your sorrows.' We stayed about two hours in the country. I walked in the garden with my uncle; I never tired of hearing him talk. He spoke French with a charming

**Author's note:* This is not a Spanish word, but is used in Peru to denote a country house.

purity and grace, I was delighted with his wit and his friendliness fascinated me.

At about seven o'clock we set out for Arequipa. My uncle rode his fine spirited Chilean mare. The skill and grace with which he rode showed that he had learned to ride in Andalusia. I was once again at the head of the large cavalcade; my uncle, on my right hand side, continually entertained me in the most friendly manner.

When we reached home, my cousin Carmen was busy acting as hostess to the many visitors who had gathered to receive Don Pio and his family. She had arranged a splendid supper, and my aunt invited all those present. Some accepted, others stayed to chat or smoke. I remained a long time with my uncle; I found his conversation irresistibly attractive. Bedtime came, however, and although it was late, I was sorry to leave him. I was enchanted by him, and, in the enjoyment of the happiness of being near him, I dared not think of what might come, so captivated was I by the spell he had cast over me.

IX

DON PIO DE TRISTAN AND HIS FAMILY

My uncle did not look like a European; the sun and climate had affected him, just as they affect everything else in nature. Yet our family is of pure Spanish blood, and is remarkable in that the family likeness is very strong. Only my cousin Manuela and my uncle were different from the rest. Don Pio was only five foot tall; though slight of build he was constitutionally very strong. He had a small head, with hair that had hardly begun to go grey, and a yellowish complexion. His features were delicate and regular; his blue eyes sparkled with wit. He was agile as a native of the Andes: despite his age (he was then sixty-four), he was more sprightly and active than a Frenchman of twenty-five. Seen from behind he looked no more than thirty, and, when facing one, forty-five at the most.

His character was a combination of a great deal of French charm with the cunning and obstinacy of a mountain dweller. His memory and intelligence were quite extraordinary: he could master anything with the greatest facility. He was friendly and full of charm, and a brilliant and witty conversationalist; he was full of gaiety, and if from time to time he cracked a joke or two, it was always in good taste. Everything he did was consistent with this attractive exterior; his words, his gestures and even his way of smoking a cigar were always those of a gentleman of good education; and it was surprising to recognise the courtier in a man who had passed twenty-five years of his life as a soldier and amongst soldiers. My uncle had the rare talent of knowing how to adapt his language to whoever he was addressing: when listening to him, one was so fascinated by the charm of his words that one forgot any grievance one might have against him. He was like the sirens of old: no one has ever had the same magic effect as he over my whole being.

To all these brilliant qualities, which made Don Pio one of the few men destined by Providence to lead others, we must add a ruling passion, a rival to his ambition and always dominating it: namely avarice, which made him behave on occasions with great meanness. On the other hand, in an attempt to conceal this blot on his character, he sometimes acted with great generosity. If this vice of his had not been evident to all, he would not have found it necessary to do this; his occasional acts of generosity might have deceived casual observers as to his real character, but not those who were closely associated with him.

Shortly after his return from Spain he married his niece, Manuela's sister. My aunt was called Joaquina de Florez, and must have been without any doubt the most beautiful member of the whole family. When I met her she was about forty, and was still very attractive. Her many confinements (she had had eleven) rather than her age were responsible for any deterioration. Her large black eyes

DON PIO DE TRISTAN, FLORA'S UNCLE AND THE LAST VICEROY OF SPAIN IN SOUTH AMERICA

were beautiful in shape and expression, and her smooth golden skin and pearly teeth made a brilliant impression on me. I felt that Mme de Maintenon must have looked like that. Although her education had been much neglected, my uncle had taken her in hand, and the result certainly did him credit. Joaquina was worthy to be a royal consort or the mistress of a septuagenarian monarch. Her great talent was to convince everyone, including her husband, who was no fool, that she knew nothing about anything but her children and her household. Her great piety, her appearance of humility, gentleness and obedience, the way she spoke to the poor and the simple people who greeted her in the street, her apparent timidity and the very simplicity of her dress, all created the image of a pious, modest person without ambition. She knew how to smile affably and how to give a flattering inflexion to her voice when addressing all parties in the race for power. Her manners were simple; though keeping herself always in check, she had a facile tongue, a persuasive eloquence, and those lovely eyes of hers filled with tears at the slightest emotion. If this woman had been in a situation to match her capacity, she would have been one of the most remarkable people of her time. She had cast her character in a Peruvian mould.

As soon as I met her, I felt an instinctive repulsion. I have always been on my guard against the charm of people whose smile is not matched by the expression in their eyes. My aunt, to an expert observer, was an example of this, despite the care with which she modulated her voice to match the smile on her lips. Her diplomacy was the admiration of all who knew her, for in Peru duplicity is most highly esteemed. Joaquina made a show of religion, observing all the superstitious practices of Catholicism with a thoroughness which was tiresome to her immediate circle; but the clergy had to be placated and the devout won over. Where her ambition was at stake, my aunt found nothing irksome. She flattered the poor with sweet words, but did not relieve their misery, though being immensely rich she could well have done so. Religion was not for her a matter of loving her neighbour; it called for no acts of devotion or sacrifice. It was there to serve her emotions; it helped to stifle remorse. More miserly than her husband, she was capable of revolting acts of meanness; her egoism stifled any tendency to generosity. Under a cloak of humility she concealed infinite pride and ambition. She loved society and all its pageantry, and had a passion for gambling and good food; she spoilt her children in order not to be bothered by them, and as a result they were very badly behaved. Entirely preoccupied with their own ambitions and avarice, the parents took little interest in them, and although Arequipa was not lacking in opportunities for education, since there were teachers of art, music and French, my uncle's children were not being taught anything, and had no skills of any sort. Yet the eldest was sixteen, and the others twelve, nine and seven.

Joaquina's sister, Manuela Florez d'Althaus, was a complete contrast. She was one of those charming creatures that art can imitate but not create, who embellish and enliven everything around them, and whose enjoyment of life seems to derive entirely from the happiness they shed around them. My cousin Manuela was to Arequipa what the ladies of fashion of the Boulevard du Gand or the Bouffes are to Paris, the model envied and imitated by all. She spared neither trouble nor expense to keep up with the new fashions: she took the relevant journals and her correspondents sent her new models as soon as they appeared. The best dressmaker, who worked full-time at her house, copied the dresses shown in the illustrations, and so faithfully that when I saw my cousin, I often seemed to be looking at one of those sweet little ladies who adorn the window display at Martinet's in the Rue du Coq. Not many women could get away with such servile imitation, but Manuela had so much grace that everything suited her, everything looked charming on her. Her pretty little features, her delightful expression, so full of wit and sprightliness, her attractive manners, her lively coquettish bearing all fitted the dresses she wore, however bizarre they were.

Like my uncle Pio, Manuela differed from the rest of the family both in features and character. She loved spending extravagantly. She felt the need for luxury and refinement in everything; she would have been really unhappy without her lace-edged cambric chemises, her fine silk stockings, her exquisite satin slippers. No fine young miss of Paris had so many scents and pomades, so many baths and such careful make-up as she; she exhaled perfumes which made one feel surrounded by magnolia, roses, heliotrope and jasmine; in her hair she wore fresh flowers of such beauty that she might have been a priestess of their cult. Her house was luxurious; her slaves were smartly turned out and her children the best dressed in the town, especially her little daughter who was a lovely child, sweet and prettily attired. Manuela had no trace of Spanish solemnity: she had the light, thoughtless gaiety of a child, an artlessness which contrasted with the destructive falsity so typical of Peruvian society. She passionately loved all forms of amusement; the theatre, balls, parties, expeditions, visits filled most of her time, and yet were not enough to satisfy her. She found time to study politics, reading all the newspapers, and was well informed on what went on both in her own country and in Europe: she had even learnt French in order to read French publications. In addition she kept up a frequent and voluminous correspondence with her husband, who was away most of the time, and with a number of other people. She wrote very well and with surprising facility. In addition to all these talents, she had a great heart, full of generosity, and a sensitivity rare in Peruvian women. She was born to live in the élite society of a great European capital, where she would have shone brilliantly, but alas! my poor cousin was reduced to wasting her rich substance in an environment whose petty intrigues were foreign to her. Her pretty clothes would have attracted a crowd of delighted admirers in a brilliant Paris salon, but they went for nothing at a party in Arequipa; she was wasting her time on such people, but her adornment was like the plumage of the birds of her country: she was born a queen and could shine in an oasis in the desert. After the portrait that I have just painted of her, it may cause surprise that she had chosen for a husband a soldier like Althaus, whose style was so different from hers, so sweet, so mannered, so scented. And yet it was a very good marriage. Manuela loved her husband deeply, put up with his bluntness without being in the least put out, and carried out his slightest wishes. Althaus loved her too; and showed it in all he did for her. He let her be the absolute mistress of the household, bought her everything he could think of to please her and appreciated her beautiful clothes. Here was proof that a marriage of opposites can sometimes work better than one of like-minds.

The first days after my uncle's arrival were spent in talking; I never tired of listening to him. He told me the entire family history, and said how sorry he was that fate had not allowed him to meet me earlier; in short, he spoke with such benevolence and affection that I forgot his previous behaviour and felt that I could count on receiving fair treatment from him. But alas! my eyes were soon opened. One day when we were discussing family matters, he seemed to be trying to discover the reason that had brought me to Peru. I told him that, as I had neither relations nor financial resources in France, I had come to seek help and protection from my grandmother, but hearing at Valparaiso that she had died, I had transferred all my hopes to his affection and sense of justice. This reply seemed to upset my uncle, and the very first words he spoke petrified me with astonishment and pain. 'Florita!' he said, 'when it comes to money matters, I know only the law and put aside all personal considerations. You ask me to show you justice: only the papers you carry will be the measure of that justice. You show me the copy of a baptismal certificate in which you are described as a legitimate daughter, but you have no copy of your mother's marriage certificate, and your birth certificate shows that you were registered as illegitimate. As such, you have a right to a fifth of your father's inheritance; that is why I sent you the account of his estate, for which I acted as executor. You saw that there was hardly enough to pay the debts he incurred in Spain, long before he went to France. As for my mother's estate, as you know, Florita, illegitimate children have no right of inheritance from their grandparents. I have, therefore, nothing belonging to you unless you can produce an attested document proving the marriage of your mother to my brother.'

My uncle went on in this way for more than half an hour, and his hard voice and the expression on his face revealed that he was in the grip of his dominant passion. He had become like the miser in Walter Scott, the father of Rebecca, counting the gold pieces in his bag one by one, then putting them all back again without rewarding the man who had restored them to him. Oh! how a man loses his stature, how debased he becomes, when he allows himself to be dominated by a passion which stifles his natural instincts! I was in Don Pio's study, sitting on a sofa, and he walked up and down, talking and talking, like a man who is trying to convince himself that he is not doing something wrong. I could see what was going on inside him, and was sorry for him. The wicked are unhappy, and one must pity them. Their vices do not originate within them; they are tyrannical masters bequeathed to them by the social institutions, from which only noble natures are able to shake themselves free.

'Uncle,' I said, 'are you quite convinced that I am your brother's daughter?'

'Indeed, yes, Florita, you are too like him for there to be any doubt.'

'Uncle, you believe in God: each morning you sing his praises and faithfully observe the rites of his religion. Do you think it is God's will that a man should abandon his brother's daughter, disown her and treat her like a stranger? Are you not afraid of disobeying that law whose divine imprint is within us, by refusing to give a child her birthright? No, no, uncle, I am sure that you will not be deaf to the call of your soul, you will not lie to your conscience, you will not deny God.'

'Florita, laws are made by men, and they are as sacred as God's commands. Undoubtedly I should love you, and do in fact do so, as my brother's child; but as the law gives you no right to what my brother would have inherited, I owe you none of that. You have only a right to a fifth of what he owned at the time of his death.'

'Uncle, my father's marriage to my mother is a well-known fact; it ended only with his death. It was solemnised by a priest, although it was not, I agree, invested with the forms required by human laws. I was the first to inform you of this fact. But would anyone in good faith use the omission of these formalities as an excuse to take the bread out of the mouth of an orphan? Surely you realise that I could have found a way to make good these omissions, if I had had any reason to doubt your fairmindedness? Do you think it would have been difficult for me to obtain, from some church in Spain, a document legalising my mother's marriage? Had I been armed with such a document, you would have been unable to refuse me my share of my father's inheritance: you would have had to pay me every penny of it. Before I left, I consulted several Spanish lawyers. They all advised me to obtain such a document, and explained how I could obtain it. Well, uncle, I rejected their advice, and my letters to you will confirm my words: I rejected it because I believed in your affection for me, and wanted to owe only to your sense of justice whatever I was to inherit.'

'But, Florita, I cannot understand why you insist on calling me unjust. Am I the trustee of your money? Have you the right to claim a single piastre from me?'

'So be it, uncle; since you take refuge in the letter of the law, you are right, and I know only too well that, as an illegitimate child, I have no right to any of my grandmother's estate. But, as the daughter of the brother to whom you owe so much, have I no right to your personal gratitude? Well, uncle, I appeal to you on these grounds. I do not ask from you or from the co-heirs the 800,000 francs that each of you have had as your share; I only ask for the eighth part of that sum, just enough for me to be able to live on. My needs are very slight, my tastes modest. I have no love of society and its luxury. With an income of 5,000 francs I can live anywhere, free and happy. This gift, uncle, will satisfy me completely, and I want to owe it to you alone. I shall bless you for it, and all my life long I shall feel an inexhaustible gratitude.' As I spoke these words, I went closer to him, took his hand and pressed it hard against my heart. My voice choked with tears; I gazed at him with an expression of unutterable tenderness, anxiety and gratitude, and waited, trembling, for his reply.

My uncle gave a start and broke his silence with: 'But

Florita, what are you suggesting? Do you imagine that I can give you 20,000 piastres? It's an enormous sum, 20,000 piastres!'

I cannot describe the sudden effect that the bluntness and the hardness of this reply had on me. What I can say is, that the sensitive state which I had been in since the beginning of the interview gave way suddenly to a fit of indignation so violent that I thought my last hour had come. I walked up and down the room for some time without being able to speak. My eyes flashed; my muscles were tense; had the thunder struck I should have heard nothing. I had no idea what my uncle was saying; I was in one of those states when the soul is in touch with a superhuman power. I stopped in front of my uncle, and seizing him by the arm I said in a tone that he had never heard before: 'So, Don Pio, in cold blood and with deliberation, you reject the daughter of your own brother, the brother who was a father to you, to whom you owe your education, your fortune and your whole position? You, who have an income of 300,000 francs, show your gratitude to my father by coldly condemning me to suffer poverty; you have a million of my money, yet you abandon me to the horrors of penury, you condemn me to despair and force me to despise you, though you are the man whom my father taught me to love, my only relative on whom my hopes depended! Ah! man without faith, honour or humanity, I also reject you, I am not of your blood, and I leave you to the remorse of your conscience. I want nothing more of you. This very evening I shall leave your house, and tomorrow the whole town shall know about your ingratitude for the memory of that brother, the mention of whose name always brings tears to your eyes; they will know how cruelly you have treated me and how you have betrayed my misplaced confidence.'

I left his study and returned to my great vaulted chamber. I was in an indescribable state of exasperation and misery. I wrote immediately to M. Viollier. When he arrived, I asked him to find me a lodging, saying that I no longer wished to stay at my uncle's. He begged me to wait for two days, as M. Le Bris was due to arrive from Islay. My uncle had meanwhile been telling the whole family about my hostile intentions. Althaus was sent to me with a peace mission, and I described to him the scene which had just taken place between me and Don Pio. 'I'm not surprised,' he said, 'and knowing him as you did you should have expected it. But, Flora my dear, before causing a scandal and bringing more trouble still upon yourself, let me see if things can be arranged. Neither Manuela nor I will dispute any rights you may have. The shares will be re-allotted, each of us will get his due and that will be that. Don Pio and Margarita's uncle (Margarita was my cousin Carmen's daughter) have two very crafty lawyers; but you could choose Dr Baldivia who is undoubtedly a match for them. If you insist on leaving Don Pio's house, I offer you ours, and though we shall be on opposite sides in the dispute, we shall be no worse friends for that.' Manuela also came and made similar offers, showed much kindness and consoled me as much as was in her power.

That night, I was unable to rest for a single moment. Fever coursed through my veins, and made it impossible for me to lie on my bed, for I could not stay still. I walked up and down, and was even obliged to go out into the courtyard to breathe the cool morning air. Oh! how I suffered! My last hope had gone! The family that I had come so far to find now showed me the many faces of their egotism; how cold they were, and as insensitive to the misfortunes of others as if they were marble statues! My uncle, who was the only one of them who had lived with my father and enjoyed his love and trust; my uncle, on whom I had lavished my affection and who had so many reasons for sympathising with my plight, now revealed himself in all the stark nakedness of his meanness and ingratitude.

Next morning, I was physically exhausted, but felt no desire either to sleep or to eat. For five days my over-excited brain kept me in this state. However, I visited the president of the Courts of Justice, a learned lawyer, and told him about my situation. He said that when my uncle had received my first letter, he had come to consult him, and that after reading it he had told my uncle that he had no need to worry about any claims that his brother's daughter might make, since she had a right only to a fifth of her father's estate. However, he advised me out of fairness to consult one of the best lawyers. I consulted two, both of whom thought that I had a case, but admitted that the outcome would be doubtful, especially as my adversary would be my uncle Pio, and the country I was in was one in which justice could be bought. My uncle would be the main party in the dispute, since he had inherited a third of a share in addition to his own on behalf of his wife, together with a legacy of 100,000 francs which my grandmother had left to Joaquina. He would be capable of sacrificing a quarter, or if need be, a half of his inheritance in order to win the case. These two lawyers, and indeed the president himself, were completely baffled by my behaviour. 'That letter, mademoiselle, that unfortunate letter,' they said, 'was your undoing; if only you had come armed with an attested affidavit as to the marriage between your mother and father, this would have been acceptable here as a genuine marriage certificate, and you would have been able to override all objections.' I did not dare to tell those gentlemen that I had counted on the *affection, gratitude* and *fairness* of my uncle; they would have thought I was a *madwoman*; *I preferred them to think that I was only silly*.

M. Le Bris came to see me; I consulted him on what I had best do. He was indignant at my uncle's behaviour; he knew him well, and had a correct estimate of his character. Being a proud man, he advised me to leave Don Pio's house immediately. He made all the offers of help that one would expect of an old friend, and I was much comforted by the kind interest that he showed.

Meanwhile, my uncle cared little as to whether or not I left his house. It was his nature to settle all disputes where possible by friendly agreement, since he knew by experience how talented he was at compromise. He therefore wrote to me to ask me if I would be willing to attend a meeting of all the members of the family, including himself, Althaus, and the old doctor who represented Margarita, the daughter of Carmen. I had not been able to face seeing him since the scene I had described. My meals were brought to my room, and I still intended to leave.

However, I yielded to Althaus's solicitations and went once more to my uncle's study. It was extremely painful to me to be again in the presence of a man who had forced me to despise him, a man whom I was inclined to love so dearly. He addressed me with greater gentleness and affection than ever; he gave an account before the two witnesses of his behaviour towards me. Althaus and the old doctor declared that it had been at Don Pio's request that I had been allotted, when my grandmother's estate had been divided up, the 15,000 francs that she had left me. The two gentlemen also told me that it was due to my uncle's generosity *alone* that I owed the pension of 2,500 francs that I had been receiving for the last five years. I was grateful for these marks of my uncle's affection and my eyes filled with tears. He noticed this, and fearing that my pride might be hurt at receiving such a sum annually as a gift, he hastened to inform the two gentlemen that it was not a *gift* but the payment of a debt. 'For,' he added, 'if, due to the lack of certain formalities connected with the marriage of her mother to my brother, Florita is deprived of her rights as a legitimate heir, she has undeniably the right, as an illegitimate child, to a maintenance allowance: I took it upon myself to pay this, and I ask her to accept me as her permanent financial adviser.' After a long conversation, during which my uncle was clever enough to persuade all of us, including myself, that he loved me as if I were his own child and that his conduct towards me had always been loyal, generous and full of gratitude for everything he owed to my father, and after moving me to tears and *touching the emotions of Althaus*, he asked me in his fondest manner to forget all that had passed between us, and begged me to stay at his house as his daughter, his friend, his wife's friend and the second mother of his children; and it was all done with such charm and apparent sincerity that I promised him everything he asked for. Joaquina then added the final touches to what he had so well begun; and the two *sirens* charmed me to such effect that I abandoned all legal action and put my trust, not in their sense of justice, but in their promises.

M. Le Bris and all my intimate friends admired my

courage and were astonished at the way I resigned myself to being fleeced; they would not have expected it from one so proud and independent. I saw their point of view: anyone as openhearted as myself would not be expected to have any fellow feeling for such people as my aunt and uncle, whose only motives were ambition and greed and whose flexible natures varied according to their momentary advantage. I was not so easily swayed; I had kept my native independence and this angelic resignation was foreign to it; but I was yielding to the hard facts imposed by my circumstances, which I could not reveal either to M. Le Bris or to anyone else. It was for my children's sake that I controlled my normal reactions. If I had taken my uncle before the courts and made a scandal, he would have been my enemy for ever; I had little chance of prevailing against the influence he could bring to bear, and by losing the case I should also lose the possibility that he might assist my children. Indeed, if I had only myself to think of I should not have hesitated for a moment; my claims were supported by a baptismal certificate, in a country where that was almost the only document needed to prove legitimacy, and I should have tried to regain the ground lost by my imprudent letter; and if I had not been recognised as a legitimate member of the family, I should have broken completely with these unnatural relatives and indignantly refused the annual pension which they had allowed me, to prevent me from dying of hunger; but I was not free to act in this manner: I had to pocket my pride and avoid jeopardising assistance which, though insufficient, was an essential subsidy for the education of my children, considering that I had little hope of winning a case against the family or arriving at a compromise. In any case, to win the case money was necessary, and plenty of it. When I left Bordeaux, M. Bertera, out of the kindness of his heart and his interest in me, had provided me with 25,000 francs worth (5,000 piastres) of letters of credit on M. de Goyeneche of Arequipa; in addition, on my arrival at Valparaiso, I had found a letter from M. Bertera, containing another credit for 2,000 piastres (10,000 francs); so I had at my disposal more money than was necessary for the legal costs; but if I failed, as there were reasons to fear, I would be in M. Bertera's debt and in no position to pay him. The same reasons prevented me from availing myself of offers from M. Le Bris: I could never accept such proposals without the certainty of being able to repay any advances made to me. I had in mind also the weakened state of my health. My five months of seasickness had impaired it, and I had not ceased being ill since I had landed in Peru. The volcanic air of Arequipa and the unsuitable food, the violent shock I had had on learning of my grandmother's death, the parting with Chabrié, and now the cruel disappointment I felt at my uncle's ingratitude, all combined to exhaust me to such an extent that I feared that I had not long to live. I considered that, such being the case, only my children mattered, especially my daughter, who would be alone in the world. I hoped that the sad prospect of my death would be enough to touch my uncle's heart, and that in my dying moments I might be able to extract a promise from him to take my children under his protection, so as to ensure them sufficient means to protect them from poverty.

Meanwhile, political events had occurred which complicated my position and made the outcome of the case even more doubtful. My uncle had returned to Arequipa on the 3rd of January, and on the 23rd of that month, news came of a revolution in Lima. President Bermudez, although supported by the intrigues of ex-President Gamarra, had been overthrown, and supplanted by Orbegoso. When the newspapers which brought this news had been read in Arequipa, meetings were held; the majority declared in favour of Orbegoso; General Nieto was appointed provincial commander of the troops; in short, a government was improvised in twenty-four hours, and without considering what the consequences of such a decision might be, the province broke away from the provinces of Yuno, Cuzco, Ayacucho and others. This revolution had spread terror through the town: each man felt his personal fortune threatened and had no sympathy to spare for others. Before this crisis, my bizarre situation had taken the general fancy; but as soon as the Arequipans had themselves to think of, they had no further thought for me. The lawyer Baldivia* flung himself into the fray in the hope of making his fortune, and sent me word that he could no longer conduct my case; I had no confidence in the other lawyers, who refused anyway to take it, fearing to get on the wrong side of Don Pio. In a land where selfishness was rife, how could I hope that, during such a crisis, these people should think of anything but their own interests? It was quite obvious that this revolution left me without the slightest chance of success. My uncle would probably return to power; such a possibility removed any hope of finding impartiality in the judges. A different future was in store for me, and I felt it would be mad, even profane, to try to resist any further in the face of a clear manifestation of Providence. I bent my head before the destiny which had weighed on me since my birth, and, like the Muslim, I cried, 'God is great!' I gave up both any idea of a legal action and any hope of a fortune, knowing full well that I had nothing to expect from my uncle's generosity, or from any pricks of his conscience, and I wrote him the following letter:

... I came to you, uncle, more in search of paternal affection and benevolent protection than to claim what was due to me. I have been disappointed in my hopes. Armed with the letter of the law, without a spark of emotion, you have destroyed one by one all the links which bound me to the family in whose bosom I sought refuge. You have not been deterred by respect for the memory of a brother whom you loved; you have felt no pity for the innocent victim of the culpable negligence of her parents. You have thrust me aside and treated me like a stranger. Uncle, such acts as these can only be judged by God ...

My first reaction of righteous indignation was to bring the hideous spectacle of these iniquities into the courts of justice, but after some days' reflection I have realised that my strength, which has so long been undermined, would

* *Translator's note:* This is Don Juan Gaulberto Valdivia, a protégé of the priest Luna Pizarro, deputy for Arequipa in the Congress in Lima and leader of the party opposing President Gamarra.

be unable to bear the horrible distress which the scandal of a legal action would cause me.

Since the legitimacy of my birth had been challenged, I ardently desired to be recognised as a legitimate child, so as to throw a veil over my father's lapse, his memory having been sullied by the state of abandon in which he had left his child. But when I went into the question of the methods which would have to be employed to defeat my claim, I say again, uncle, I recoiled in horror. For in fact you would have had to prove that your brother was a dishonest man and a cruel father; that he was dastardly and cowardly enough to deceive an unprotected young woman whose misfortune should have been respected in the foreign land to which she had fled from the terrors of the revolution, and that, exploiting her love and inexperience, he covered up his bad faith by the farce of a clandestine marriage. You would also have had to prove that your brother had allowed the child that God had given him to languish in poverty and suffer the insults and scorn of a barbarous society; and despite the fact that he had *recommended his daughter to your care in his last words*, you would have had to sully his memory by claiming that his negligent behaviour was premeditated. Oh! even if I were certain to win the case, I would not pursue it. I feel that I have the courage to bear poverty with dignity as I have done until now; I am ready to pay this price so that my father's soul shall rest in peace.

Flora de Tristan

I admit that after sending this letter I felt relieved; my pride needed the satisfaction of telling the family what I thought.

My uncle showed the letter to the family. Joaquina alone was offended. Her husband pointed out to her that I ought to be forgiven owing to my over-excited and distressed state, and he showed me that he knew how to make allowances himself by not complaining of the hard words I had addressed to him. That evening, Don José, the house chaplain, came and told me in confidence (but I realised that this was on orders) that the family was busy getting together a fund so that I could be in a position to buy a small property where I could live decently.

My cousin Carmen, Manuela, Althaus, Don Juan de Goyeneche, in fact everybody except M. Le Bris, criticised me strongly for acting as I did towards my uncle, and especially towards my aunt. 'That was the wrong way to set about it,' they said, 'if you wanted to get something out of them. Since you did not want to go to law, you should have adopted a soft approach, made up to your uncle, flattered Joaquina, waited patiently for the moment when Don Pio could have made a public exhibition of his great generosity to you. Instead of that, you have wounded them where they are most vulnerable and have shown up their avarice to the world. How do you expect them not to hate you, with a hatred that will be the more dangerous for being concealed?' They were right: another woman in my circumstances would have got 100,000 francs out of my uncle and the gracious protection of Joaquina, provided she had not got a character like mine, openhearted and proud, nor my invincible loathing of flattery. If my uncle had agreed like a gentleman to give me 100,000 francs, I should have been fully satisfied, would have accepted his generosity and have been deeply grateful to him; but when to obtain such a sum I would have been forced to betray my independent nature, I preferred to remain poor, finding the price too high when my freedom of thought and God-given individuality were at stake, to exchange them against a little gold, which I could not have looked at without feelings of remorse.

Althaus told me that my uncle had undertaken, in the presence of the whole family, to guarantee the pension of 2,500 francs which he paid me. I sent word to thank him, without putting too much trust in his word, but keeping it in mind so that I could remind him of it were I to need some slight help for my children.

It was then that I appreciated all the truth contained in the words of Bernardin de Saint-Pierre, when he compares misfortune to the Himalayas, from whose summit all the surrounding mountains appear no more than little hills, and the beautiful countries of Kashmir and Lahore are spread out below. I had reached the high point of my grief, and I must say – and what a consolation in one's distress it is – that having reached this high point, I found in grief itself sources of inexpressible and indeed celestial joy, which I had never imagined to have existed. I felt carried away by a superhuman force, which bore me into a higher sphere, from which I could see the things of this earth as they really are, freed of the deceptive trappings in which men's passions have dressed them. At no time in my life have I been so calm: if I could have lived in solitude with books and flowers, my happiness would have been complete.

X

THE REPUBLIC AND THE THREE PRESIDENTS

I would find it difficult to explain to my readers the causes of the revolution which broke out at Lima in January 1834 and of the civil wars which followed. I have never been able to understand how the three claimants to the presidency were able to convince their supporters of the justice of their claims. The explanations which my uncle gave me on the question were not very intelligible. When I questioned my cousin Althaus on the subject he replied with a laugh: 'Florita, ever since I had the honour to serve the Republic of Peru, I never knew a president whose right was not very questionable. At times there were up to five claiming to be legally elected.'

In brief, here is what I was able to gather. The wife of President Gamarra, realising that she could no longer maintain her husband in power, got her supporters to put up as candidate one Bermudez, a hanger-on of hers, and he was elected president. Her opponents alleged, for reasons unknown to me, that Bermudez's candidature was invalid, and they put up Orbegoso in opposition. It was then that the troubles began.

I remember that the day the news reached Lima I was ill, lying fully clothed on my bed, discussing the vanity of human life with my cousin Carmen. It was about four o'clock. Suddenly Emmanuel burst into the room and said with a bewildered look: 'Do you know what's happened? The courier has just brought the news that there has been a frightful revolution in Lima, a terrible massacre! People here are so shocked that there has been a spontaneous reaction. Everyone is assembled in the cathedral square, and General Nieto has been appointed commander-in-chief of the province. There is such confusion that there's no knowing what to believe and who to listen to. My father has sent me to fetch Uncle Pio.'

'Well then,' said my cousin coolly, shaking the ash from her cigar, 'go and tell Don Pio de Tristan all about it. Such matters are of interest to him, since he can expect to have to pay one side or the other. But it's of no interest to us. Is Florita not a foreigner? And as for me, since I've not got a penny in the world, what difference does it make to me whether they are killing themselves for Orbegoso, Bermudez or Gamarra?'

Emmanuel left us, and a few minutes later Joaquina came in. 'Holy Virgin!' she said, 'have you heard of the new misfortune that has descended on our country? The city is in rebellion, a new government is being installed, and the wretches at the head of the insurrection are going to put pressure on the landowners. God, what a disaster!'

'You are right,' said Carmen. 'In such circumstances one is almost pleased not to be a landowner; for it is hard to give one's money for fighting a civil war when one could use it to help the unfortunate. But it can't be helped, it's "the other side of the coin".'

My uncle and Althaus arrived. They were both clearly worried; my uncle, because he was afraid they would make him donate some money; my cousin, because he could not decide which side to back. They both trusted me, and sought my advice in this difficult situation. My uncle, coming quite close to me, spoke unrestrainedly: 'My dear Florita, I am very worried; advise me. Your ideas about everything are so sensible, and you are really the only person here with whom I can speak about such serious matters. This man Nieto is a dishonourable scoundrel, a spendthrift and a weakling who will let the lawyer Baldivia lead him by the nose: and Baldivia is very capable but an intriguer and a dyed-in-the-wool revolutionary. Those brigands will put pressure on us, how much God knows. Florita, an idea occurs to me: if tomorrow morning early I were to go and offer those robbers 2,000 piastres, and also propose a financial levy on all the other landowners, do you not think that it would make them believe that I was on their side, and that it might deter them from taxing me so heavily? Dear girl, what do you think?'

'Uncle, I consider your idea excellent. Only I think that the sum that you are offering is not enough.'

'But, Florita, do you think that I am as rich as the pope? Would the equivalent of 10,000 francs really not be enough?'

'Dear uncle, remember that their demands will be relative to the amount people can afford. You must realise that if you, the richest man in town, give only 10,000 francs, their total cash return will be meagre; and I think I am in a position to tell you that they mean to take everything they can get hold of.'

'How do you mean? Do you know something?'

'Nothing definite, but there are indications.'

My contacts with Baldivia had given me an idea of his character. When I learned that he was in the new government, I assumed that the landowners would be exploited, and it was this that made me speak so confidently to my uncle.

When he had left, Althaus came up to me and said: 'Florita, I don't know what to do. Which of these three rascals should I support as president?'

'Cousin, you have no choice. Since Orbegoso is recognised here, you must march under his flag and under Nieto's command.'

'That's exactly what maddens me. Nieto is an ass, presumptuous like all fools, and will let himself be led by that crook lawyer Baldivia; whereas on Bermudez's side, there are some soldiers I could fight with.'

'That may be so, but Bermudez is at Cuzco and you are at Arequipa. If you refuse to work with them, they will ruin you, squeeze you dry and generally harass you.'

'That's what I fear. How long does Don Pio think that this government will last? I haven't asked him, because he has lied to me so often that I don't believe a word he says.'

'At least, cousin, you can believe his actions: what should decide you is that Don Pio expects this government to last long enough to offer it money. Tomorrow he will take 4,000 piastres to Nieto.'

'He told you that?'

'Yes, dear friend.'

'Oh, then that alters matters. You are right, cousin. When a shrewd man like Don Pio offers Nieto 4,000 piastres, a poor soldier like me should accept the post offered him of chief of the general staff. Tomorrow, before eight, I shall go to the general. What a devilish profession mine is! I, Althaus, forced to serve under a man whom I wouldn't even have promoted to corporal when I was a lieutenant in the Army of the Rhine! – You pack of thieves!' he went on. 'If I can succeed in getting paid for even half the work I have done for you, and which you are incapable of appreciating, I swear I'll leave your accursed country and never return.' There was no stopping Althaus now, and he embarked on a diatribe against all three presidents: ex-president Gamarra, the pretender Orbegoso, and the man with the power of the military behind him, Bermudez. He despised all three. But he soon began to see the funny side, and to joke delightfully about them.

When Althaus had gone my thoughts took a more serious turn. I could not help deploring the sad fate of Spanish America, where no stable government has yet emerged to protect persons and property. The Spanish Americans are not at the present time fighting for principles but for bosses who reward them by robbing their fellow men. There will come a day when Providence will unite all these peoples under the banner of Labour. Let us hope that then, remembering their disastrous past, they will have a healthy detestation of men of blood and pillage!

I was still dozing when my uncle came into my room next morning. 'Florita,' he said, 'I have thought of what you said. I fear that 2,000 piastres will not be enough; but 4,000 is a huge sum!'

'Yes, indeed; but Althaus told me yesterday that they were regarding the money only as a loan.'

'Ah, so this lot also go in for big words! They talk about loans, the insolent rascals! Bolivar also called his extortions loans; but who has refunded me, or even thought of refunding me, the 25,000 piastres that the great "Liberator" took from me when he came here? General Sucre also took our money under the guise of a loan, but I've not seen any of the 10,000 piastres that he "borrowed" from me. Ah, Florita, such impudence makes me lose my normal calm. They come to our homes and rob us by force of arms, and, adding insult to injury, they record the stolen sums under the heading of loans: it's insolent beyond words.'

'Uncle, what time is it?'

'Eight o'clock.'

'Well then, I urge you to go now, because I know that the proclamation making the landowners liable to the tax will be promulgated at ten o'clock.'

'Really? Then I've no time to lose. I've decided on 4,000 piastres.'

And so, I thought, by a balancing stroke of Providence, the sum that he unjustly refuses to give me is torn from him by force. If I could believe in divine retribution, should I not find an example here? Has not my uncle been wounded in his tenderest spot? – as if God had decreed that the unjust should be victims of injustice.

My uncle returned in a happy mood. 'Ah, Florita, how wise I was to follow your advice. Imagine, those rascals have already drawn up their list. The general gave me a very good reception, but that man Baldivia seemed to have guessed my reason for coming. He looked as if he was thinking: "You've brought your money for fear that we were going to ask you for more. It won't do you any good." Fortunately, I'm as sharp as he is.'

At ten o'clock the *bando* (an order proclaimed by the town crier) was published; in all my life I've never heard such an uproar! Althaus came to my room, laughing: 'Cousin, aren't you lucky to have no money! Today those who have are looking terribly down in the mouth, and I should hate to see such a nice person as you with a similar expression. I am now chief of the general staff of Generalissimo Nieto: and it's already saved me 800 piastres. That amiable Dr Baldivia had put down Manuela Florez d'Althaus in his *bando* for the modest sum of 800 piastres; but as everything in these happy times is done under the authority of the military, the *bando* came to my office, and before signing it I had the good idea of reading the names of the victims. When I reached that of my respected wife, I simply crossed it out and went to see the general. Speaking very loudly, I said that I found it strange that my wife had been put down for 800 piastres when neither his wife nor the wives of the other top members of the government had been made to contribute one single *real*. Dr Baldivia tried to reply, saying that "the niece of Don Pio – " but I interrupted him vehemently with: "Not in this case the niece of Don Pio, but only the wife of Althaus, chief of staff. And if dog is eating dog, I'll change my skin and go and bark elsewhere." I said this in a quiet voice, but banged my sword on the ground and jangled my spurs to such effect that the monk took his pen to strike out my wife's name. Finding it already crossed out, he pursed his lips, went pale, and from his expression I felt he was weighing up how determined I was; but as at Waterloo I stood firm as a rock, and looking him in the eyes I said: "Comrade, in this affair we each have our task: yours is to write *bandos* milking the citizens of their money, and mine is to see that they are carried out. I think that my sword will be just as useful as my pen on this occasion." The comrade took the point, and I assure you, Florita, that this piece of barrack-room behaviour, as you will no doubt call it, was very effective.'

At about noon, Carmen came in with an expression of glee on her face. 'Florita, I've come to fetch you. Dear friend, get out of bed. You really must come and sit at my sitting-room window and enjoy the sights in the Calle de Santo Domingo. There are things going on that you must put in your diary: I've already made a note of the two most remarkable ones. Now, wrap yourself up in your cloak and put your large black veil over your head; I'll cover the window-sill with rugs and cushions. You'll be as good as in bed, and we'll have as much fun as two queens.'

'But, cousin, what is going on in the Calle de Santo Domingo?'

'What's happening? The funniest thing ever. You will see all the landowners, with moneybags tucked under their arms and long, pale faces, walking along looking like people on their way to an *auto-da-fe*. Quick, Florita, we're missing all the fun.'

Yielding to her entreaties, I installed myself at her window. Carmen was right. There was material here for interesting observations.

My cousin was filled with secret venom, very common amongst those who dare not fight openly against a society which victimises them. She took every opportunity to avenge herself against the hated system. So she addressed everyone who passed by, enjoying twisting the blade in the wound. 'What a great weight you're carrying, Señor Gamio. Where are you carrying those big bags of piastres? You've enough there to buy a pretty little *chacra* [country estate] for each of your daughters.'

'Why, don't you know, Doña Carmen, that they've had the iniquity to tax me 6,000 piastres!'

'Really, Señor Gamio? But that's frightful! The head of a family, and such a methodical, economical man, who does without everything in order to save sacks and sacks of money, what a revolting injustice!'

'Ah yes, you know how I've deprived myself in order to save. Well, all my savings gone at once: they're taking it all!'

'And, Don José, if only this were all they were going to take!'

'What, do you think they will ask for more?'

'Don José, we live in times when honest folk are not free to talk; one must pray to the Holy Virgin for the poor people who have money.'

Señor Gamio, with tears in his eyes, trembling with fear, left Carmen's window with despair in his heart. The next to come by was Señor Ugarte, a man as rich as my uncle, but much more miserly. Normally, he dressed in blue stockings, worn shoes and a patched coat; on that day, in the grip of a miser's woe (perhaps the strongest woe of all), he had put on, in the hope of disguising his wealth, the raggedest clothes he had. Garbed in multi-coloured rags, he looked grotesque. When I saw him I could not help bursting out laughing. I hid my face behind my veil, whilst my cousin, who was more used to controlling her emotions, engaged him in conversation: a poor rich man, looking like a beggar, the possessor of a fortune of five or six million.

'Señor Ugarte, why do you exhaust yourself carrying such weighty sacks? Have you no negro or donkey to save you the trouble?'

'What are you thinking of, Doña Carmen – entrust moneybags to a negro? Help me put the sacks on your window-sill: there are 10,000 piastres there, Doña Carmen, and almost all in gold.'

'Oh! sir, I care not what colour they are, but surely it is hard to give up all that beautiful bullion, which was hidden away in some cellar, to give it to people who are going to put it into circulation?'

'Give it? Say rather that they are stealing it. For, by the Holy Virgin in Heaven with her Blessed Son, if they hadn't threatened to put me in jail and if I wasn't afraid that, while I was in jail, my wife wouldn't steal my money, I would have burnt at the stake rather than give them a penny. My poor money, my only joy, they're taking it all!'

The poor creature in a paroxysm of grief began to weep as he looked at his sacks, like a mother over her dead child. My cousin drew back into the room so as to be able to laugh unrestrainedly. I on the other hand regarded the unfortunate man as an object of pity; I felt he was victim of a mental disease, and madness interests me and excites my compassion. Next, I saw him only as a vile slave of gold, a man without pity for his fellow men, holding himself aloof from the world, a stranger to all the warmth of our natures, and felt the greatest contempt for the miserable fellow who, six times a millionaire, was dressed in dirty rags. This civil war, I thought, was decreed by

Providence. The extortions of the military government will at least have the immediate effect of putting into circulation coinage whose only function is to be circulated, until the time comes when a general need for order and security brings about the establishment of a benevolent government.

My cousin had now come back to the window, and she offered Ugarte a cigar, knowing that it was the best way of consoling him. Ugarte never offered anyone a cigar: he had always left his at home, so that he could sponge on others and save a few pence.

'Here, Señor Ugarte, here's a fine Havana cigar for you, a contraband cigar; it cost two pence.'

'But señora, that's quite a present you are giving me; I really enjoy a good cigar; but you realise that I can't pay so much for one.'

'Alas, señor, with a quarter of one of these moneybags, you could buy Havana cigars as big as the towers of Santo Domingo. But after being robbed in this way you'll never be able to smoke good cigars again.'

'And the worst of all, Doña Carmen, is the injustice of it: demanding 10,000 piastres of me, me, a poor man without a coat to his back. My enemies call me rich. Me rich! Holy Virgin! – because I've got two or three small estates which cost me more than they bring in? Everybody knows that for the last six years I haven't received one piastre from my farmers. What little cash I had I've lent to people who don't pay me back. It's got to the point that often my wife hasn't enough money to go marketing with.'

'And yet, señor, since ten o'clock this morning (and it's now only midday), you found these bags of gold lying about somewhere.'

The poor fool looked at my cousin in terror. There was a sombre madness in his face and he began to tremble. It was clear that he was suffering horribly. And then this beggarly figure, bending under the weight of his bags of gold, hurried away as fast as his burden allowed.

'Carmen, you are very wicked.'

'But is it not revolting to see a millionaire, dressed in pauper's rags, pile up money that he will never enjoy, burying it and so depriving the poor of work? In this town there are five or six rich men, and each one tries to be meaner than his fellows; they are like leeches sucking the gold and silver out of society and giving nothing back.'

Carmen's indignation was well founded. In countries where there are banks which issue paper money, thereby allowing industrialists to satisfy the needs of the labour force, a miser is merely a fool and is universally mocked. But in backward countries where gold has kept all its power, the miser is a public enemy who stops the circulation of money and makes work burdensome or even impossible because too much is demanded of the worker for too little. It is therefore not surprising that the masses, exploited by the greed of the few, welcome and support with all their strength levies imposed by those in power: they are only taking their revenge for their daily deprivations. The invention which in modern times has had the most potent results is perhaps, after printing, that of paper money. By competing with gold it has diminished its power; it has made it possible for intelligent hard work to be rewarded by wealth – in a word, it has destroyed usury and the enslavement of talent. In all countries where there is no system of public credit to put money, or the symbol that represents it, within the reach of labour, the rich will be as much hated by the people as they were under the Romans, or as the Jews were in the Middle Ages, and the masses will always be prepared to support any regime which despoils them of their riches.

We were still discussing the thoughts provoked by the avarice of Señor Ugarte when we saw Don Juan de Goyeneche approaching. He was in such a state that I thought he would collapse. Carmen invited him inside. 'I am going to see Don Pio,' he said; 'I hope he will be able to lend me some money, otherwise God knows what will become of our family. Do you know, ladies, that those people (Doña Carmen, is there any danger of our being overheard? Look out of the window in case anyone is listening), do you know that they have had the effrontery to demand 20,000 piastres from our venerable brother, the bishop? From my sister they want 5,000 and from me 6,000. So there go

31,000 piastres, at one fell swoop, out of our resources! Ah, Florita, how much would I give to change places with our brother Mariano! He lives in tranquillity in Bordeaux, peacefully enjoying his income. I have long regretted having bought all his properties from him, and more than ever since this revolution I repent my utter stupidity in having chained myself to this country.'

'Cousin,' said Carmen, 'you must be philosophical about it. The wheel of fortune turns, and out come the winning and the losing numbers. One can't win all the time. Your father came to this country with nothing; he made a vast fortune; your brother Don Emmanuel, now Count of Guaqui, has twenty millions of his own, so they say; all that comes from Peru. Do you really think, Don Juan, that if your father had remained in the Basque Country, one of your brothers would be a bishop and the other a Spanish grandee?'

He got up to go, realising that Carmen, who hated him, was not going to give him any comfort. It was clear that Carmen had a secret satisfaction in having her revenge on these skinflints who had disapproved of her way of living, whilst accepting her twopenny cigars and coming to her dinners and her parties. She tried to insist on my returning to the window, but I found the sight of avarice in the clutches of tyranny repugnant: it showed humanity in too contemptible a light, and I resisted.

'At least, Florita, come and see our neighbour Hurtado. He has loaded his 6,000 piastres on to a donkey. He's a philosopher: let's see what he has to say.' I gave in to my curiosity in order to hear what an old philosopher had to say about giving up his piastres.

'Bravo, Señor Hurtado,' said Carmen, 'at least you are not tiring yourself by carrying your bags to the town hall.'

'Carmen, a philosopher should only bend under the weight of his wisdom. My donkey is meant to carry burdens, and I cannot see why gold and silver alone should be exclusively carried by men, when iron, copper and lead, much more useful metals, are loaded on to beasts.'

'Neighbour, I see that you are contributing without rancour, which is easy for anyone who, like you, "possesses a tomb''.* But poor Don Pio de Tristan, Juan de Goyeneche, Ugarte and Gamio, as you realise, cannot accept it so easily.'

'Yes, Carmen, you are right, I possess a tomb, for true wisdom is more inexhaustible than the richest tomb of the ancient Incas.'

'Neighbour Hurtado, you are going to make me angry once more: it's the same every time I talk to you. You are about to try and convince me that it is your wisdom which has provided the funds to buy the seven or eight houses that you own in the town, your fine country property, your great sugar-mill; that it's with your wisdom that you have brought up your eleven children, educated them all and given a dowry to your daughters; and it's your wisdom which has kept your daughter the nun at Santa Catalina's in so much luxury that it scandalises the whole convent, and your wisdom which has made donations to monasteries and built a church in the village of your country estate. Let us hear no more about your wisdom: heavens, at that price everyone would become wise.'

'Yes – if people were capable of wisdom; but I have looked everywhere in vain, I see no wise men but only fools. Goodbye, neighbour. Dear Mademoiselle Florita, now that you are better, come and see me. You have, my dear girl, all the qualities for the attainment of wisdom, which is why I so much enjoy talking to you.' And he walked on.

Everyone at Arequipa was really convinced that old Señor Hurtado had found a tomb from which he financed his vast expenditure. I myself think that, like the old man in La Fontaine, the treasure he had found was his capacity for work – and this he called his 'wisdom'. That venerable man was economical without being miserly, and a very hard worker: his power of concentration on the task in hand was very great and far superior to that of the rest of his countrymen. He had worked throughout his life and successfully carried through his many enterprises. This in

* *Author's note:* Of people the origin of whose wealth is a mystery, the Peruvians say that they 'possess a tomb', because the ancient Peruvians were buried with their treasures, and, at the time of the Conquest, they hid their wealth in tombs.

my opinion sufficiently explains the origin of his fortune, without having to postulate the miraculous discovery of a 'tomb'. Had he made such a discovery, there would still be cause for rejoicing, because he made such a noble use of his wealth. But people are jealous of men of superior intelligence; when they are unable to deny their success, they are reduced to inventing a miracle to explain it. Anything rather than acknowledge their superiority.

At this point my uncle sent for me, and I returned to my room. Despite the letter I had written to the family, he continued to show complete confidence in me, telling me of his most intimate worries, consulting me about everything with a frankness and friendliness which I could not understand. Did he fear my resentment and was he trying to forestall the effects of it? I venture to think that this must have been the explanation. I might, through my contacts, be of service to him. Don Pio had a special talent for making use of anyone, however humble, and for allaying the resentment of his enemies.

Since the recent events the town had completely changed its character: the monotonous calm and deadly boredom of pre-revolutionary days had changed to a continual bustle and noisy clamour. The government that had taken power in Orbegoso's name had to use the money collected from the landowners to equip an army strong enough to oppose that of Bermudez. I was very well informed about everything that was happening in the general staff; Althaus, always open with me, and feeling the need to ridicule his illustrious superiors, recounted everything in the greatest detail. The presumptuousness, incapacity and carelessness of these men were incredible. What Althaus had no access to came to me through Emmanuel, and as a result I was the best informed person in town. If Nieto and Baldivia had had the capacity required by their positions they could certainly, with orderliness, economy and hard work, have carried out all the necessary measures by using the enormous sums levied from the unfortunate landowners; but money easily come by goes equally easily. Whenever a ship arrived at Islay, the general at once gave orders to discover what arms and munitions were on board, and to buy any available swords, rifles, powder,

GRAN MANSCAL LUIS JOSÉ DE ORBEGOSO

ammunition, cloth etc. Obviously, such methods soon emptied the till. Baldivia was no wiser, nor did he forget his own interests. He founded a newspaper at Arequipa, which was expensive to run, and made himself editor in chief with a salary of 1,000 piastres a month, plus a fee for every article he wrote for it.

Hardly a month after the promulgation of the famous *bando*, Althaus came into my room laughing so uncontrollably that I asked: 'Why all this laughter, cousin? Has the generalissimo committed a few more blunders? Out with it, so that I can join in the joke.'

'Well, dear friend, this morning our amiable, far-sighted general sent me instructions to go and put in order what he called his "Grand Armoury", into which I have until now not been allowed. There were good reasons why he had surrounded the place with mystery. Can you guess what I found there?'

'Swords, presumably, and rifles?'

'Yes, swords, but you would never guess how many: there are 2,800 swords in that armoury that he has just bought – and I defy Nieto to muster more than six hundred to eight hundred men! There are eighteen hundred rifles, and what rifles! There's no danger that they'll ever kill their brothers with these Birmingham small-arms. This sort cost twenty-two francs each here, a nice shiny English rifle, very cheap! A simple barge-pole would be more lethal than ten of these rifles. And the swords: excellent for cutting turnips. And I haven't mentioned the stacks of blue cloth, the colour of a French grenadier's uniform, and thousands of belts and shoulder-straps that I found in a corner – but not one ammunition pouch to fit on to them. Devil take it, the news of the revolution in Lima must have been brought by carrier pigeon to all those tricksters, the English and French sea-captains, and they've come to plague Peru with their cast-off goods. You might expect all these weapons to be properly stored so as to keep them in good order – that the rifles, for example, would be protected from rust. Not at all: everything is heaped up anyhow in the old chapel, which leaks all over the place – just thrown there like so many bundles of hay. But never mind, wet or not, those rifles will never fire a shot!'

Althaus stayed for more than two hours, joking about the sayings and doings of the distinguished leaders of the republic, with such originality and humour that I could not help laughing with him. 'Althaus,' I told him, 'you ought to advise them. You can see that they have no idea what to do in the serious circumstances into which their rashness and ignorance have led them.'

'Advise them? Ah! Florita, I can see that you still do not understand the people of this country. They are presumptuous fools who are convinced that they have an inborn wisdom. In the first years of my residence in South America I was, like you, upset at seeing them make so many mistakes, and I explained to them frankly that if they did things otherwise the results would be better. Do you know what happened? The idiots became my implacable enemies; they no longer trusted me and hid everything from me – like the armoury here. If they hadn't urgently needed the skills I possess they would have thrown me out like a leper. I suffered much at the beginning from such people, but then I made the best of it and stopped worrying. I let them commit their follies and made a joke of them, having learnt during my stay in France the power of ridicule when it's used at the right time and in the right way.'

'But Althaus, what you have just told me is most alarming; such folly could have serious consequences for the people of Arequipa. If Nieto buys all this rubbish from the European sea-captains, he will be forced to make new financial levies. The way things are going there will be no end to it.'

'That's exactly what will happen: Baldivia, that dashing monk, is already drawing up his second *bando*. This time Don Pio will not escape. Ugarte and Gamio will be sucked dry; but it's the bishop and his family who will be hit especially hard. Ah! burghers of Arequipa! You want a republic? Well, my friends, we are about to show you that a republic costs a republic!' And he went on to pour ridicule on that system of government. Absolutism was inborn in the *Baron* Althaus, and the sample of republican organisation that he was contemplating was hardly likely to convert him.

The Spanish American cities, separated from one

another by great stretches of uncultivated and uninhabited territory, still have few common interests. The most urgent need was to create municipal administrations suitable to the intellectual level of the population and capable of progressing with them; these could have been joined into a federation which was simply an expression of the existing links between them. But, in order to throw off the Spanish yoke, armies had to be created and, as always happens, the power of the sword predominated. If the population of these republics had been less dispersed, their opinions would have been more united and they would not, for these last twenty years, have offered the distressing prospect of wars endlessly renewed.

Independence, when it came, confounded all prophecies. England spent enormous sums in order to promote it, and it is clear, now that Spanish America is free, that the motive which was instilled into the people to encourage them to throw off the Spanish yoke was not a desire for political liberty (for which they were far from ready), nor for freedom of trade, since the masses were too poor to profit from it. It was hatred against the Spaniards for the privileges they enjoyed that was made the issue at stake.

With the example in mind of North America, where freedom has achieved such striking results, people are puzzled to see how the South remains so long a prey to political convulsions and civil wars. It is important to remember the differences in climate and moral temper between the two. In South America, needs are few and easily satisfied. Wealth is still very unequally distributed and mendicity – the unseparable companion of Spanish Catholicism – is almost a profession. Before independence, enormous fortunes had been made in public service, in trade (especially in illicit trade) and in mining; very few of these fortunes were based on agriculture. The mass of the population were in rags and are no better off since. Whereas in English America, the customs and usages had developed under the influence of liberal ideas, both in politics and religion. There were no great distances between the centres of population, and the climate was such that the people had many needs. They had preserved the European habit of hard work, and since wealth could only be acquired by agriculture or by normal trade, it was fairly well distributed.

It is surprising that, human prudence being what it is, all the rich did not leave Spanish America at the same time as the Spanish government; it was obvious that they would become the victims of the ensuing commotions. It was their wealth that financed the wars, and these will never cease until there are no longer any large fortunes left to plunder. The development of the mines is in rapid decline; a number have been flooded as a result of the wars, and as soon as peace is re-established the inhabitants will be forced to rely almost entirely on agriculture. This will have a civilising effect, and will result in a gradual growth of notions of order and rational liberty.

When the news of the events in Lima reached Arequipa, the men who caused the city to side with Orbegoso were not motivated by a concern for the welfare of the public, or by any conviction that this president was better than his rivals. They saw an opportunity to seize power and to acquire wealth, and they took it. Baldivia, who had a great influence over General Nieto, induced him to seize the military command of the whole province, then, under the general's protection, he put himself at the head of the civil government and distributed the posts to men of his own creation. The two men – or in reality Baldivia alone – ran everything for the three months before the arrival of San Roman.

As Althaus had warned me he would, Baldivia promulgated his second *bando* a month after the first. This time, my uncle Pio was taxed 6,000 piastres. He protested, but had to pay 'on this very day', as the *bando* put it, adding that anyone in arrears would be sent to prison. The bishop had to pay 30,000 piastres! – his brother and sister 6,000 each; Ugarte, 10,000 – he suffered a fit of madness and his wife had to take him to the country. Poor Gamio nearly died. One of my women cousins, called Gutierrez, was the only one who showed any character. She firmly refused to pay, and they failed to succeed in forcing her to. The whole town was so enraged that Nieto dared not walk abroad; and Baldivia, that bold man, who had for some time taken to dressing as a layman, prudently returned to his monkish garb. The people had some respect for it, and he was nervous of the landowners' reaction. After this second financial levy, which was spent no more wisely than the first, they requisitioned horses, then mares, then mules: and finally they took even the donkeys! Such extortions caused a state of exhaustion in the citizens of Arequipa: they grumbled but had not the courage to resist. Then came a general call-up, under Nieto's orders. It was the last straw. The Peruvian people are anti-military; they all abhor the status of soldier; the Indian prefers to commit suicide rather than serve in the army.* At first the people refused outright to obey the general's order; Baldivia then resorted to persuasion, and in a series of articles in his newspaper he so cleverly played on their pride that all the young men enrolled of their own accord. The clever monk, exploiting their vanity and their ignorance, compared them to Spartans, Romans and, finally, to the 'Parisian Immortals' of 1830!

Such is the Peruvian character: vain, boastful, know-all, swashbuckling – all in words: but incapable of resolution or perseverance in any courageous course of action.

My life was quite varied and busy, what with the bustle of the town, my many friends and my intimate conversations with my uncle, Althaus and Emmanuel; but my heart was not in any of this, and from then on I was conscious of a terrible void and was gripped by deep depression. Those who have loving natures cannot live by the events of daily life alone; they must have emotional ties. I realised, but too late, that I had yielded too easily to the promptings of my imagination when I came to Peru in search of tranquillity and happiness, when I could only find these in the loving surroundings that were now denied me. I was still young and passed for an unmarried woman; I could therefore have expected to be loved by some man who might have married me in spite of my lack of means. I can positively assert that several gentlemen of Arequipa

* *Author's note:* My uncle told me that during the twenty years that he spent at war in Peru, every time there were rivers to cross or the route lay along the edge of a precipice, he lost many Indian soldiers who flung themselves into the rivers or over the cliffs, preferring such a death to the life of a soldier.

gave me clear enough indications of their intentions for me to have no doubts about this. If I had been free, I would have responded to the affection and gratefully accepted the protection of one of them; but I felt the weight of my chains, even at the immense distance that separated me from the man who was my master; I therefore had to stifle the warmth of the nature that God had given me, and appear cold, indifferent and even unfriendly. I am openhearted to a fault, and I longed to confide my troubles, yet when I wanted to weep on the bosom of a friend, I had to remain isolated from my fellows, living under a continual strain. When I set out I certainly did not foresee what I would have to suffer as a result of posing as an unmarried woman. On board ship this was to some extent mitigated by my affection for Chabrié; but from the time I broke with him, I made up my mind to avoid having such friendships in future; they were too dangerous both for me and for the other participant.

This was no life: living is loving, and I could only feel alive if I could satisfy the need, and this was impossible. When, as a substitute, I tried to concentrate all my affections on my daughter, I realised that this too had its dangers. I dared not think of the child, and constantly drove the thought of her out of my mind, for fear of giving myself away by mentioning her in conversation. How difficult it is to forget eight years of one's life, especially for a mother. Joaquina's youngest was my daughter's age; she was a nice child and mischievous; her talk often reminded me of my poor Aline, and when this happened, my eyes would fill with tears. I avoided taking part in her games and would retire to my room with feelings that only a mother can understand. You wretch, I would say to myself, what have you done? Grief has made you a coward, a brute. I ran away, unable to bear the burden. I left my daughter in the hands of strangers. The poor child may be ill, dead even! Then my imagination would exaggerate the dangers she was in and my guilt towards her, and I would fall into a fever of despair.

My surroundings increased my unhappiness. I ignored the children, and would have preferred never to see them. I was so cold towards both my uncle's and Althaus's that the poor little things dared not speak to me or even look at me. That house, where my father was born, which should have been my home and where I was treated as an outsider, was a continual irritant to my wounded heart. The presence of its owners reminded me continually of the vile injustice that they pitilessly practised against me. Their hospitality had a bitter taste, and I would have run any risks or danger to escape from the den of these brigands who had so robbed me. But thoughts of France were fraught with the horrors I had suffered there: I knew not where to go nor what to do! There was no refuge nor rest anywhere on earth. Death, which for some time I had believed to be imminent and which I had welcomed as a gift from God, failed to come to my rescue: my health improved. I could see no glimmer of hope, and there was not a soul in whom I could confide my troubles. A deep depression took hold of me; I fell silent and took to brooding over sinister courses of action. I hated life; it had become a burden too heavy for me to bear. It was then that I had to struggle against a violent desire to destroy myself. I have never approved of suicide, always considering that it results from an inability to support pain. To hold life in contempt when one is suffering has always seemed so natural to me, that I have felt that to commit suicide is the action of a coward; but grief has its moments of anger, which common sense is too weak to resist when not supported by faith. At that date, I believed in human reason. I was not yet resigned to letting life take me where it would; I was either borne up by hope or cast into despair, according to whether I saw the future as fair or foul. I had to fight hard to overcome this disgust of life, this desire to die. There was a demon which ceaselessly reminded me of my past miseries and depicted my future misfortunes, and pointed a murderous dagger at my heart. I spent eight days and nights in the throes of death, and again and again felt its icy grip on my body. I finally emerged from this long struggle, by letting this infernal power take possession of my soul.

I decided that I too would enter the social battlefield; after having been the victim of society and its prejudices for so long, I too would try to exploit it, I would live on the lives of others, I would live for myself alone. Like the rest of the world, I would not be deterred by any scruples. I am in the midst of a society in process of revolution, I said to myself; let me see what part I can play in this, and what tools I can find to use.

At this period I did not believe in Catholicism, but I believed in evil; I had not understood God's omnipotence and his infinite love of the beings he has created; my eyes were not yet open. I did not realise that suffering and joy are two inseparable sides of life; that one inevitably brings the other in its train and that is the means by which all things progress; that all beings have their phases of development through which they must pass; blind agents of Providence, they all have their mission to fulfil, from which they cannot depart without causing an affront to divine omnipotence. I thought then that it depended on our will to play the part that we wished to play. Until then I had only felt emotional needs; ambition, greed and other artificial passions had seemed to me but the fever of sick brains. I had always aspired to a life ruled by tender affection, in circumstances of modest well-being; and these aspirations had been denied me. I had been enslaved to a man (whom I have already described) at an age when all resistance is useless; born of parents whose union was not registered according to legal formalities, I was forced when still very young to forego all the tender emotions and the possibility of a life free of poverty. Loneliness was my lot; it was only furtively that I could appear in society; my father's inheritance had fallen into the clutches of a millionaire uncle. My cup was running over, so I turned in open revolt against an order of things which had so cruelly victimised me, by sanctioning the servitude of the weaker and the expropriation of the orphan. I made the decision to participate in the intrigues of ambition, to rival the monk in audacity and guile, and to be, like him, pitiless.

It was then that hell entered into my soul! Hell exists whenever we deviate from the way that Providence has mapped out for us, and our torments are even greater the further we depart from it. Vainly we try to change our natures. There are few people, I think, whose will power is greater than that with which God has endowed me; and yet, quite determined as I was to harden my heart and become ambitious, I could not succeed. I concentrated on Baldivia, studying him until I understood his burning desire for domination and his hatred of the bishop; but I could not appropriate any of this feeling to myself; I realised that to be like the monk would be repugnant to me. I then imagined myself in Althaus's place, and knew that the strong emotions he sought in life would cause me acute pain. As for my uncle, I could never understand what enjoyment he could get from spending his life engaged in base intrigues, in petty schemes.

I nevertheless persisted in the plan I had made not only to become involved in politics but to play a major part. To encourage me, there was the example of Señora Gamarra, who had become the prime mover of the republic. Gamarra and she, having toppled Orbegoso, now ruled in the name of Bermudez; Señora Gamarra ran everything and commanded the armed forces; and in the names of Bermudez and Orbegoso, the struggle would now be waged between Señora Gamarra and the monk Baldivia. It was necessary to take the latter's place, and so rally all the supporters of Orbegoso. It was only by the sword that such a plan could succeed. I deeply resented having to work through another person, feeling as I did capable of acting on my own. I would have to find an army officer whose energy and popularity with the soldiers made him a suitable instrument; I would have to make him fall in love with me, encourage his ambition and use him in all my schemes. I began to make a serious study of the officers who came to my uncle's house and those I chatted with familiarly each evening at the Althaus's. I had not, however, succeeded in destroying all my better nature, and the good principles that I retained rebelled against the career into which I obstinately insisted on entering. When alone, I was assailed by sinister thoughts of the many victims who would have to be sacrificed before I could gain power and retain it. I tried to comfort myself with the thought of the illusory plans for the public good that I had in mind; but in vain: a secret voice kept asking me how I was so sure of their success that to attain them I was prepared to commit murder, and – in my miserable situation – how could I point the finger at those whose destruction I would have to plot? I could see the ghosts of my slaughtered enemies rising up against me: my woman's heart was overwhelmed, my hair stood on end in horror and I suffered in advance the pangs of remorse.

When I felt there was no escape from the internal torment which wracked me so violently and from the tiresome political conversations, I would call on my cousin Carmen and ask her to come for a walk in the country. Carmen was full of an inexhaustible kindness to me that I shall always remember with gratitude; she would agree to come, although it was a tiresome chore to her. As there was no promenade in Arequipa, the women stayed at home. The care they took of their feet also tended to make them sedentary; they thought that walking would make their feet grow fat. A favourite walk was to the water-mill, which we sometimes entered. I liked looking at this rustic establishment, which was in general very inferior to ours. Other days we would visit the chocolate mill, quite close to the flour mill. There my pleasure was to find the progress of civilisation; the cocoa was ground, the sugar was crushed, and it was all mixed together to form chocolate. The machine had been imported from England: it was a very fine one, run by water power. The manager was full of attention to me, because of the interest I showed, the questions I asked him about his machine and the attention I paid to the explanations he gave me. I always left with a small packet of very good cocoa and a charming bouquet that he gallantly presented to me. When the river was low enough for us to cross by jumping from rock to rock or by being carried over by our negresses, we would climb the hill which rose from the far bank and from which the whole valley of Arequipa could be seen. Sitting beside Carmen, legs crossed in the Oriental fashion as was the custom of the country, I delighted in remaining for hours at a time in that spot, gently day-dreaming, chatting to Carmen while she smoked her cigar.

When, during our conversations, Carmen spoke of the misfortunes of her country, I was doubly distressed. It was clear to me that if someone with a generous and strong nature were able to seize power, the disasters could be ended and an era of prosperity might ensue for that unfortunate country. I thought of all the good I could do if I were in Señora Gamarra's place, and was more determined than ever to attempt it.

Among the officers who came to my uncle's and to Althaus's I only met one who might have come up to my expectations, and though he was the one I found most repugnant, I would not have hesitated a moment to try and make him fall in love with me, so convinced was I of the saintly nature of the part I could have played; but it seems that God had reserved me for a different mission: that officer was married. When I was quite convinced that there was no one at Arequipa whom I could use, I was forced to abandon my plans. However, one hope remained, and I clung to it. I decided to go to Lima.

I informed my uncle and the whole family that I had decided to return to France, adding that, wishing to visit the Peruvian capital first, I proposed to embark for Lima. This news surprised everybody: my uncle seemed to be deeply affected; he advanced strong arguments to dissuade me from my intention, but did not offer me a situation of any greater independence than the one I already enjoyed in his house. Althaus was truly upset; his wife was in despair, and the two members of the family who expressed most regret were Emmanuel and Carmen. I was profoundly sorry at the thought of leaving my cousin Carmen; the others did not need me, but for her I had become a necessity. However, my uncle asked me to await the outcome of the political crisis before going, and I agreed.

The monk had succeeded, with the help of money and of his newspaper propaganda, in organising an army as follows:

Infantry	1,000 men
Cavalry	800 men
Battalion of Immortals formed from the flower of Arequipa's youth	78 men
Chacareros (peasantry) from the neighbourhood	300 men
	2,178 men

There was in addition a National Guard, formed of three to four hundred veterans, exclusively for the defence of the city.

The general had set up a camp, both in order to present a warlike appearance and to get his troops out of barracks and accustom them to hard living. The camp was badly placed from a military point of view. It was about a league from Arequipa, and being near a village had the serious disadvantage of being surrounded by *chicherías*, taverns selling *chicha*, an alcoholic drink made from fermented crushed maize.* The headquarters was in the house of a certain Señor Menao. Althaus had tried to discourage Nieto from setting up this camp, pointing out the risks to the soldiers' health during the wet season, and the enormous amount it would cost. The general, stubborn as ever, had pooh-poohed such arguments, and also ignored the wise counsels of his chief of staff as to the positioning of the camp. Nieto's objective was to make a show, to create an image of a great military leader in a warlike setting; it tickled his stupid vanity to parade his authority among the tents with a large entourage of officers. He liked to be at the head of his brilliantly uniformed staff: from the town to the camp and back to the town again they rode continually, a cavalcade of heroes which gave us much cause for amusement. The general, riding a fine black horse, looked like an impersonation of Murat, so varied and sumptuous were his uniforms. Baldivia, usually dressed in his monk's habit and mounted always on a white horse, played the role of a Peruvian La Fayette. The crowd of officers who accompanied them, gleaming with gold, their plumes nodding, were no less ridiculous.

Thanks to Althaus, and with the general's agreement, I had a horse at my disposal whenever I wanted to visit the camp. The townsfolk were without horses, as they had had to surrender them or else hide them to avoid requisition. Only my uncle had kept his Chilean mare, because she was so spirited that no officer wanted to

* *Author's note:* When there is no mill for grinding the maize, the women chew it and spit it into a vessel in which it is then fermented.

ride her, and she would have been the cause of accidents amongst the cavalry. To visit the camp was one of my favourite pastimes; I went either with my uncle or with Althaus or Emmanuel, who was now an officer. The general always gave me a good reception, but the monk seemed to guess my thoughts and the contempt I felt for him. As soon as he saw me, his face, always shifty-looking, hostile, impudent, took on a special expression: it was clear that he knew how much I disliked him. He would greet me with cold politeness, and listen carefully to anything I said without appearing to pay any attention, but he never joined in the conversation. From Emmanuel I heard that my visits were not at all popular and that my hilarious conversational asides with Althaus were offensive to them: but how could I avoid laughing at such ridiculous officers? Nieto, setting up a camp for only eighteen hundred men (the *chacareros* and the Immortals were not included) had taken more space than a European general would have required for fifty thousand. On a knoll to the left of Señor Menao's house, they had constructed a redoubt which was defended by five small mountain guns. It was the first time I had ever seen any, and they reminded me of waste water pipes. This redoubt was overlooked by a naturally fortified position which the enemy could easily occupy if he approached along that particular road: and as Arequipa is an open town which can be reached by ten different routes, it was not easy to predict which one they would choose.

The infantry camp, which was on lines close to the redoubt, was a very poor affair. The unfortunate soldiers slept in small ill-fastened tents, made of so light a canvas that they could not keep out the rains, which were frequent at that season. The cavalry, under the command of Colonel Carillo, took up more space. They were on the other side of the redoubt. The general made me gallop in front of the horses, which were in one long row and widely distanced from each other. Things were no better arranged here than with the infantry – indeed they were a pathetic sight. At the far end of the camp, behind the soldiers' tents, the *ravanas* were quartered, with all their cooking gear and their children; washing was hanging out; the women, as they washed clothes or sewed, made an infernal din, shouting, singing and chattering.

The *ravanas* are the camp followers of South America. In Peru, a soldier can have as many of them as he wishes: some have as many as four. They are therefore a numerous company, and march several hours ahead of the men in order to have time to obtain food, cook it and set up camp. When this advance guard moves off, one realises what these unfortunate women have to put up with, the life of danger and hardship that they lead. They are armed; they load their cooking pots, tents and other baggage on to mules; a crowd of children of all ages trails after them; they set their mules off at a fast trot, and run behind them. In this way they climb snow-covered mountains and swim across rivers carrying one or even two children on their backs. When they arrive at the appointed place, they first choose the best camp site, then unload their mules, put up the tents, feed the children and put them to bed, light the fires and start the cooking. If there is a village nearby, a group of them goes there to forage for food. They descend on the village like hungry beasts and ask the inhabitants for food for the troops. If the response is favourable they do no harm; but if they are obstructed, they fight like lionesses, and their courage and ferocity overcome all resistance. They then plunder the village, take their booty back to the camp and share it out between them.

These women, who provide for all the needs of the soldiers and wash and mend their clothes, receive no pay. Their only reward is to be given the right to steal with impunity. They are of Indian race and language, and speak no Spanish. They are not married, belong to no one, yet are claimed by anyone. They are creatures apart; they live and eat with the soldiers, stop where they stop, are exposed to the same dangers and lead a life of even greater hardships. When an army is on the march, its survival almost always depends on the courage and determination of these women who travel four or five hours ahead. When one thinks that in addition to all these trials they have to be mothers, with all that involves, it is surprising that they survive at all. It is remarkable that whilst the Indian male prefers to commit suicide rather than be a soldier, the

Indian women take up the life voluntarily and undergo all its hardships with a courage of which their menfolk are incapable. There is no more striking proof of the superiority of women amongst primitive peoples. Would the same not be true of more civilised races, if both sexes received the same education? Let us hope that the time will come when the experiment will be tried.

Various meritorious generals have tried to find a substitute for the system of *ravanas* to prevent the women from accompanying the army; but the soldiers have always successfully resisted these attempts. They have too little confidence in the military services provided in their place to give up their *ravanas*.

These women are hideously ugly, which is not surprising, given what they go through: they have to endure both the burning sun of the *pampas* and the icy summits of the Andes. Their skin is therefore sunburned and chapped and their eyes bloodshot; they have, however, very white teeth. Their only garments are a short woollen skirt reaching no further than the knee, and a sheepskin, hanging down back and front with a hole in it for the head. They disregard the rest: feet, arms and head are always bare. They are on the whole fairly peaceful amongst themselves, though jealousy can sometimes lead to murder. This is not surprising when one thinks that there is no authority to restrain them. If, under the same conditions, the same number of men were living together without any form of discipline, the murders would undoubtedly be much more frequent. The *ravanas* worship the sun but do not observe any religious practices.

The headquarters building had been transformed into a gambling den. The large downstairs room had been divided in two by a curtain. One side was occupied by the general and the senior officers, the other by the subalterns. Everyone, in both rooms, played faro for enormous sums.* Althaus wanted me to see the officers of the republic in their glory, and so took me, at eleven o'clock at night, to

* *Author's note:* The Peruvians are great gamblers. Colonel Morant, in a game at Charillos, near Lima, lost 30,000 piastres in one night.

the house of Señor Menao. We did not go inside, but, unseen, we peered in at the window. What a sight! We saw Nieto, Carillo, Morant, Rivero and Ros sitting round a table with cards in their hands and a heap of gold in front of them. On the table were bottles and glasses full of wine or liqueurs. Their expressions showed the gambling passion at its most extreme: some showed concentrated rage, some the unquenchable greed that feeds on whatever winnings luck provides. They were all smoking cigars, and the dim light which filtered through the smoke made them look like figures in an inferno. The monk was not gambling, but walking slowly up and down. He would sometimes stop and look at them, and folding his arms would seem to be saying: 'What can I expect from such collaborators as these?' With his long black robe and his sinister expression he looked in these surroundings like the incarnation of evil, chafing at the obstacles which vice can put in the way of successful crime. The muscles of his face worked in an alarming manner, his little black eyes shone darkly, his upper lip expressed scorn and pride. Then he regained his calm with an appearance of resignation. We watched the scene for a long time; no one saw us: the slaves on duty were asleep, the brave defenders of the fatherland were engrossed in their game, the monk in his thoughts. As we left, Althaus and I talked of the misfortunes of a country in the hands of leaders such as these.

Towards the end of March the news came from Lima that President Orbegoso was preparing to come and take over the command of the Arequipa provincial army. Nieto was plunged into despair by this: the president was coming to wrest from him the glory which he would be bound to acquire by confronting San Roman. Our gallant general could not rebel, as he had not enough influence to set himself up as head of a party under no one's protection; so, in order to prevent what he considered as an affront, he resorted to a typical ruse. He arranged secretly for a confidential letter to be sent to someone who was bound to pass it on to San Roman. The letter said that Nieto was in a pitiable state, without weapons or ammunition, and incapable of putting up a defence. Once this letter had been dispatched, the general with the greatest impatience daily expected the arrival of the enemy forces.

For the last three months the expected arrival of the famous General San Roman had dominated all conversations. For the first two months his name produced the same effect on the population as the word 'bogeyman' on the imagination of small children. Orbegoso's supporters depicted him as a ferocious, evil man, capable of personally cutting the throats of the unfortunate Arequipans for his own pleasure, and of burning and sacking their town to satisfy his party's vengeance, and so on and so forth. The general public enjoyed exchanging stories about San Roman, both in order to scare each other and also because as a race they have a tendency towards exaggeration and fantasy which leads them inevitably to extremes. But there were also individuals, such as the monk and the general, and their supporters, whose particular interest it was to spread these rumours.

The entire hopes of each of the two parties depended on the army which supported it, and the battle between the two armies would alone decide the issue. Victory in arms meant complete success, defeat total failure. Orbegoso's followers had been everywhere unsuccessful, and their only hope now lay in the valour of the Arequipans, on whom all eyes were therefore turned. Señora Gamarra, on the other hand, felt that the authority of the government which she had set up could not be maintained whilst a centre of armed resistance remained; to be mistress of Lima she must first be mistress of Arequipa; if, with the three battalions that remained at her disposal, she could subdue that town, she could return to Lima without opposition from Orbegoso. It was therefore vitally important for the army chiefs, the authorities of the city and all those interested in supporting Orbegoso in Arequipa, to foster exaggerated ideas about the disasters which would follow a victory by San Roman, so that the people would be in a mood to defend themselves to the last man. Handwritten leaflets were for this purpose circulated daily, composed by the monk but unsigned, in which it was said that San Roman had promised his soldiers that they would be allowed to sack the town. There followed a description of the massacres, rapes and atrocities which would take place, and these struck terror amounting to despair into the timid hearts of the inhabitants. The monk therefore achieved his objective, for despair fills even a coward with courage. The general harangued his soldiers; the prefect and the major issued proclamations on the same lines; and then finally the monks from various monasteries, under duress, preached resistance to the death in their churches.

All these speeches and sermons produced the desired effect on the public. During the first month after the insurrection, the possibility of San Roman's sudden arrival with the three best battalions under his command caused so much anxiety that the defence measures were zealously organised. During the second month the Arequipans, confident in the effectiveness of these measures and in the eventual victory which the monk assured them would be achieved by their valour, got used to the idea of the coming struggle and steadfastly awaited the enemy. But in the third month their impatience knew no bounds. San Roman's delay in arriving seemed to prove that he was afraid of them, and this increased their courage, but – as always happens to the inexperienced – they suddenly passed from a state of terror to one of over-confidence, a boasting and bragging which filled all reasonable people with anxiety. Defeat would be calamitous, but the results of victory would be no less fraught with problems, with these men who were both cowardly and foolhardy in control. From the moment when, blindly over-confident, they fancied that the battle was already won – before even having met the enemy – they vied with each other in folly, all of them, from the general down to the most junior official at the town hall: it was pathetic! I then realised that whatever happened would be disastrous for the country, that the success of Nieto would bring, as inevitably as that of San Roman, enormous taxes, the plunder of property and pillage of every sort.

On the 21st of March Althaus said: 'Florita, apparently the general has at last got some correct intelligence. San Roman will be here tomorrow or the day after. You will find it incredible, but in spite of spending a vast sum on spies, we have not until now had a single piece of genuine information about what goes on in the enemy camp. The general will not let me take a hand in this – his silly pride is hurt when I give him good advice, and he hides what he can from me.'

Two days before this the troops had returned to barracks. This had been made necessary because they had become exhausted by the hardships and privations they had had to undergo during their useless sojourn under canvas. Now, one would think that, if the general trusted the intelligence he received, he would quickly re-deploy the troops, either into the positions they had just left or into new ones dictated by new circumstances. He would take all possible precautions to prevent any surprise attack by the enemy, to avoid confusion among the troops and panic among the public. And finally, he would take measures to prevent any disorders which might be expected as a result either of victory or of defeat. Any military leader of sense would have done all this. But General Nieto thought of none of these things. Without taking any action whatsoever, leaving everything to take care of itself, he went with all the other leaders to Tiavalla to celebrate Holy Week. Next day at about four o'clock in the afternoon, a spy rode in at speed with the news that the enemy was at Cangallo – everyone knew about it! Nieto was urgently sent for; the Immortals formed up, the troops emerged in a disorderly fashion; the *chacareros* were so scared that they refused to obey orders and the bigwigs at the town hall committed folly after folly: confusion reigned.

It was at this point that the ignorance and uselessness of these presumptuous leaders, both civil and military, who were in authority over these unfortunate people, became apparent. Everything that happened that evening and during the night that followed would be incredible to any European. I therefore omit all details, but say only that the confusion was such that, if San Roman had realised it, he could have seized the town on that day, marching his troops into the barracks without a fight: no one was in a fit state to fire a single shot to prevent it. He would have finished the war in three hours. It is a great pity that he did not do so, as much bloodshed would have been spared and much irreparable damage avoided.

XI

THE CONVENTS OF AREQUIPA

As I have already said, Arequipa contains a great number of convents and monasteries, more even than most Peruvian cities. They exude so calm, so religious an air compared to the bustle of the world outside, that one might conclude that if peace and happiness exist on earth it must be in these habitations of the Lord. But alas! the disillusioned seeking repose will not find it in these cloisters. In those vast structures, whose cold, dark exteriors bespeak a tomb-like silence within, there are instead nothing but conflicts, contained but not resolved by the enforcement of discipline. Like volcanoes, the calm exterior veils the boiling lava inside.

Even before I had been in any of these convents, whenever I passed by their open porches or along those great black walls some thirty or forty feet high, my heart seemed to stop; I felt such compassion for the unfortunate victims buried alive under such great heaps of stone that my eyes filled with tears. During my stay at Arequipa I used often to go and sit on the roof of our house. From there I could enjoy the view stretching from the volcano to the pretty river beneath it, and from that smiling valley to the two magnificent convents of Santa Catalina and Santa Rosa. The latter especially attracted my attention and occupied my thoughts: for it was here that a fascinating drama had occurred, the heroine of which was a beautiful, loving and unfortunate – oh, how unfortunate! – young woman. She was related to me, and I was drawn towards her but, forced to obey the fanatical prejudices of the society in which I lived, I could only see her in secret. Although, at the time of my arrival in Arequipa, it was two years since she had escaped from the convent, the effect that her escape had produced was still fresh in people's memories. I had therefore to be very careful about showing any interest in this victim of superstition; I might otherwise have done her harm, by reawakening the fanaticism of her persecutors. Everything that Dominga (that was her name) had told me of her strange story made me most anxious to see the inside of the convent where the poor creature had languished for eleven long years. And so, when towards evening I climbed up on to the roof to watch the spectacle of the sun casting its beautiful but sad radiance over the charming valley of Arequipa as it went down behind the three volcanoes, turning their snows to crimson as it did so, my eyes were always drawn towards the convent of Santa Rosa.

In my mind's eye I could see my cousin Dominga in the heavy ample robe of the Carmelite nuns, with a long black veil, leather shoes with brass buckles, a black leather scourge hanging down to the ground, a heavy rosary which the unfortunate girl pressed from time to time, asking God to help her in her plan, and then crushed, desperately and angrily, in her clenched fist. I seemed to see her at the top of the tower of the beautiful church of Santa Rosa, where she used to go every evening, with the excuse of inspecting the bells and the clock, for which she was responsible. From the top of this tower she could take a long look at the narrow little valley where she had spent her childhood hours – at her mother's house, and at her brothers and sisters running and playing in the garden. How lucky they were, those sisters of hers, to be at liberty to run and play! And what lovely coloured clothes they wore, what beautiful hair they had, adorned with flowers and jewels. How she envied their elegant shoes, their big silk shawls and their light gauze scarves! She would then feel herself stifled under the weight of her own heavy clothes. How she hated her chemise, her stockings and her long, full robe, all in coarse wool. The hard shoes chafed her feet, and her long black veil, which the order strictly insisted should be kept always lowered, was to her like the lid of a coffin closed on someone unconscious, but still alive. In my imagination I could see her flinging back this terrible veil with a convulsive gesture, hear her groans and watch her trying to get her arms through the bars which covered the windows of the bell tower. The poor prisoner only wanted a little of the open air which God gave to all his creatures, a little place in the valley where she could move her cramped limbs; she would have liked to sing the songs of her mountains, dance with her sisters, and like them put on little slippers, a light white scarf, and a few wild flowers in her hair. Alas! she wanted so little, but a terrible, solemn vow, which no human power could break, deprived her for ever of fresh air, gay songs, clothes to suit her age and the changing seasons, and the exercise necessary to her health. The poor girl, at the age of sixteen, in the prey of a fit of resentment and wounded pride, had decided to give up the world. Not knowing what she did, she had even cut off her long hair, and throwing it at the foot of the Cross, had sworn, by the crucified Christ, that she would take God for her husband. The story of the *monja* (nun) made a great sensation at Arequipa and throughout Peru, and I have found it worthy of inclusion in my narrative. But before recounting the tale of my cousin Dominga, I ask the reader to follow me into the convent of Santa Rosa.

In normal times, these convents were inaccessible. No one could go in without the permission of the Bishop of Arequipa, and since the *monja* escaped, he firmly refused all applications. But in the crisis which enveloped the city, they offered sanctuary to the frightened population. My aunt and Manuela thought it wise to retire into one, and I used this opportunity to study the details of monastic life. Santa Rosa was always in my mind, and I put pressure on these ladies to decide in favour of it rather than Santa Catalina, which they would have preferred. I had great difficulty in overcoming their prejudices, but finally succeeded. At about seven in the evening we went to the convent, after sending a negress ahead of us to announce our arrival.

I doubt if there has ever existed, even in the most monarchical of states, a haughtier or more discriminating aristocracy than the one I encountered with amazement when I entered Santa Rosa. The hierarchies of birth, title, colour and wealth reign supreme, and have real significance. When one sees the nuns all walking in procession together dressed in the same uniform, one assumes that equality applies in everything; but as soon as one enters a courtyard, one notices how the aristocrats lord it over the plebeians, the white women over the coloured, and the rich over the poor.

Santa Rosa is one of the largest and richest of the Arequipan convents. It is conveniently planned: there are four cloisters, each round a spacious courtyard. Thick stone pillars support the rather low vaults of the cloisters. The small low doors of the nuns' cells open on to them. These cells are large and brilliantly whitewashed. They are lit by a window with four panes which, like the door, gives on to the cloisters. The furniture consists of an oak table and stool, an earthenware jug and a pewter mug. Above the table is a large crucifix. The figure of Christ is in yellow ivory, blackened by time; the cross is in black wood. On the table there is a skull and a little hour-glass, a breviary and sometimes other prayerbooks; nearby, hanging on a large nail, is a black leather scourge. Except for the Mother Superior, no nun is allowed to sleep in her cell, which is only to provide a place for meditation, self-communion and repose in silence and solitude. They eat communally in a vast refectory, dining at midday and supping at six. Whilst they eat, one of them reads aloud passages from the holy books. They all sleep in dormitories, of which there are three.

These dormitories are vaulted, L-shaped, and entirely windowless. A ghostly lamp is placed in the angle of the L, but its light hardly penetrates more than six feet away, so that the two wings of the dormitory remain in total darkness. Not only outsiders, but even the servant-maids are forbidden to enter these dormitories. But if at evening one makes a furtive incursion under the dark cold vaults of these long halls, the scene recalls a descent into the catacombs and the effect is so lugubrious that it is difficult to suppress a revulsion of fear. The 'tombs'* are on each

* *Author's note:* The enclosures to which each nun retires for the night are called 'tombs'.

side of the dormitory at twelve to fifteen feet from each other. They are raised on a dais and look exactly in shape and arrangement like tombs in the crypt of a church. They are hung with black woollen cloth, like that used for funeral hangings. The interior is ten to twelve feet long by six wide and six high. Inside there is a bed made of two thick oak planks fixed on four iron legs. On the planks is a large linen sack filled, according to the degrees of saintliness of the occupier, with cinders, pebbles, thorns even, or with straw or wool. I, in fact, entered three of these tombs, and the sacks were all straw-filled. At the end of the bed is a small piece of furniture, in black wood, which is table, prie-dieu and cupboard all in one. As in the cells, there is a large crucifix facing the head of the bed. Underneath it, there is a skull, a prayerbook, a rosary and a scourge. It is expressly forbidden to introduce any light into these 'tombs' in any circumstances. When a nun is ill, she goes to the infirmary. My poor cousin Dominga slept in one of these 'tombs' for eleven years.

The life of the nuns is arduous in the extreme. They rise at four for matins, followed almost uninterruptedly by a succession of religious services which they must attend. These last until midday, after which prayers begin again and continue until the evening. In addition there are numerous saints' days involving processions and other ceremonies. Such is their life. Their only recreation is to walk in their beautiful gardens. There are three of these, in which they grow exquisite flowers with loving care.

When nuns take the veil in the Carmelite order, they make a vow of poverty and silence. When two of them meet, one must say: 'Sister, we must die,' and the other must reply: 'Sister, death is our deliverance,' – not another word. However, they do talk, and talk a great deal, but only during their walks in the garden or when they are in the kitchen supervising the servants, or when they pay duty visits to the top of the towers. They also talk in their cells, paying long surreptitious visits to each other. In short they talk whenever they think they can do so without breaking their vow, and to lull their consciences they keep utterly silent in the courtyards, the refectory and especially in the dormitories, where human voice has never sounded. I am not one to blame them for their slight violations of the rule of the holy order of Carmelites. I find it natural that they should want to exchange a few words after long hours of silence. But, for their own welfare, I would wish that they would confine their conversation to the flowers they grow, the good sweetmeats and excellent cakes they make, their magnificent processions and the rich jewels of their Virgin, or even their confessor. Unfortunately, these ladies do not confine themselves to these subjects. Criticism, scandal and backbiting are predominant. It is unbelievable what small jealousies, what unworthy rivalries they feel for each other and the cruel malice with which they continually treat each other. There is no softness in the relations between these nuns: dryness, harshness and hatred are the keynotes. Nor are they any stricter in observing their vow of poverty. No one should have, according to the rule, more than one servant; however a number of them have three or four slaves who live in the building. In addition they all keep a slave outside the building to run errands, buy anything they need and communicate with their families and the outside world. Some of the nuns are very wealthy and make valuable gifts to the convent and its church; they send gifts of fruit and sweetmeats or handiwork made in the convent to friends in town and sometimes people they are fond of receive even more valuable presents. Santa Rosa of Arequipa is considered one of the richest religious houses of Peru; yet the nuns seemed to me to be more unfortunate than those of any of the convents I was able to visit.

I must say, however, that the Mother Superior received me with the greatest courtesy. She was sixty-eight, and had been in charge of the community for eighteen years. She must have been very beautiful, and had now a face of great nobility; everything about her expressed great strength of will. She was born in Seville, and came to Arequipa at the age of seven. Her father sent her to Santa Rosa for her education, since when she had never been outside it. She spoke Spanish with remarkable purity and elegance, and was as well educated as a nun can be. All the questions that she asked me about Europe indicated that she had been much concerned with the political events which had shaken Spain and Peru for the previous twenty years. Her political opinions were as fanatical as her religious ones, and the latter were extreme beyond all reason. Speaking of Dominga, she said: 'That girl was *possessed of the devil*; I am happy that the devil chose my convent, for this will be an example that will stimulate faith; for, my dear Flora, I will confess to you a small part of what distresses me: every day I see how the faith, the true faith that alone can believe in miracles, is weakening in the hearts of the younger nuns.' This austere and strict woman was obeyed and respected by the nuns, whom she ruled with a rod of iron; but even after so many years in charge, she had commanded the sincere affection of none of them.

The three days spent in this convent had so fatigued my aunt and cousins that they refused to remain any longer, whatever the risks they might have to run outside. I on the other hand during this short stay had collected many useful observations and had not been at all bored. The solemn nuns saw us off as ceremoniously and correctly as they had welcomed us, and we passed through the vast oak door which was bolted and barred like the gateway of a fortress. No sooner had the gatekeeper closed it behind us than we started to run down the long wide streets of Santa Rosa, shouting: 'Lord, what a joy to be free!' The ladies were weeping, the children and the negresses were gambolling in the street, and I admit that I too breathed again.

The day after we entered Santa Rosa, Althaus had sent to tell us that the news was false, that the Indian who brought it was in San Roman's pay and that the latter would not be arriving for another fortnight. We therefore thought that we could return home; but the evening of the day we came out there was another alarm, and this time my relations all retired into Santa Catalina. It seemed that San Roman was definitely at Cangallo. His arrival so close to Arequipa (four leagues) made the danger imminent; as soon as the news had spread, the disorder in the town and in the camp was hardly less than at the first alarm caused by the spy. The convents and the churches had now become furniture stores. For the last fortnight the inhabitants had been hiding all their movable possessions in them, and their empty houses looked as if they had been pillaged. I had my trunks carried to Santo Domingo with my uncle's effects. It was midday when the enemy was reported to have reached Cangallo, and my uncle was expected at about six or seven o'clock. The flat roofs of the houses were full of people gazing in all directions. But they were to be disappointed. The enemy had halted.

Althaus came from the camp and said: 'Cousin, it is true this time that San Roman is at Cangallo; but his soldiers are exhausted and I am quite sure that he will stay there three or four days to recover.'

'So you think he won't come today?'

'I think he won't be here for four or five days, so you can join Manuela. In any case you will be able to watch the battle from the top of the convent, quite as well as from the roof of your uncle's house.' I followed his advice and went to Santa Catalina to join my relatives.

Again I found myself inside a convent, but what a contrast to the one I had just left! What a commotion, what excitement when I entered! 'La Francesita, la Francesita!' everyone was calling. Hardly had I got through the door before I was surrounded by a dozen nuns all talking at once, shouting, laughing and jumping with joy. I stood for at least a quarter of an hour in the entrance, which is under a tower, almost suffocating from the heat in the crush caused by these boisterous nuns and the crowd of negresses and *sambas* which surrounded me. I was seriously beginning to think that I was going to faint – my legs were giving way, I was bathed in perspiration and the din they were all making so deafened me that I no longer knew where I was. Then the Mother Superior arrived to welcome me. She was a cousin of the Superior of Santa Rosa, and related to our family in the same degree. As she approached, the noise decreased a little and the crowd opened to let her pass. I really felt quite ill. The good lady realised this, scolded the nuns severely and ordered that all the negresses should withdraw. She then took me into her cell, which was large and beautiful, and there, after inviting me to sit down on rich rugs and soft cushions, she sent for a selection of excellent cakes made in the convent, served on an exquisitely made Parisian tray, with Spanish wines in crystal decanters and a superb gilt goblet, elegantly cut and engraved with the arms of Spain.

When I had recovered a little, the good lady insisted on accompanying me to the cell which she had chosen for me. What a darling cell it was! and how many young women of the world would have liked it as a boudoir! Imagine a small vaulted chamber, ten to twelve feet wide by fourteen to sixteen feet long, carpeted from end to end in fine English carpet with a Turkish design. In the middle of one wall was a small door with a pointed arch; on each of the shorter walls there was a small window in the same style, with curtains in cherry-coloured silk fringed in black and blue. At one side of the room there was a little varnished iron bedstead with a mattress in English ticking and cambric sheets edged with Spanish lace. Opposite stood a divan, also in English ticking, covered with a rich rug from Cuzco. Near the divan, there were cushions for visitors to sit on and pretty tapestry stools. In the far wall there was a niche, in which stood a beautifully made console table with a white marble top which did duty as a little altar. In it were several pretty vases full of natural and artificial flowers, silver chandeliers with blue candles, a little prayer-book bound in purple velvet and fastened with a little golden chain. Above the console was a small, beautifully carved oak crucifix, and above that a picture of the Virgin in a silver frame. On either side of her stood St Catherine and St Teresa, also in rich frames. A charming little rosary with small beads had been draped over Christ's head. Finally, to complete this elegant furniture, in the middle of the room stood a table covered in an ample cloth, and on the table a large tray with tea and four cups, a cut-glass decanter, a tumbler and refreshments. This charming retreat was the Mother Superior's *retiro*. This lady had taken an enthusiastic liking to me for the only reason that I came from the country 'where Rossini lived'. In spite of my remonstrances, she insisted on my installing myself in her *retiro*. She stayed quite late with me; we talked mostly of music and then of European affairs, which were of great

A BED-CHAMBER AT AREQUIPA IN THE OLD STYLE

A PERUVIAN GARDEN

interest to all these ladies; then she retired surrounded by a crowd of nuns, for they all cherished her like a mother or a friend.

During ten years of travel I have sampled many bedrooms and many beds; but I do not remember ever having such a delicious sensation as when I got into the charming little bed of the Mother Superior of Santa Catalina. I was childish enough to light the two blue candles on the altar, and I picked up the rosary and the pretty prayerbook and read for a long time, stopping frequently to admire all the objects around me or to take a deep voluptuous breath of the perfume which came from my lace-fringed sheets. That night, I almost wanted to be a nun. Next morning I rose late, the kind Superior having said that it was unnecessary for me to get up at six (as we had been made to do at Santa Rosa) to hear mass. 'It will be enough if you come to the eleven o'clock mass,' the good lady had said, 'and if your health does not permit it, I will give dispensation from that also.' The first day was spent in visiting the nuns: they vied with each other to see me, touch me, speak to me; they asked innumerable questions. 'How do they dress in Paris? What do they eat? Are there any convents?' But above all, 'What music is being played?' In every cell we found a large group gathered; everyone spoke at once, with plenty of laughing and joking. Everywhere we were offered cakes of all sorts, fruit, jam, cream, candy sugar, syrups and Spanish wines. It was a continuous banquet. The Superior had organised a concert for the evening in her little chapel, at which I heard the finest passages of Rossini very well played by three pretty young nuns as enthusiastic as their Superior. The piano came from the best maker in London, and the Superior had paid 4,000 francs for it.

Santa Catalina also belonged to the Carmelite order but, as the Superior told me, 'with many modifications'. Yes, I thought, and what modifications! They did not wear the same habit as at Santa Rosa; theirs was white, very full and trailing on the ground. Their veil, normally a 'Carmelite' pale brown, was black on the great feast days. I do not know if their rule insisted on their wearing only woollen cloth, but in fact only their robe was woollen. It was very finely woven, silky to the touch and brilliantly white. Their headdress was of black crêpe, and so prettily pleated that I wanted to have one as a curiosity; its graceful shape made them look charming. The veil was also of crêpe; they only wore it at church or on ceremonial occasions. It was clear that these pious ladies made no vow of silence nor of poverty, for they talked volubly and almost all spent a good deal of money. The convent church was large; the ornaments were rich but rather neglected. The organ was very fine, the choirs and the music generally were looked after with special care. The internal arrangements of the convent were extremely bizarre. It consisted of two sets of buildings, the old convent and the new. The latter had three small elegant cloisters; the cells were small, but airy and very light. In the middle of each courtyard there was a circular flowerbed and two beautiful fountains which kept everything cool and clean. The walls of the cloister were covered with vines. A steep road led up to the old convent, which was a labyrinth of little streets and alleys going this way and that, with a main street running through the middle nearly as steep as a stairway. The smaller streets and alleys led to the cells, which were like small independent dwellings, very peculiarly designed, rather like country cottages for the nuns who lived in them. Some I saw had an entrance courtyard large enough to keep poultry, with the kitchen and slave quarters around it; then a second courtyard with two or three rooms; then a garden and a little *retiro* with a terraced roof. For the last twenty years, the nuns of this convent had not eaten or slept communally: the refectory was unused, and so was the dormitory, but for form's sake each one kept a bed there, which was white as ordained by their rule. They were not forced, like those of Santa Rosa, to attend an endless succession of church services. On the contrary, after fulfilling their duties, they had plenty of time left for housekeeping, for looking after their clothes, for charitable occupations and indeed for their amusements. There were three very large gardens in which only vegetables and maize were grown, because each nun grew flowers in the garden of her cell. In general they led a very busy life; they did all sorts of needlework, took student-lodgers and in addition kept a free school for the daughters of the poor. They were active in many kinds of charity: they gave linen to the hospitals, dowries to girls and distributed daily bread, maize and clothes to the poor. The revenue of this community was enormous, but the ladies spent sums in the same proportion. The Mother Superior was then sixty-two. She had been appointed and dismissed on several occasions. The priests who were governors of the convent were opposed to her easy-going nature, but each time the nuns – who loved her because of it – were able to reinstate her, because they had the right to appoint their Superior by vote. This amiable lady, the complete opposite of her cousin at Santa Rosa, was so thin and delicate that she seemed to disappear altogether inside her long voluminous robe.

The ladies of Santa Catalina lived more or less as they pleased; the Superior was too kind to thwart them in any way. The aristocracy of wealth, which takes precedence everywhere even in democracies, was the only one that existed, so far as I could discover, in that convent. In this respect they were progressive. Of all these ladies, three were considered the leaders of society. The first, who came to the convent at the age of two, was about thirty-two or thirty-three when I was there; she belonged to one of the richest families of Bolivia and had eight negresses or *sambas* as servants. The second was a girl of twenty-eight, tall and slim, beautiful with that lively, bold beauty of the women of Barcelona: she was indeed of Catalan origin. This charming girl, an orphan with 40,000 francs a year, had lived at the convent for five years. The third, a sweet girl of twenty-four, good-hearted, gay, full of laughter, had been a nun for seven years. The eldest, Margarita, was the convent apothecary; the second, Rosita, was the gatekeeper; but the youngest, Manuelita, was too frivolous to carry out any duties whatever.

From the day following our arrival, each of these three friends had let it be known how much they wanted to hear from our lips the true story of poor Dominga; there was a rumour current in the convent that the three of them had joint plans for a similar and no less sinful escapade. Rosita was the same age as Dominga and was particularly interested in her, as she had known her well when they were children. My cousin, Manuela Althaus, who was very willing to tell the story perhaps for the twentieth time, agreed to satisfy their curiosity.

Manuelita welcomed us at her pretty little dwelling in the 'old convent'. The dinner was one of the most splendid (it was certainly the best presented) that I attended during my stay at Arequipa. We ate from fine Sèvres porcelain, the cloth was damask, the silver elegant and, for dessert, the knives were silver-gilt. When dinner was over, Manuelita charmingly invited us to withdraw to her *retiro*. She closed the garden door and gave orders to her chief negress that we should not be disturbed for any reason whatever.

This little *retiro* was not as pretty as the Superior's, but it was more original. As I was a foreigner, I was made the guest of honour. I was urged to occupy the whole divan, and I lay on it comfortably supported by silk cushions. The three nuns, looking elegant in their long pleated robes, sat close to me; Rosita, cross-legged in the local fashion, sat on a cushion and leant against the foot of the divan; Manuelita sat beside me and played with my hair, which she plaited in a dozen different ways; and solemn Margarita in the middle showed off her beautiful full-fleshed white hands by playing with her ebony rosary. My cousin, the principal actress, sat facing her audience in a big old-fashioned armchair, with a plump cushion under her feet.

She began by explaining why Dominga had become a nun. 'She was more beautiful than any of her sisters; at fourteen, her beauty was ripe enough to inspire love. A young Spanish doctor was attracted by her, and, learning that she was rich, tried to make her fall in love with him. This was not difficult; she was a young innocent; she had an affectionate nature and loved him as a girl of her age can love, sincerely and with complete trust. The poor child was convinced, in her simplicity, that he loved her as much as she loved him. The Spaniard asked for her hand; her mother accepted the proposal, but feeling that her daughter was too young, wanted the marriage to be postponed for a year. He, like almost all the Europeans who come to these parts, was consumed by greed. He only wanted to become rich, and seeing in Dominga a means of attaining that end, he had speculated on the innocent credulity of a child. Only a few months after he had proposed, he left her for a widow who was quite undistinguished but much richer than Dominga, betraying the true love of the child without the least thought of the profound sorrow he would inflict on her by abandoning her. His betrayal wounded her cruelly. Her whole family had known about her intended marriage and her wounded pride was too much for her to bear. She felt humiliated, and all attempts to console her merely revived her sorrow, which was only seeking oblivion. In her despair she saw the convent as the only refuge. She told her family that God had called her and that she had decided to become a nun. Her whole family tried to dissuade her, but she was utterly determined; her broken heart made her impervious to any pleading. They tried everything, but she was deaf to every appeal, remonstrance or advice. The only result of her family's opposition was her decision to enter the strictest of the Carmelite orders. After a novitiate of a year, she took the veil at Santa Rosa.

'It seems', continued my cousin, 'that Dominga in the fervour of her religious zeal was happy for the first two years of her stay at Santa Rosa. After that she began to tire of the severity and of the exalted moral standards demanded, and her second thoughts on the matter made her regret bitterly the fate she had chosen. She did not dare to speak of her unhappiness and tedium to her family, who had so strongly opposed her decision, and in any case, what good could it have done?

'Poor Dominga kept her sorrows to herself and, expecting no help from anyone, resigned herself to suffering until death should come to relieve her. Each day spent in the convent, which she now regarded as a prison, weakened her health which had once been so robust. A deathly pallor replaced the rosy cheeks which had been her special charm when she had lived in the world. Her eyes, once beautiful, became dull and sunken, like those of a penitent exhausted by the austerities of the cloister. One day, towards the end of her third year, when it was her turn to read in the refectory, Dominga found, in a passage of Santa Teresa, a hope of liberation.

'This passage says that the devil has many ingenious ways of tempting a nun. The saint describes as an example how a nun of Salamanca fell to the temptation of trying to escape from the convent. The devil suggested to her the idea of putting the corpse of a woman into her own bed, so as to make everyone believe that she was dead, and give herself time, with the help of a messenger of the devil, in the form of a handsome young man, to hide from the constables of the Holy Inquisition. From then on hope returned to Dominga, and her tedium fled: she hardly had enough time to think up ways of carrying out her plan. The austere religious duties were no longer tiresome, because she saw an end to her captivity. She gradually changed in her relations with her fellow nuns, seeking opportunities to talk to them, in order to get to know them really well. It was especially the gatekeepers that she sought to make friends with. These sisters carried out their duties for a period of two years only. After each changeover, she made great efforts, by offers of service and acts of kindness, to win over the new one. She was also particularly generous and kind to the negress who acted as messenger for her outside the convent, so as to win her complete devotion. She was so careful and determined that she left nothing undone which could help to further her project. However, eight years went by before she could carry it out. It would be too long to describe all her anxieties, and how she passed from hope to fear and back again.

'Finally, in desperation, she made up her mind to confide her plan to one of her fellow nuns whom she specially loved and who had just become gatekeeper. Fortunately her confidence was well placed and now, sure of the assistance and silence of the gatekeeper, she concentrated on the means of obtaining what she needed for her plan to succeed. She had also to confide in the negress, her messenger, for the plan depended on her collaboration for its success. To do so was dangerous, but as in everything else connected with her escape, Dominga showed great courage and resourcefulness. She could only communicate with her negress in the parlour, and through the iron bars of a grill. She might be overheard by one of the silent nuns who ceaselessly patrolled the parlour and kept an ear open for what was being said.

'This is the plan that Dominga had worked out, and which she ventured to explain to her negress, at the same time offering her a large recompense for the danger she would be likely to run. The negress would have to find the corpse of a woman and bring it at nightfall to the convent. The gatekeeper would let her in and show her where she could stow the corpse. Dominga would come and fetch it during the night, place it on her bed and set fire to it, then escape whilst the flames consumed both the corpse and the 'tomb'. It took the negress a long time to find a corpse. It would have been dangerous to ask for one at the hospital, where they in any case would only have handed one over to a surgeon and for a specific use, since there is no medical school in Arequipa. It was most unlikely that she would be able to find a corpse at her own home; so without the co-operation of a young surgeon who was let into the secret, Dominga's friend would have finished her two years' service as gatekeeper without the opportunity for escape arising. One dark night, the negress stifled her feelings of horror by thinking of the promised recompense, and loaded onto her back the corpse of an Indian woman who had died three days before. At the convent gate she made the agreed signal. The gatekeeper, trembling with fear, let her in. The negress put down the corpse at the spot silently indicated by the gatekeeper and then went round the corner of the street to wait for her mistress.

'Some time later, the gatekeeper bolted her door but did not lock it; she then, as was the rule, carried the key to the Superior, and retired to bed in her own 'tomb'. Around midnight, when Dominga judged all the nuns to be sound asleep, she came out of her 'tomb', in which she left her little dim lamp burning, and went to fetch the corpse. It was a very heavy load for so delicate a person – but what can the love of freedom not achieve? The horrible burden seemed to her as light as a basket of flowers. She placed it on her bed, dressed it in her own nun's clothing and put on a complete set of clothing which she had managed to procure. She then set fire to her bed and fled from the convent, leaving the door wide open.

'No one', my cousin continued, 'suspected the truth. The gatekeeper, who naturally was wide awake, followed Dominga to the door and bolted it, and in the confusion caused by the fire in the 'tomb' cleverly regained the key from the Superior and locked the gate in the usual way. Everyone was convinced that Dominga had burned to death. The remains of the corpse were unrecognisable, and it was buried with all the ceremony usual for a nun's funeral. Two months later the truth began to leak out; but the nuns of Santa Rosa refused to believe it; and when it became common knowledge that Dominga was alive, they still maintained that she was dead, and that the story of her escape was a slanderous lie. They only became convinced when Dominga herself gave proof of her existence by claiming from the Superior the return of her dowry of 10,000 piastres.'

We retired to bed, leaving the ladies plunged in deep thoughts which we felt it indiscreet to interrupt. 'I would be prepared to bet,' I said to my cousin, 'that before two years are out these three nuns will no longer be here.' 'I think so too,' she replied, 'and I should be very pleased. These three ladies are too beautiful and too agreeable to live in a convent.'

We left Santa Catalina next day. We had been there for six days, and all this time the ladies did everything they could to make our stay as pleasant as possible: magnificent dinners, delicious tea parties, walks in the gardens and all the interesting corners of the convent. Within the limits of what the convent could offer, they did what they could to amuse us. We were seen off by the entire community, pell-mell, without any ceremony or etiquette, but with such true and such touching affection that we and they dissolved into tears at the genuine grief we felt at separation. How different from our departure from Santa Rosa! This time we were sorry to leave and stopped several times in the street to look back at the towers of the hospitable refuge that we had just left. The children and the slaves were sad, and we went on talking for a long time about the generosity of those good nuns.

Not a day passed during the week following our departure without their sending us all sorts of presents: their generosity was extraordinary. I had so pleasant a memory of the welcome I had received there that before I left Arequipa I went more than once to chat with my old friends there in the parlour. Then again they showered me with little gifts, and commissioned me to send them music by Rossini from France.

XII

THE BATTLE OF CANGALLO

On Tuesday the 1st of April we left the convent of Santa Catalina. My aunt, worrying about her husband and her household, was anxious to return home. In any case, everyone was saying that San Roman, impressed by the strength and quality of Nieto's troops, would not dare to come any closer, and would stay at Cangallo until Gamarra had sent him reinforcements from Cuzco. The general shared this popular view, and, still fearing the arrival of Orbegoso, was impatient at the enemy's delays and yet made no preparations to receive him. The monk in his newspaper already proclaimed victory; and the wits of Arequipa composed songs in honour of Nieto, Carillo and Morant and elegies about San Roman, so farcical and silly that I was reminded of the street singers in Paris after the revolution of July 1830.

That same Tuesday was a holiday, and the soldiers were paid. Nieto, to court popularity, gave his soldiers the day off. They took full advantage of this, spending the day at the *chicherías*, drinking *chicha* and singing the songs I have mentioned above at the tops of their voices, and the night in drunkenness and disorder. In this they were doing no more than follow the example of their officers, who spent the time together drinking and gambling. So convinced were they that San Roman would not hazard an advance before the arrival of reinforcements, that no preparations were made and no precautions taken. Those on outpost duty were equally negligent. On Wednesday the 2nd of April, whilst the defenders of the fatherland slept off the excesses of the night before, it was suddenly announced that the enemy was approaching. The population took to the roofs of the houses, but remained unconvinced, since statements made by the general had so often proved to be wrong.

I had settled myself on the parapet quite comfortably, with a large red sunshade and Chevalier's field-glass. I was rapt in the contemplation of the volcano and the valley and had forgotten San Roman, when I was suddenly brought down to earth by a negro calling out: 'Madam, here they come!' I heard my uncle coming up the stairs and, directing my field-glass towards where the negro was pointing, I distinctly saw two black lines silhouetted along the top of the mountain nearest to the volcano. These two lines, no wider than a thread, were advancing across the desert, curving now one way, now another, at times forming zig-zags but never breaking, rather like migratory birds in ever changing formations, composed of black dots seen against the sky.

When the people saw the enemy, they set up a shout of joy. The situation created by the monk and Nieto had become intolerable, and they wanted to escape from it at all costs. In Nieto's camp there was also great jubilation: officers and men alike went back to drinking *chicha* and singing songs of victory, celebrating the demise of the enemy they were going to wipe out to a man. At about three o'clock, Althaus rode into the courtyard at a gallop, and seeing us all on the roof, he called to me in a voice of great anxiety. I came down, and promised my uncle to return with the news.

'Ah, cousin,' said Althaus, 'I have never been in such a situation as this. They are all quite mad. Just imagine: the idiots are all drunk; there's not a single officer capable of giving an order nor a single soldier able to load his rifle.

If San Roman has a good spy we are lost; in two hours he will be master of the city.'

San Roman's little army took nearly two hours to reach the bottom of the mountain. It took up a position to the left of the volcano, on a hillock called La Pacheta. This overlooked Nieto's fortified positions: it was the very one that Althaus had foreseen would be occupied by the enemy. San Roman deployed his troops in extended lines to give a false impression of numbers; but it was obvious that the ranks were only one or two deep. He formed a square with the seventy-eight men who made up his complete cavalry: in a word, he did the best that a good tactician could do to give the illusion that he was four times stronger than he was. The *ravanas* lit numerous fires on the top of the hillock, set up their camp with a great din and made such a noise that their shouting could be heard down in the valley.

But once the two armies were face to face, each feared the other, convinced of the superiority of its opponent. Nieto, at the sight of San Roman's professional-looking array, felt that his elegant 'Immortals' would not be able to stand up to his adversary's experienced soldiers; San Roman, on the other hand, realising Nieto's numerical superiority, felt that he had made a rash move, and this made him lose his head. Although a good soldier, San Roman was no wiser nor less presumptuous than Nieto. From his spies' reports, he had thought that he was heading for an easy victory: he even expected to win without a fight. Several of his officers have since told me that they were so sure that they would be in Arequipa that evening, that when they left Cangallo that morning they had been preoccupied only with making themselves look smart, so that they would be ready on arrival to pay visits to the ladies. The soldiers, just as confident, had thrown away their unconsumed rations and overturned the dixies, shouting: 'Brew up the soup in Arequipa barracks – here we come!' And now their 'ladies', the *ravanas*, despite all the activity they displayed in order to give the impression of preparing a meal, had not a single cob of corn between them to cook, no food at all to offer to their men, and to cap it all, the camp site was completely waterless. When

San Roman realised his position, he was plunged in despair and cried like a child, as we later learned; but fortunately for his cause, he had three young staff officers whose courage, determination and intelligence saved the situation. Señores Torres, Montaya and Quirroga, whose qualities made them worthy of serving a better cause, took over command, rallied the soldiers' morale and silenced the insolent grumbling of the *ravanas*; and, giving an example of how a soldier should behave on such occasions, they cut with their swords leaves from the cacti which grew abundantly on the mountainside, chewed them themselves to quench their thirst, then distributed them to the men and to the *ravanas*, who all took them and fed on them without complaining. But the officers realised that this resource could only be effective for a few hours, and they decided to risk battle, preferring to die from the sword than from thirst. Lieutenant Quirroga asked the men if they wished to retreat without fighting, to flee shamefully in the presence of the enemy and then face, on their return to Cangallo, death by hunger and thirst, like mules in the desert, or whether they preferred to show what they could do against that bunch of braggarts who, despite their numbers, were incapable of resistance. The men, who in other circumstances would have fled at the sight of the enemy's numbers, gave a rousing reception to this military harangue and chose to go into battle.

It was nearly seven in the evening and I had just returned to my post. Calm seemed to reign in both camps; it was assumed that, given the lateness of the hour, the battle would not begin until dawn. Suddenly I saw what appeared to be a standard-bearer break away from San Roman's square of cavalry, followed immediately by the whole squadron, and at the same time from Nieto's army, Colonel Carillo's dragoons advanced to meet them. Both squadrons advanced at the charge. When they were within range there was a burst of rifle fire, followed by another and then another: the battle had started. There was much noise from both camps, but the smoke was so thick that the actual carnage was concealed from us.

Night fell, and we remained in complete ignorance of what was going on. At about nine o'clock a man from the battlefield passed along the Calle de Santo Domingo. We stopped him, and he told us that all was lost; the general had sent him to tell his wife to take refuge in the convent of Santa Rosa. He also said that there was a terrible disorder in our army. Colonel Morant's artillery had fired on our dragoons, mistaking them for the enemy, and had killed a large number of them.

The news spread through the town, and panic seized the population. Those who had decided to stay at home now regretted their temerity and hurriedly left: we saw them running like mad, laden with their silver dishes and their silver chamberpots.* One woman was clutching a little jewel case, another a *brasero* (brazier). The negresses and *sambas* carried rugs and their mistresses' dresses all hugger-mugger; the children cried, the slaves shouted, the masters swore, confusion reigned: it was an appalling scene. The rich, the slave-owners, the master race were in the grip of terror, whilst the Indian and the negro, rejoicing at the approaching catastrophe, were savouring thoughts of revenge. The native Indians uttered threats, and the whites were cowed. The slaves disobeyed; their cruel laughter and their fierce, dark looks disconcerted their masters, who dared not strike them. Perhaps it was the first time that these black faces and these white faces had betrayed the depths to which they were capable of sinking. I remained calm amongst all the chaos and watched, with a disgust I could not conceal, that display of all that is worst in human nature. Never before had I felt such contempt for humanity as in watching the agony of the misers, fearing the loss of their wealth more than that of their lives; the cowardice of the white population, incapable of any action of self-defence; the Indian's hatred, no longer disguised by crawling obsequiousness; the thirst for vengeance of the slave who, so lately, had kissed the hand that struck him. I continued to address my *samba* as usual, and though she was mad with joyful excitement she obeyed me, because she could see that I was not afraid. Neither my aunt nor I would again enter a convent, so my cousins went off again with their children.

* *Author's note:* In Peru, all the chamberpots are in silver.

After the tumult of the horrible scene I have described, came a deathly hush; in less than an hour the entire population succeeded in squeezing somehow into the convents, monasteries and churches. I do not think that there was more than a score of inhabited houses left in the town.

Our house had become a general meeting place, because of the security offered by the proximity of the church of Santo Domingo, and because it was hoped that Althaus would get some news through to Don Pio. We had all gathered in my uncle's study, a high vaulted chamber which faced the street. There was no light, so as not to attract the attention of passers-by, but the cigars which the smokers kept constantly alight that evening glowed in the dark, creating a scene worthy of Rembrandt. Through the clouds of smoke that filled the room, I watched four Dominican monks with broad, stupid faces, dressed in white robes, with heavy black-beaded rosaries and coarse silver-buckled shoes. They flicked the ash from their cigars with one hand, whilst with the other they fingered their scourges. On the other side, pale and thin, sat the three poor millionaires, already known to the reader: Juan de Goyeneche, Gamio and Ugarte. There were about a dozen people in the room. My aunt sat in a corner of one of the sofas, her hands clasped together, praying for the dead of both sides. My uncle walked up and down the room, talking with decisive, animated gestures. I sat on the window seat, wrapped in my cloak, from where I could watch what went on both in the street and in the room. I learned a great deal that night: these people are unique in their taste for the marvellous and for exaggeration. As that long night wore on, we were regaled with story after story, terrifying, fantastic, and all told with unbelievable self-assurance and dignity.

But the stories stopped and the conversation changed whenever news arrived, true or false, of what was happening on the battlefield. When a wounded soldier, limping towards the hospital, said that the Arequipans had lost the battle, a buzz of voices began, in the most comic manner, to recriminate against that coward, that rascal, that fool Nieto: San Roman was great, good and glorious. The Dominicans prayed to heaven for the death of that 'dog' Nieto, and began to plan the brilliant reception they would give the great San Roman. But when a quarter of an hour later another soldier came by shouting, 'Long live General Nieto! Victory is ours! San Roman is beaten!' the good fathers clapped their fat hands and cried: 'What a great general, how brave, how clever he is! Down with that miserable Indian, that *sambo* San Roman!' My uncle was embarrassed by these chattering fools, as ridiculous as they were contemptible, but his eloquent pleas for silence went unheeded, so deeply ingrained is it in the people of that country to stamp on the fallen without restraint and without pity, and to exalt the victor to the skies.

At about one in the morning, Althaus sent one of his aides to tell us that there had been no fighting since eight o'clock; that the enemy, fearing the number of their adversaries, had not dared to enter unfamiliar ground in the dark; that we had lost some thirty or forty men, including one officer; that Morant's tragic mistake was the cause, and that the troops were in fearful disorder. My cousin sent me a pencilled note, in which he said that he considered the battle to be lost.

At about two o'clock, feeling very tired, I retired to bed; as I did not wish to miss anything, I asked my aunt to wake me at dawn. By four o'clock I was on the rooftop, watching as dawn broke the magnificent view of the domed roofs of all the churches and convents of the city. Everywhere there were people – men, women, children, of all shades of colour ranging from white to black, all dressed in the costumes of their respective races but at this moment made equal by the same thought which preoccupied them all; they had become as one, the same expression was on all faces. The domed roofs and the clock towers had become alive, a collective soul dominated them all. Every roof, every tower was entirely covered with motionless figures, all in the same attitude, leaning forward, mouths gaping, eyes straining in the direction of the two armies: a sublime sight!

But by now my back was turned: I was lost in my musings, and had forgotten the fight and the fighters. A long, low sound, which rose from the rooftops like a moan from a tomb, brought me back to consciousness. This mass of human beings, moved by the same feelings, spoke with one voice. From these thousands of throats came the same cry, a thrill of pain: I was moved to tears by the sound. Without having to turn my head to look towards the battlefield, I knew what it meant: the killing had begun, or was about to begin. This cry of pain was succeeded by a deathly hush, and the stillness of the figures on the rooftops betokened a rapt attention. Suddenly there was a second cry, accompanied by gestures of relief, which reassured me: there would be no killing after all. I turned to look, and saw great activity on the battlefield. I asked my uncle to let me look through his field-glass. I saw officers running from one army to the other, firing pistol shots into the air; then General Nieto, followed by his officers, advanced to meet a group of officers from the enemy camp. I saw them mingle in mutual embrace. We then assumed that San Roman's army had surrendered and that everything would be settled.

As we were speculating about the outcome, Althaus galloped into the courtyard, shouting at the top of his voice: 'Hey, you up there! Come down quickly, I've got news for you!' I was the first to arrive in the courtyard; I ran to him and kissed him for the first time. He was not wounded but, Good Lord! what a state he was in! Normally so neat and clean, he was covered with dust, mud and blood. His features were unrecognisable; his eyes, red and swollen, protruded from their sockets; his nose and lips were puffed up; his skin was covered with scratches and bruises, his hands black with gunpowder and his voice so hoarse that I could hardly make out what he said.

'Ah cousin,' I said, grieving for him, 'I hated wars even before seeing you in such a state; after all I've seen since yesterday, I think no punishment too severe for those who begin them.'

'Florita, you will win the argument easily today, for I cannot speak. But please don't dignify with the name of "war" an absurd scrap like this one, conducted by greenhorns who have no idea how to aim a gun. Here I am, looking like a common thief! And to crown it all my dear wife has hidden away every single one of my shirts!'

Althaus made himself as comfortable as he could, drank four or five cups of tea, ate a dozen pieces of bread and butter and then began to smoke. All the time, he complained of his wife, laughed and joked as usual and told us everything that had happened since the previous night.

'Yesterday,' he said, 'the engagement was a mere scuffle – but what inextricable confusion resulted from it! Fortunately the Gamarrists lost their nerve and retreated. I had to work all night to restore order amongst our men. This morning we were drawn up on the battlefield, expecting to see the enemy descend on us from their advantageous position when, instead, we saw a man bearing a flag of truce, who in the name of San Roman asked to speak to General Nieto. The latter, forgetting all questions of dignity, was all for accepting this invitation on the spot. The monk disagreed, and so did the rest. To cut the matter short, I said, "As chief of staff, it's up to me," and without waiting for approval I spurred my horse forward towards the man with the flag. He told me that San Roman wished to speak personally to the general, and as I could get no more out of him, I went back to the general and said: "If you ask me, we should send them bullets rather than conversation: bullets always speak for themselves." That idiot Nieto ignored my advice. He wanted to show his magnanimity, to see his old comrades and his brothers-in-arms from Cuzco; the monk ground his teeth and foamed with rage. But he had to yield to the man whom he had appointed and whom he had hoped to use. Nieto silenced him with the words: "Señor Baldivia, I and I alone am in command here." The ecclesiastic, furious, gave him a look which clearly meant: "Wait till I get you, I'll strangle you with my own hands." However, not wishing to be left out, he gave up his opposition and accompanied the soft-hearted Nieto. They are now in conference with the enemy, with the two journalists Quiros and Ros in attendance. But now that I am refreshed and a little cleaner I shall return to the camp, where I shall sleep until the message comes either to fight or embrace the enemy.'

The news that Althaus had brought soon became public knowledge in the town and inside all the convents. It was felt that the parley between the two commanders would result in peace, and this hope was generally welcomed. I went to bed, telling my *samba* not to wake me unless the enemy were actually inside the courtyard. It was Thursday the 3rd of April.

I was still asleep at six that evening, when Emmanuel and my uncle came in. 'What news do you bring us?' asked my uncle.

'Nothing definite. The general stayed with San Roman from five in the morning until three o'clock; but when he returned, he had nothing to say about this long conference, except that he thought that everything would be settled. One of the aide-de-camps told us that the meeting of the two commanders had been very moving: they had lamented the misfortunes of the fatherland and the death of the officer Montenegro: standing over his body, they swore "Unity and Fraternity". In fact the whole day had been given over to making fine phrases. The Gamarrists are acting like simpletons, as gentle as lambs; and Nieto, soft-hearted as ever, has allowed San Roman to send his men and horses to water at the spring called Agua Salada; he has ordered food to be taken to them and treats San Roman and his army like brothers.'

Emmanuel urged me to visit the camp. My uncle wanted to come too and we set off. The *chicherías* and the House of Menao had all been more or less destroyed, and the camp was in disorder. It looked as if the enemy had occupied it. The maize fields had been ruined, and the poor peasants had had to leave; their huts were occupied by *ravanas*. At the headquarters, I saw those handsome officers, usually so elegant, now dirty and red-eyed, with hoarse voices. Most were asleep, stretched on the ground: and so were the men. The *ravanas'* quarters had suffered most. Morant's artillery had hit it in the confusion and had destroyed everything. Three of the women had been killed and seven or eight severely wounded. I met neither the general nor Baldivia: they were sleeping.

When we got home, my uncle said: 'Florita, I don't like all this. I know the Gamarrists, and they're not the sort of people to give in. Some of San Roman's officers are very good men. Nieto cannot compete with them in cunning.

I'm sure there's a trap hidden under all this camaraderie.'

Next day, Nieto went again to see San Roman. He sent him wine and ham, and bread for the troops. It was generally expected that at midday a *bando* would be issued in which the results of the two-day talks would be communicated to the army and the people. Two o'clock came, and still no *bando*. Then noisy complaints began to be voiced against the man who had been appointed by the people as commander-in-chief of the province, who for the last three months had had at his disposal the wealth, the liberty and the life of the citizens, and who abused such confidence by behaving like a president, or rather a dictator. This behaviour of his exasperated the people beyond measure against him; some thirty thousand souls who had been forced to abandon their normal occupations and habits and squat in monasteries and churches were impatient to know what was to be their fate; they could stand it no longer. The few who had remained in their houses, as we had done, were in considerable discomfort, as everything was hidden in the convents: we were short of linen, spoons, chairs, even beds. But this was nothing compared to what was suffered by those unfortunates huddled together in the monasteries and convents: they were short of clothes and the necessities for preparing food. Men, women, children and slaves were crowded together under horrible conditions.

Apart from these real hardships they suffered the moral torture of not knowing which of the two rivals they should support – which they should exalt with praise and which they should cover with their scorn and malediction. Not able to predict the outcome, they had to wait; and to wait in silence was, for this nation of *habladores*,* a cruel penance.

At about three o'clock the rumour spread that everything was settled, that San Roman had recognised Orbegoso as the legitimate president and had made peace with his brother-in-arms from Arequipa, but that his entry into the city had been postponed until the following Sunday, so that he could attend a thanksgiving High Mass.

* *habladores* – chatterers.

The population was delighted to hear this news, but their joy was, alas, short-lived. At five, an aide-de-camp came with a message from Althaus to the effect that negotiations had been broken off between the two commanders, and that he himself would come and tell us all about it that evening. When the people heard this, their indignation was held in check by fear, and the result was a kind of stupor: they were petrified.

We were all in my uncle's study, still not knowing after so much contradictory news what turn events would take and awaiting Althaus with great anxiety, when the poor general passed by, with the monk and a few others. I went to the window and called: 'General, would you be kind enough to tell us if the battle is going to take place?' 'Yes, mademoiselle,' he answered, 'definitely tomorrow at dawn.' Struck by his tone of voice, I pitied him; while he talked with my uncle I examined him carefully. Mental agony was written all over him: his whole body revealed it; his haggard eyes, the veins of his forehead knotted like rope, his tensed muscles, his distorted features all showed clearly how the rash fool had been basely tricked! He could hardly stay in the saddle; great drops of sweat ran down his temples; his voice was so harsh that it hurt one to listen to it; with his hands he kneaded the reins of his horse. I decided he was mad. The monk was sombre but calm; I could not look him in the eye – he froze me. They stopped only a few minutes. When they had left, my uncle said: 'That poor general is a sick man, Florita; he will never be able to command the army tomorrow.'

'Uncle, the battle is already lost; that man is no longer in his right mind. His limbs are no longer under his control. He must be replaced, or tomorrow he will commit greater follies than ever.' Allowing myself to speak my mind, I begged my uncle to go and find the prefect, the mayor and the senior officers of the army, and make them realise the critical situation into which Nieto had brought them, so that they could immediately call a meeting to deprive him of his command and appoint another general in his place. My uncle gave me a startled look and asked me if I too had not gone off my head, wanting him to 'compromise himself' by acting in this way. And such men regard themselves as republicans! While we talked, Althaus arrived. He told me later that the whole army was angry with the general – there was talk of tearing off his epaulettes. 'Here's the story in a nutshell,' he said: 'San Roman had no food supplies, and cajoled Nieto into letting him have some, promising him that he would recognise Orbegoso as president; our credulous general believed in promises which were made simply as a matter of expediency. Finally Nieto returned: we had been waiting most impatiently. Morant asked him: "Do we fight, and is it this evening?" "Tomorrow, sir, at dawn." He brought three of San Roman's officers with him; he had them arrested, and now, this evening, he proposes to have them shot. I tell you, the man is mad. He should be replaced, but the choice of a successor is very difficult. And what procedure should we adopt? As you see, all the citizens who should be dying for their country are hiding in the convents; your uncle has gone to bed. The Goyeneches, the Gamios and the rest do nothing but weep. Well, I ask you, what the devil can one do with this nation of milksops? I am completely convinced that we shall lose the battle, and I dislike this idea, for I hate Gamarra.'

Althaus shook hands, and reassured me about his safety, saying: 'Don't worry on my account. The Peruvians know how to run, but not how to kill.' And he went back to the camp.

I was wakened before dawn by an old *chacarero*, with a message from Althaus, to the effect that San Roman, under cover of darkness, had left his position in order to retreat in the direction of Cangallo, and that Nieto had started in pursuit with his entire army, even including the *ravanas*. When dawn broke, I climbed out on to the roof but saw no sign of either camp: so at last they had gone off to do battle.

At nine o'clock, gunfire was heard; it was frighteningly rapid. The watchers were utterly silent, like a man on the way to the scaffold. After half an hour, we saw a cloud of smoke rising behind La Pacheta: the village of Cangallo was at the foot of that mountain, and we presumed that the battle was there. At about eleven, a number of soldiers appeared on the top of La Pacheta: hardly half an hour had passed since they disappeared behind it, and now we only saw scattered men, some on foot, others on horseback. With the aid of old Hurtado's excellent field-glass, I could see clearly that some of these unfortunates were wounded: one sat down to tie up his arm with a handkerchief, another bandaged his head; yet another lay prone across his horse. They all made their way along the narrow difficult track down the mountainside.

By half past twelve, the Arequipans realised the disaster that had struck them. The spectacle of a rout was played out before our eyes, as grand as a mighty storm, and just as terrifying. I had witnessed the revolution of July 1830, but I was then excited by the heroism of the people and had no thought for danger; at Arequipa, I could only think of the calamities that threatened the city.

Carillo's dragoons, on their fine horses, with the Peruvian flag on the end of their lances, suddenly appeared on the top of La Pacheta. They galloped down the mountain in utter panic and disorder. After them came the *chacareros*, riding on mules and donkeys; then the infantry, running amongst the horses and the mules, and throwing down their packs and their rifles in order to gain speed; finally, the artillery, to protect the rearguard. And last of all came the unfortunate *ravanas*, with one or even two children on their backs, driving before them the laden mules, the oxen and the sheep that Nieto had insisted must accompany the army.

At the sight of all this, the watchers uttered a cry – a horrible cry, a cry of terror, which I can still hear. Then suddenly the crowd disappeared; the roofs were just empty roofs, silence fell and the alarm bell from the cathedral alone was heard.

At about half past one, the wounded began to arrive. Again, there were distressing scenes. At the corner of our house, more than a hundred women gathered: they were waiting for the unfortunates to pass by, and were tortured by the fear of recognising a son, a husband or a brother amongst them. As every casualty arrived, these women put up a howl of despair so anguished that it was a torment to hear them. What I suffered that day!

We were all worried about Althaus, Emmanuel, Crevoisier, Cuello and others, and could not understand why the general did not come to occupy the town to defend it, as the plan had been in case of defeat. More than an hour had passed since the defeat, and surely the enemy would be here at any minute. Cuello arrived; he was dying, a bullet had pierced his side and he had been bleeding for three hours. He was taken to the hospital, and I went there to help his sister make him as comfortable as possible.

As I returned to my uncle's room, I saw Emmanuel galloping up; we all surrounded him, impatient for news. Neither Althaus nor any other officer had been wounded, but both sides had lost a number of men. Emmanuel said that the general intended to abandon the city, as it was impossible to defend it against the enemy. Nieto had sent him to spike the guns on the bridge and throw the rest of the ammunition into the river.

He told us all this in five minutes, and asked me to pack Althaus's personal effects so that everything could be ready for his flight. I hurried to his house; with the help of his negro, whom I almost had to beat before he would obey, I loaded a mule with a mattress and a packed trunk. My *samba*, with a negro belonging to my uncle Pio, led the mule and the rebellious slave on to the road, in order to make it easier for Althaus to leave the town. Having achieved this first objective, I had tea and food prepared, realising that my poor cousin would be in urgent need of sustenance. I heard a great clatter of horses and ran to the door: it was the general, with all his officers, galloping through the town; the army would follow. My cousin came in: I had a spare horse standing ready for him. When he saw it, he jumped off his own, came to me, took my hand and said: 'Thanks, dear Flora, thanks. Has my luggage gone ahead?'

'The mule has already gone, but it would be a good thing if your two aides went to catch it up, because that damned negro refuses to follow you.'

'Have you something for these gentlemen to drink? They are dead tired.'

I gave them good claret, and they each took two bottles, and filled their pockets with sugar, chocolate, bread and everything I could find in the house. Their horses were also given wine, and when all were somewhat refreshed, they left.

From shouting words of command, Althaus was too hoarse to speak. As he hurriedly drank his tea he told me briefly that this time it was Carillo's dragoons who had lost the battle. They had become confused in their movements and had fired on Morant's artillery, convinced that they were the enemy. 'As I've said before, Florita, until those amateur soldiers learn military tactics, they'll go on making blunders. Now the general refuses to defend the city. I don't know why he's panicked like this. He can only think of running away and has no plan drawn up. When we reached the house of Menao, we had great difficulty in persuading him that he must at least give the troops time to rally: this is why we have so many deserters. When we reached the *chicherías*, we did our best to round up the deserters, but were unsuccessful. The cowardly rascals, with the help of the *ravanas,* are hiding somewhere – gone underground, I think, like moles. What I do find surprising, cousin, is that the enemy is so slow to arrive: I can't understand it.'

At this point Emmanuel arrived in the courtyard. 'I've come to fetch you,' he said to Althaus. 'Everyone is leaving. The monk has loaded the rest of his cash on his horse. The general has gone to say goodbye to his wife, who gave birth to a baby last night. I'm going to give my poor mother a good hug. Come on, cousin, we're all waiting for you. Let's go.' Althaus embraced and kissed me, and asked me to look after his wife and children. I kissed dear Emmanuel, and the two left at speed.

When I returned to the Calle de Santo Domingo it was entirely deserted. Everywhere the houses were strongly barricaded. The city seemed utterly calm; but blood stained the streets, and this evidence of murder done and this solitude gave eloquent witness to the disasters which had already befallen and others which were yet to be feared. I went to my uncle's room and gave an account of what I had learned from Althaus and Emmanuel. Everyone assembled there was indignant with the general, but no one took any action whatsoever.

At five o'clock, I went up again on to the roof. All I

could see was a great cloud of dust raised by Carillo's dragoons as they fled across the desert. They were heading for Islay, where they knew that there were two ships waiting to take them beyond the reach of San Roman. I sat for a long time in the same spot as that morning. How the city had changed! It was now wrapped in a deathly hush. The inhabitants were all praying, resigned it seemed to being massacred without putting up any resistance. My uncle asked me to come down and go to the church of Santo Domingo, where he and his entire household were going. I realised for the first time that I had not eaten all day. I drank a cup of chocolate, took my cloak and went to the church.

At frequent intervals the watchers on the towers were asked if they saw anyone coming from the direction of La Pacheta. They answered each time: 'No one at all.' At last, at seven o'clock, three Indians turned up at the gate of the monastery. They said that the enemy had reached the *chicherías*, but that San Roman did not wish to enter the city until the authorities had gone out to invite him to do so. At this news, great excitement developed in Santo Domingo. The prefect and all the authorities of the town had taken refuge there, and they insisted that it was up to the reverend fathers to carry out this peaceful mission. The monks, who were not exactly courageous, objected strongly to this proposal, and a great debate ensued. It was partly due to me that the monks decided to accept. I knew that they were all strong supporters of Gamarra. I spoke to the prior, Don José, who was my aunt's chaplain, and was persuasive enough to convince them. Four or five civil servants from the town hall accompanied them. They set off, and an hour later we saw them returning followed by two regiments, one of cavalry and one of infantry. And so the Gamarrists were the victors. On Saturday the 5th of April, at eight in the evening, they took Arequipa.

XIII

A TEMPTATION

When I woke, I found my family and friends in a state of excitement. They said that soldiers had been wandering round the town during the night, robbing whoever they met, and two people had been killed.

It was Sunday. The Cabero ladies were anxious not to miss the nine o'clock mass, so we went, escorted by two monks. The church was a most disgusting sight. It was scandalous to see men, women, children – even dogs – all crowded together, with beds, impromptu kitchens, chamberpots, all enveloped in a cloud of smoke. In one corner the mass was being sung, in another people were eating and smoking. I went to see my uncle and aunt who were installed in the prior's cell with seven or eight other people. I was still unable to persuade my uncle to return home: he remained afraid that his house would be pillaged. Not at all afraid, I returned home alone and settled down to write up the three days that had just passed. That evening my uncle still insisted on remaining at the monastery. I spent the night at home without other company than my *samba,* who said: 'Don't be afraid, miss, if the soldiers or the *ravanas* come to sack the house, well, I'm Indian like them, I speak their language. I shall tell them: "My mistress is not Spanish, she is French, don't hurt her." I'm sure that then they'd do you no harm, for they only attack their enemies.' So spoke a fifteen-year-old slave.* But no slave has ever loved his masters, however kind. On the second day I was still alone when two officers came and asked to speak to Don Pio. I did not wish to

* *Author's note:* She belonged to my aunt.

admit that my uncle was in hiding. They were shown into my room, and I told them that Don Pio was away, and asked them what they wanted of him.

'Señorita, we should like your uncle, as one of the local notables, to come and speak to Colonel Escudero, who has replaced San Roman, killed in battle. We are the victors, and the Arequipans are putting a strain on our moderation by continuing to treat us as enemies. Ever since we entered the town, all the houses have been barricaded, our troops are without bread, our wounded have been left dying on the battlefield, and all the while the inhabitants insist on remaining in the convents, as if we had come here to massacre them. You are the first person to whom we have explained our needs; but you realise, señorita, that this state of things cannot endure.'

I talked for a long while with these gentlemen, and found them very correct. When they had left, I went immediately to Santo Domingo to inform my uncle and the others who had taken refuge there. As soon as they heard that San Roman was dead and Colonel Escudero appointed in his place, they began to calm down, since the latter was well known and much loved in Arequipa. Nearly everyone left the monastery and returned home, and my uncle went straightaway to visit Escudero. When he returned, he said: 'We are saved. I personally have nothing to fear. Escudero owes me a great deal and is devoted to me. Since San Roman's death has left the army without a commander, would you believe that he offered to have me appointed?'

'Would you accept?'

'Certainly not. In such crises, one must stay in the background. When everything has finally calmed down, I shall see if I can get myself into a suitable post. I'm too old to be a military commander.'

'But it seems to me, uncle, that it's just in difficult crises like this that men like you should be ready to contribute their talents and their experience.'

'Florita, it is lucky for you that you are not a politician, because your devotion to duty would be your undoing. Rather than offer my services to these dunces, I prefer to let them get embroiled in troubles and difficulties. The more of these they have, the more they'll need me. They'll come to me on their bended knees, and I'll be able to make my own conditions.' I looked at my uncle, and could only say: 'Poor Peruvians!'

At this juncture, my uncle went to Escudero and offered him a loan of 2,000 piastres. He advised the Goyeneches, Ugarte and others to follow his example. The bishop offered 4,000 piastres, his brother and sister 2,000 each. The others gave in proportion. During all the troubles, the foreigners and their property were untouched. When Escudero arrived, M. LeBois and two heads of English firms made him a small loan to subsidise the needs of his troops, who had not had a distribution of bread for three days: but this loan was voluntary.

On the third day, Escudero issued a *bando* ordering all house doors to be opened within three hours, and left open as usual,* adding that any doors remaining closed would be broken open by soldiers. This order forced those who had remained in the convents to return home.

We learned from Althaus that, on Sunday, the 6th of April, Nieto and the entire army had arrived at Islay; they had spiked the guns, burnt the customs registers and forced the administrator, Don Basilio de la Fuente, to leave for Lima. They themselves, after laying waste the neighbourhood, had embarked for Tacna in three Peruvian ships.

Escudero had made his entry into Arequipa during Sunday night, so that no one knew exactly how many soldiers he had with him. First, San Roman's death was announced; four days later they spread the rumour that he was only wounded; then after a week he came to Arequipa, where he also arrived during the night.

Here is the explanation of all this, given me personally by Escudero. San Roman, after fooling Nieto for three whole days with the only objective of getting provisions for his troops, withdrew to Cangallo, not expecting Nieto to follow. Before going into battle, he intended to consult Gamarra and obtain reinforcements from him. When he

**Author's note:* At Arequipa, all house doors are normally left open at all times.

reached Cangallo, he found Escudero with four hundred men sent him by Gamarra. San Roman's men were giving a welcome to the newcomers, when Nieto's army suddenly apppeared on the heights of La Pacheta. A great confusion ensued. San Roman had allowed his men to bathe and some were naked; when they saw the Arequipans they thought they were done for. If it had not been for Escudero, who rallied them, they would have all taken flight. Battle was joined and they fought courageously, but they soon ran out of ammunition and began to panic. When San Roman saw his soldiers in this confusion, he thought the battle was lost and that the best thing he could do was to run away himself. With a few of his staff, he galloped off as fast as his horse could carry him. And so it was that these two brave champions fled in terror from each other, running without stopping for a day and a night, until there were *eighty leagues* between them! Nieto's terror drove him as far as Islay, forty leagues to the south, and San Roman's to Vilque, forty-two leagues north. It was by a miracle that a part of San Roman's army rallied and advanced on Arequipa. One of the officers of that army, whom Nieto had kept imprisoned in the town hall, saw the retreat of the Arequipans from the roof of the building. Taking advantage of the moment of panic, he jumped on the first horse he could find in the town hall courtyard and, knowing the country well, he took a short cut and arrived at Cangallo in an hour. He shouted to the men on the run to stop, and told them that Nieto, convinced he was beaten, had abandoned the city and was fleeing towards the port. If it had not been for this officer the two armies, believing that they had lost, would have continued to run in opposite directions, and the town would never have seen either defenders or attackers again.

When Escudero told me all this, I thought of Althaus, for whom military science was the supreme arbiter of success and failure, and I was sorry that I could not show him, using this as an example, how unpredictable are both men and science.

A messenger had to be sent all the way to Vilque, to alert San Roman that he had won the battle. He only returned to Arequipa a week later. He was supposed to be wounded in the thigh to explain this delay, but he was nothing of the sort.

My uncle, who had a talent for keeping in with all parties, was – if not in the confidence of the Gamarrists – in any case very close to them. Every day they came to dinner, and morning and evening the house was full of them. Conversing with them, I was surprised to find how superior they were to Nieto's officers. Señores Montoya, Torres, Quirroga and especially Escudero were all most distinguished men.

Escudero was one of those adventure-loving Spaniards who leave their dear motherland to seek their fortune in the New World. Well versed in many things, he was at home as a soldier, a journalist or a trader. He was able to cope in an emergency with remarkable facility, and excelled in anything he put his hand to as if it had been his lifelong speciality. He had a keen wit, an inexhaustible imagination, a merry nature and a persuasive eloquence. This extraordinary man was the secretary, friend and adviser of Señora Gamarra. For three years he had been intimately associated with her in this way, and was the envy of a host of rivals. He had devoted himself to her cause, writing articles to support her objectives and to counter the continual attacks made upon her; he acted under her orders, accompanying her on her hazardous expeditions and never flinching at the bold plans conceived by a woman whose ambitions were Napoleonic in scale.

Ever since his first visit to us, I became friendly with Colonel Escudero; our characters were in harmony; he treated me with great confidence and revealed all that had happened in the Gamarrist army: I realised, from what he told me, that San Roman had committed as many follies as Nieto. Listening to Escudero, it seemed clear to me that he was tired of the restraints imposed on him by his all-powerful mistress, and that he was only looking for a pretext to escape from them. He visited me daily; we had long conversations together. I had plenty of time to get to know him well, and I realised that he was probably the only man in Peru who could assist me in fulfilling my ambitions. I was distressed by the misfortunes of a country that I had come to consider as my own; it had ever been my passionate desire to contribute to the well-being of mankind, and an active, adventurous career had always attracted me. I felt that, if Escudero were to fall in love with me, I would have a strong influence over him. I was then once again tormented by conflicting emotions, I was torn once more between opposing forces of the mind. The idea of becoming the close associate of this man, so brilliant, so bold, so debonair, entranced me. If while following the ups and downs of fortune with him I were to fail, what would it matter, I wondered, since I had nothing to lose? The voice of duty would perhaps have been powerless to save me from this temptation, the strongest I ever felt in all my life, if another consideration had not come to my aid. I was apprehensive of the moral depravity which usually accompanies the exercise of power. I was afraid of becoming hard and despotic, as much a criminal as those in power already. I dreaded becoming powerful in the country where my uncle lived: I had loved him so well, and still did so, yet he had hurt me so much. I did not want to be in a position to be able to take revenge, and I can say here, before God, that I sacrificed the career that I could so easily have made to the fear of having to treat my uncle as an enemy. This sacrifice was all the greater because I found Escudero attractive. In the eyes of many he was ugly, but not in mine. He was from thirty to thirty-three years old, of medium height, very slim, with a sunburnt complexion, very black hair, very bright but soft eyes, and teeth like pearls. His tender gaze and his melancholy smile gave him a noble and poetic quality which moved me deeply. I felt that with such a man I would have been able to achieve the impossible. I am convinced that if I had become his wife I would have been very happy. Amid the turmoil of our political life, he would have sung me a ballad or played the guitar as free of care as when he had been a student at Salamanca. Once again, I had to exert all my moral courage not to succumb to the temptation offered by such a future. I was *afraid of myself*, and I felt it was prudent to take flight to avoid this new danger. I therefore resolved to leave for Lima immediately.

No one could understand why I wished to leave so

suddenly. In vain did they insist that the road to Islay was infested with deserters living only on brigandry, and in vain did they exaggerate the dangers I would have to face. I was deaf to all warnings. I felt that no danger was so great as the one which threatened me were I to remain in Arequipa. To escape that, I would have crossed all the deserts of the earth. The pretext I gave was that I must leave in order to arrive in Europe before the bad weather set in; and as deep down my uncle and his family were quite glad to see me go, they did not insist further. An Englishman of my acquaintance, Mr Valentine Smith, was intending to travel to Lima. I asked him if he would accept me as a travelling companion, and he welcomed my proposal. We made a deal with an Italian captain whose ship was at Islay, and it was fixed that we should sail on the 25th of April.

Before I left, I had to go through the drudgery of goodbye visits. According to etiquette I ought, as on my arrival, to have called on everyone; but I went only to see the main families with whom I had close relations, and sent cards to the rest. These visits gave me an opportunity to discover the extent of the harm done by the war to this unfortunate city. In every house I found people in mourning and in tears. But it seemed to me that, worse than the sorrow caused by death, were the discord and hatred which the civil strife had aroused within the families. Deep rifts had occurred between relatives, between brothers. The search for liberty had nothing to do with these political quarrels: each man had espoused the cause of the leader from whom he had most to expect.

When I went to say goodbye to the bishop and his family, I witnessed a striking example of the misfortunes which beset those benighted people who rely on factors outside themselves for their happiness. The Goyeneches had never felt happy except when sitting on heaps of gold, and a loss of part of their wealth had impaired their intellectual faculties. The bishop looked like a skeleton, so thin, aged and cadaverous had his face become. As he sat ensconced in his great armchair, clad in silks, covered with gold, and giving practically no sign of life, he seemed to be attending his own funeral. I was moved by the spectacle, though, as I realised on reflection, the distress which caused it was itself absurd. How important to him must money be, I wondered, for him to be so deeply affected by losing it? After all, he spent little on himself, nor did he relieve the unfortunate. I was baffled: avarice poses moral problems that I have never been able to solve. If this prelate had distributed his wealth to the poor, his enemies could have done nothing to harm him; the apostolic virtues would have protected him more effectively than the gold which defiled him, and no one, not the monk Baldivia nor General Nieto, would have dared to disturb his repose.

I also wanted to pay a visit to San Roman. I had not yet seen him. He kept to his quarters, because the myth of his broken leg had to be maintained. Fearing that I would speak too candidly, my uncle did his best to prevent me from going to see him, and would only come with me when Escudero offered to be my escort. He warned San Roman of my visit, and urged him not to be shocked at my frankness. When we entered the drawing-room at Gamio's house, we saw a group of officers standing there, gesticulating and talking very loudly. As soon as they saw us they retired rapidly into the adjoining room. I wanted to follow them, so as to catch the victorious general on his two legs; but my uncle guessed my malicious intent and held me back, saying: 'Wait till they announce us.'

Two or three officers came towards me, saying, 'Señorita, the general is most flattered by your visit; he is fortunately feeling rather better. You will find him lying on a couch.' I went into Señora Gamio's bedroom. San Roman apologised for not rising to receive me. He was not lying, but sitting, with his leg supported by a stool. This man, so feared by the Arequipans, was not particularly frightening to look at. He was aged about thirty; his expression was frank and merry; but his hair, beard and the colour of his skin showed that he had Indian blood in his veins, and this made him very ugly in the eyes of Spanish Peruvians.

Our conversation was somewhat unusual, joking and serious at the same time. He was a good talker, but he had a defect that had fatal effects on the caution which my uncle had urged me to observe: he kept bursting into laughter at the slightest thing. This extreme hilarity contrasted with the seriousness of his entourage, but it put me at my ease, and I also laughed a good deal.

'Is it really true, mademoiselle,' he said, striking an arrogant attitude, 'that the Arequipans are afraid of me?'

'So afraid, colonel, that I had given you the nickname of *Croquemitaine*.'

'And what does that mean?'

'It is a word used by nurses in France to frighten little children. "If you're not good, if you don't do what you're told," they say, "I'll call the bogeyman, and he'll come and eat you," and the child is frightened and obeys immediately.'

'Aha, it's a nice comparison. Nieto is the nurse, the Arequipans are the children and I'm the man who eats them up.'

'So you're going to eat them up, those poor Arequipans?'

'Heavens, no! On the contrary, I've come to restore order and encourage work and trade, so that they can all have something to eat.'

'It's a noble aim, colonel. I should be interested to learn the system that you intend to adopt in order to attain it.'

'Our system, mademoiselle, is that of Señora Gamarra. We shall close our ports to the many foreign vessels which are competing to infest our country with all sorts of goods which they sell so cheaply that the poorest negress can strut about decked out in finery. You will realise that industry cannot develop in Peru with such competition, and as long as the people get cheap goods from abroad, they will not make an effort to manufacture them themselves.'

'Colonel, industrialists cannot be trained like soldiers, and factories cannot be built, as armies can, by force.'

'It is not as difficult as you think to carry out our plan. Our country can supply all the raw material – flax, cotton, silk, incomparably fine wool, gold, silver, lead and so on. As for machines, we'll import them from England, and we'll get workmen from all parts of the world.'

'A bad system, colonel! Believe me, it is not by isolating yourselves that you will foster the love of work and competitiveness.'

'Mademoiselle, I believe that necessity is the only spur that will force these people to work. Note also that our country is in a much more advantageous position than any in Europe, as it has neither a vast army nor a fleet to support, nor a large national debt to bear; it is therefore in favourable circumstances for industrial development; and when peace has been restored, and we have outlawed the consumption of foreign goods, there will be nothing to stop the successful development of the industries that we shall establish.'

'But you must realise that, for a long time to come, labour will be dearer here than in Europe. You have only a small population; will you use it to produce textiles, watches and furniture? What will then become of agriculture, still so backward, and the exploitation of the mines, which you have been forced to abandon for lack of labour?'

'So long as we are without factories, the foreigners will continue to take our gold and our silver.'

'But colonel, gold and silver are products of the country, and more than anything else would lose their value if you could not exchange them against foreign produce. I say again, the time to establish factories has not yet come for Peru. Before you can do this you must stimulate in the population a taste for luxury and the comforts of life, create needs, so that they will wish to work; and it is only through free trade in foreign merchandise that you will attain this. Whilst the Indian goes barefoot, dresses only in sheepskin, lives on a little maize and a few bananas, he will never work.'

'Well done, mademoiselle, I see that you zealously defend your own country's interests.'

'Oh, I'm not forgetful of my Peruvian origins. I ardently desire to see this country prosper. Educate the people, open up good communications, leave trade free and you will see prosperity arriving with great strides. It is only by using this very simple means that your brothers in North America have astonished the world by the speed of their progress.'

We talked for a long time. My gaiety and my gravity so charmed the victorious general that, when I got up to leave, he rose at the same time to see me out, forgetting his 'broken' leg. I was wicked enough to let him walk a few steps, despite the alarmed faces of the officers present, and then said: '*General,* please go no further, your wound is very dangerous. Stay well wrapped in your cloak, don't talk political economy, smoke good cigars and in time, if you follow this treatment, I hope you will be cured.' San Roman thanked me for my sincere interest, and limped back to his couch.

That evening, Escudero came to see me. When I saw him I burst out laughing so heartily that he could not help laughing with me. We had understood one another. 'Dear Florita,' he said, 'we are all the same – sometimes actors and sometimes spectators of an eternal comedy. Maybe, at Tacna, at this very moment, General Nieto has his arm in a sling. Good heavens, these little deceits are very innocent ones.'

'Yes, no doubt, colonel. But agree with me that when one has publicly announced that one has a broken leg, one should remember not to stand up straight on two to show young ladies to the door.'

'It's most unfair of you to reproach poor San Roman for having forgotten that his leg was supposed to be broken, when you know quite well that it was all the fault of your gazelle-like eyes, whose power you well realise. You are most unfair, Mademoiselle Flora.'

'Colonel, unfairness doesn't enter into it. I found San Roman's situation laughable, and you too have just been laughing at it.'

'It's different for me: I am like your friend Althaus, I laugh at everything. But then I've not just conquered the conqueror, like Florita the Fair.'

'Really? Oh, that's a point in his favour. I was afraid that he wasn't too pleased after all the frank remarks I made about his silly policies.'

'He liked you so much that he said to me: "If I were free, I'd propose marriage to that young lady. I can't understand how you bachelors can let her escape."'

'He seems to think well of himself, does Mr Bogeyman.'

Before leaving Arequipa, I also wished to say goodbye to my cousin the *monja* of Santa Rosa. I had to go there alone. The courage and perseverance of the young nun were universally admired; but she lived an isolated life, and though she was connected with the richest and most influential local families, no one *dared* visit her, so great was the power of superstitious prejudices over the minds of this ignorant and credulous people. Dominga was criticised for her fondness for fine clothes and luxury, as if she had to continue in the outside world the absurd austerities that she fled from in the cloister. It seemed to me quite natural that the poor recluse should compensate in this way for the eleven years of captivity, of tortures and privations of all sorts that she had to suffer in Santa Rosa.

She looked exquisitely beautiful that evening. She wore a pretty silk dress in pink and black check, a little black lace pinafore, black net mittens which half exposed her plump and dimpled arms; her shoulders were bare, and a string of pearls adorned her neck. Her ebony-black hair, shining like the finest silk, was draped over her bosom in plaits woven with pink satin ribbons; her beautiful face bore traces of melancholy and suffering, which lent an indefinable charm to her whole person. When I entered she ran towards me, saying in a tone which touched me to the heart: 'Is it really true, dear Florita, that you are going back to France?'

'Yes, cousin, I'm off, and have come to bid you goodbye.'

'Ah, Florita, how lucky you are and how I envy your lot!'

'But dear Dominga, are you so unhappy here?'

'More than you can imagine, much more than I ever was at Santa Rosa.' As she said this, she wrung her hands in despair, and raised her large sad eyes to heaven as if to reproach God for her cruel destiny.

'But Dominga, you are free, you are so beautiful and so elegantly dressed, are you really more unhappy than when you were a prisoner in that gloomy convent, buried under your nun's veil? I admit that I do not understand.' The young woman, tossing her haughty head and looking at me with a sardonic smile, said:

'I free? Where have you ever found that anyone weak who is the prey of vile prejudice, was ever free? Here,

Florita, in this drawing-room, dressed in this pretty silk dress, Dominga is still the *monja* of Santa Rosa. By courage and determination I succeeded in escaping from my "tomb"; but the woollen veil that was my burial veil is still over my head, dividing me from the world for ever. I fled from the cloister in vain: the people's cries of protest have sent me back there.' She embraced me closely, and I felt her heart beat as if it would break; but she wept no tears. A long silence followed: we both felt that one word from either would let loose so many painful thoughts. I made no attempt to comfort her: no comfort can be given for such a sorrow. I caressed her hair, and cut a lock of it which I keep preciously. Poor Dominga! How I felt for her in her sorrow!

At about ten o'clock, there was a knock at the door. It was the young doctor who had helped her obtain a female corpse. She took his hand and said with emotion: 'Florita is leaving . . . And I . . .'

'You too,' interrupted the young man. 'You too will leave soon! Be patient a little longer, and you will soon see my fair land of Spain and my good mother, who will love you like a daughter.' At these words, poor Dominga sighed as if hope were reviving; she smiled again, and with both love and doubt in her voice, she said:

'God grant it, Alfonso, but alas, I fear that I shall never be able to enjoy such happiness!' This final scene made me realise how much my cousin had suffered.

The time of my departure approached. In my uncle's household they went about with long faces; but I had read their thoughts and their regrets were as insincere as the tears shed by an heir about to inherit from a dying man. It was clear to everyone from the extremely simple clothes I wore that this rich family had given me nothing to supplement my penurious state; it was obvious that in Don Pio's house, Mariano's only daughter was being treated like a stranger. Yet I was calm, resigned; I showed my displeasure by neither word nor expression. Since the scene I had had with my uncle, I had allowed myself not the slightest allusion to the lot which had been meted out to me. But this dignified behaviour of mine made them as ill at ease with themselves as with others. My presence was a perpetual reproach to them all, and my uncle, who was genuinely fond of me, felt some remorse.

The day before I left, he repeated the promise that he had made in the presence of the whole family to pay me a pension of 2,500 francs as soon as normality had been restored, and he handed me a letter for M. Bertera in which he instructed him to pay me regularly and in advance.

XIV

I LEAVE AREQUIPA

On Friday the 25th of April, Mr Smith came to fetch me at seven in the morning. I was ready to mount my horse and my face showed no sign of perturbation, but I felt deeply moved at leaving the place, for it was the house where my father was born. I had hoped to find a home there, but for the seven months that I had stayed I remained no more than a visitor. I was glad to leave a house where I had been tolerated but not adopted, where I had suffered mental tortures and where despair had been my counsellor. I was glad to leave – but where for? I had no idea. I had no plans, and, tired of disappointments, I had no objectives. Spurned wherever I went, without family, without fortune or profession or even a name of my own, I was setting off at random, like a balloon which lands wherever the wind wills. I said farewell to the walls of the house, calling on my father's spirit to come to my aid; I embraced my aunt, and was sorry for her in my heart for her coldness towards me; I kissed her children and was sorry for them too, for they would in their turn suffer days of affliction. I said goodbye to the many servants gathered in the courtyard, I mounted my horse and left that temporary home for ever, to put myself in God's hands. My uncle, my cousin Florentino and a number of friends came with me to see me off.

We rode in silence. Those who were close to me admired my great courage and were alarmed by it. M. Le Bris and M. Le Viollier were sad, and my uncle seemed so too, but I took comfort from a secret voice within me. I felt, instinctively, that God had not abandoned me. At Tiavalla we stopped, and I looked back towards Arequipa and its charming valley. Then I looked at my uncle. We had come to a point where the road was narrow and I had gone ahead, and so we passed through the village. When we were out in the country again, I stopped to wait for my uncle ... but he was no longer there. M. Le Bris told me that, to spare me the pain of a final parting, he had taken advantage of a twist in the road to return to Arequipa unseen by me. It was finished: I was never to see my uncle again. I found the thought extremely painful. Despite the fact that he had hurt me so much, that it was due to his hardness and ingratitude that I was forced to wander homeless, like the birds of the forest, without any more security than they, that he had behaved unjustly towards me and that his avarice had been greater than his affection or his pity, well, despite all this, I loved him! I loved him *against my better judgment,* so lasting and so powerful are the early impressions of childhood! I was so upset, that I hesitated a moment as to whether I should return to Arequipa, just to see my uncle again, to beseech him to love me, to forget that he had deprived me of what was mine, so strong was the need that I felt for his affection. Ah! Who can explain the fancies of the human heart? We love, we hate, as God dictates, more often than not without being able to discover why. And how unfortunate are the effects of social organisation! If I had not been obliged to contest my inheritance with my uncle, we should have sincerely loved each other. I had no sympathy with his character as a man of politics, but I liked all the rest. I have never met a man whose conversation was more instructive, whose manners were more attractive, and who had a merrier wit.*

* *Translator's note:* Don Pio remarried, having become a widower, at the age of eighty, and according to Paul Gauguin,

At Congata we found a good breakfast waiting for us, which we owed to the gallant attentions of the very attentive Mr Smith. We stayed at Señor Najarra's until the heat had lessened somewhat; at about midday the sea wind began to blow, and we set off. When I left my two best friends, Messieurs Le Bris and Viollier, I was deeply moved. For the last seven months they had been extremely kind, and I felt sincerely attached to them.

Mr Smith's servant was a very intelligent Chilean, and my uncle had lent me a reliable factotum to look after me until I sailed. In addition, owing to the kind and gallant attentions of Colonel Escudero, I had a security guard. Lieutenant Monsilla, with two lancers, had been appointed by him to protect me. This journey was much less arduous than the last. I had armed myself with everything necessary to protect myself, as far as possible, from sun, cold, wind and thirst, in a word, all the discomforts of the desert. I had two good mules, so that I could change my mount. In addition, Mr Smith was so extremely kind as to put his spare horse at my disposal. My aunt Joaquina had lent me two saddles, an English one for the horse, and another more suitable for the mules; lastly, Mr Smith's attentions were no less valuable than those I had once received from Don Balthazar, for he had ten years' experience of this sort of journey.

When we reached the top of the first mountain, we halted. I dismounted and went and sat at the same place where seven months before I had been laid down half dead. I stayed there for quite a time, enjoying the view of the delightful valley of Arequipa: I was saying farewell to it. I was thinking what a strange shape the city took on from this angle, and my thoughts ran on until it came to me that if I had been free and able to become linked with a man of my choice, I could have led as happy a life there

reared another family. Aline Gauguin, Flora's daughter, brought her two small children, Paul and Marie, to Peru, and received warm hospitality from Don Pio and his son-in-law Echenique who was vice-president and later president of Peru. They stayed for five years. Don Pio died in 1860, aged ninety-one. He left a generous inheritance to Aline, but she never received it.

as in most European countries. The thought saddened and moved me. 'Mademoiselle,' said Mr Smith, who had been on the move since he was sixteen and could not conceive how one could become fond of any one country, 'don't be sorry at leaving Arequipa: it's a pretty town all right, but the one I'm taking you to is a real paradise. This volcano is fine, I wish we had one like it in Dublin; the Andes are splendid, but you will agree that they are the cause of the cold, volcanic wind which would make the jolliest, sweetest man in England turn bilious. Lima for ever! If you can't be a member of parliament with £10,000 a year, come and live in Lima.' So Mr Smith's natural gaiety and wit soon turned my thoughts into other channels.

When travelling from Arequipa towards Islay, the sun is on one's back and the wind in one's face, so one suffers much less from heat than when going in the opposite direction. I stood the trip very well and without undue fatigue, for, my health having improved, I was more resistant than on my earlier journey. At midnight we arrived at the *tambo*. I lay down on my bed fully dressed whilst the supper was being prepared. Mr Smith had a marvellous talent for coping effectively with all the troubles attendant on travel. He dealt with everything – the cooking, the muleteers, the animals – all with admirable speed and tact. He was a young man-about-town of thirty, who did everything with elegance; even in the desert, he was the drawing-room dandy. Due to his care, we had a very good supper, after which we sat and chatted, for no one wanted to sleep. We set off again at three in the morning. The cold was so intense that I wrapped myself in three ponchos. When dawn came I was overcome with a drowsiness that I could not shake off, and I asked Mr Smith to let me sleep for just half an hour: I lay down, and without giving the servant time to spread a rug, I slept so soundly that they dared not rouse me to make me more comfortable. They let me sleep for an hour, and I felt very well after it. We were by then out in the *pampa*, and I mounted the horse, so as to cross this vast area at a steady gallop. Mr Smith was sure that I could not keep up with him; to encourage me he challenged me time and time again, and I accepted, making it a point of honour to be always fifteen or twenty yards ahead of him. This stimulation had the desired affect: I soon became an excellent horsewoman. I galloped my horse so well, without exhausting it, that Lieutenant Monsilla could not keep up with me, and the two lancers were left even farther behind. At last Mr Smith himself had to ask me to have pity on his fine Chilean mare, which he was afraid of overtiring.

At midday we arrived at Guerrera, where we made a stop. We ate in the cool shade of the trees, then made our beds on the ground and slept until five o'clock. We climbed the mountain slowly and reached Islay at seven. Don Justo got a big surprise when he saw me. Full as ever of kindness and hospitality towards all strangers, he looked after me well. Islay was a changed town since I last saw it. This time I was not invited to any balls. Nieto and his brave soldiery had pillaged everything during the twenty-four hours that they had stayed there. Apart from requisitioning food, they had gone to great lengths to extort money from the unfortunate inhabitants. The town was wrecked. Good Don Justo said again and again: 'Ah, mademoiselle, if I were not so old, I would leave with you. The endless wars which lay this country waste have made it uninhabitable. I have already lost two sons, and expect to hear news of the death of the third, who is in Gamarra's army.'

I stayed three days in Islay waiting for our ship to sail, and it would have been a dull time had it not been for Mr Smith and the officers of an English frigate anchored in the bay, to whom he had introduced me. I have never met, I am sad to say, men so distinguished in their manners and their minds as the officers of the frigate, *The Challenger*. They all spoke French, and had lived for some years in Paris. They wore smart clothes at all times, remarkable for their extreme cleanliness and elegant simplicity. The captain was a superb man, as handsome as a god. He was only thirty-two, but was overshadowed by a deep melancholy: his actions and his words betrayed a hint of sorrow which was painful to see. I asked one of his officers why this was, and he said: 'Ah, yes, mademoiselle, he is indeed very sad, and the misfortune that causes it is extreme. For the last seven years he has been married to the most beautiful woman in England. He loves her madly, and is equally loved by her, yet they must live apart.'

'But who insists on their separation?'

'His profession of naval officer is the cause. As he is one of the youngest frigate commanders, he is always sent to distant posts for three or four years at a time. We have been in these parts for three years, and it will be fifteen months before we return to England. You can imagine how cruelly he suffers from so long an absence!'

'Say rather, how cruelly they both must suffer! But has he no money of his own, since he stays in a career which is a torment to himself and the woman he loves?'

'No money! He has an income of £5,000 a year of his own, and his wife, who is England's richest heiress, brought him £200,000; she is an only child, and will have twice that sum again when her father dies.'

I was dumbfounded. 'Then, sir, explain what power it is that condemns your captain to live apart from his wife for four years and waste away on board his frigate, whilst his lovely wife spends her life in sorrow and in weeping?'

'He must reach a high rank. Our captain only obtained her father's consent to marry this rich heiress on condition that he followed his profession until he became an admiral. The young man and the girl both agreed to this; they gave their word, and to carry out his promise he must sail the seas for at least ten years more, for with us seniority determines promotion.'

'So your captain feels obliged to live for ten years more apart from his wife?'

'Yes, he must do so to fulfil his promise; but when these ten years are up he will be an admiral, will become a member of the House of Lords and perhaps a minister of the Crown: in short, one of the first men of the realm. It seems to me, mademoiselle, that to arrive at such a fine position is worth a few years' suffering.'

But I was thinking how, for the trappings of greatness, mere baubles, men trample underfoot all that is most sacred! God himself had been pleased to bless these two people: beauty, wit and wealth, they had it all, and their mutual love should have given them as much happiness as our natures are capable of enjoying. Happiness seeks to spread itself; all around it, its gentle influence makes itself felt. Their happiness would have made others happy. But what happens? This prospect of an earthly paradise is shattered by the vanity of a silly old man, who insists that the best twenty years of the life of these young people should be sacrificed, and spent instead in sorrow and distress, in all the torments of separation. When they are reunited, she will have lost her beauty, and he his illusions; his heart will be devoid of love, and his mind of freshness, for twenty years of trials, fear and jealousy wither even the noblest natures. But he will be an admiral! A noble lord! A minister! – and all the rest. Stupid vanity!

The story of the captain of *The Challenger* plunged me into the most bitter thoughts. Wherever I looked there was moral suffering; everywhere it seemed to result from ungodly prejudices which put mankind at odds with Providence, and I raged at the slow progress of human reason. I asked the handsome captain if he had any children. 'Yes,' he told me, 'a daughter as beautiful as her mother and a son who, they tell me, is very like me: I have never seen him. He will be four by the time I meet him, if God permits me ever to do so . . .' And the poor man stifled a sigh. He was still capable of feeling, because he was young, but at fifty he would probably become as hard as his father-in-law, and would perhaps demand sacrifices from his son and daughter as cruel as those imposed on him. This is the way that the prejudices which distort our nature are passed on; and the vicious circle is only broken by the appearance of one of those beings whom God has endowed with a firm and energetic courage, willing to undergo martyrdom rather than bear the yoke.

On the 30th of April, at eleven in the morning, we sailed out of the Bay of Islay; on the 1st of May, at two in the afternoon, we anchored off Callao. That port did not appear to be as busy as Valparaiso. Recent political events had had a deadening effect on business, which was at a low ebb, and there were fewer ships than usual. From the sea, we could see Lima on its hill, amidst gigantic Andean peaks. The size of the city, and the number of church towers, gave it a look of fairy-like grandeur.

We stayed in Callao until four o'clock, when the coach

for Lima was due to depart. I had plenty of time to look at the town. Like Valparaiso and Islay, Callao for the last ten years had been developing so fast that when the ships' captains returned after an absence of two or three years they could hardly recognise it. The finest houses belonged to English or American merchants. They had large warehouses. Commercial activity ensured continual movement between the port and the city, which was two leagues inland. Mr Smith took me to his agent's office, and I found in that English house all the luxury and comfort peculiar to the English. The servants were all English; like their masters, they dressed as if they had been in England. Like all the houses in Lima, the house had a verandah, a convenient feature in hot countries: one can walk round the house, out of the sun, and enjoy the fresh air. This one was embellished by attractive English blinds; I sat there some time and could watch at my ease everything that went on in the long wide street which forms the entire township of Callao. It was Sunday. The sailors in their best clothes were walking up and down. I saw groups of English, Americans, French, Dutch and Germans, indeed a mixture of almost all nations, and snatches of all languages came to my ears. As I listened to these sailors talking, I understood the fascination which their adventurous life must have for them, and the enthusiasm of the 'true sailor' Leborgne. When I was tired of the street scene, I glanced into the large drawing-room whose windows looked on to the verandah. Five or six Englishmen, with calm, cold, handsome faces, very correctly dressed, were gathered there. They drank grog and smoked excellent Havanas as they swung in Guayaquil hammocks which hung from the ceiling.

Four o'clock came at last, and we got into the coach. The driver was French, and everyone I saw there spoke French or English. Two were Germans, great friends of Althaus, so I was immediately among friends. This was the first time I had been in a carriage since I had left Bordeaux, and it was so pleasurable that I was entirely happy for the two hours that the journey lasted: I felt I was back in a civilised country again. The road was bad as we left Callao, but after a league or so it became fairly good, very wide and smooth without much dust. At half a league from Callao, to the right of the road, there were very extensive ruins of Indian buildings. The town that had stood there had ceased to exist when the Spaniards conquered the country. It would no doubt be possible to discover from Indian tradition what town this was and what caused its destruction, but up till then the conquerors had not been interested enough in the history of the people to try to find out. A little further on, to the left, was the village of Bella Vista, where there was a home for sailors. At about half way our driver stopped at a tavern kept by a Frenchman. When we had passed this, the city rose up before us in all its magnificence. The surrounding countryside was many shades of green, covered with a lush vegetation. Everywhere there were large orange trees, tall palm trees and many other tropical trees with their varied foliage; this was more wonderful than anything one had dreamed of.

Half a league from the entrance to the town, the road was lined with tall trees forming a truly majestic avenue. At the edges there were quite a number of people walking; also many young men rode by us on horseback. I was told that this avenue was used as a promenade by the people of Lima. Amongst the ladies, many were wearing the *saya*: this costume looked so strange that I watched it fascinated. Lima was a closed town, and at the end of the avenue we arrived at one of the gates. The two pilasters were made of brick, and the pediment bore the Spanish royal arms, which had been defaced. Officials inspected the vehicle, as at the gates of Paris. We crossed a large part of the town. The streets were wide, and the houses entirely different from those at Arequipa. Though Lima looked so grand from a distance, it was disappointing from within; it failed to keep its promise. The fronts of the houses were mean, their windows without glass; the grilles of iron bars suggested suspicion and constraint, and the lack of activity in almost all the streets was depressing. The coach stopped at a house of some distinction. I saw a tall, fat lady approaching from within, and recognised her immediately from the description given me by the officers of the *Mexicain* as Mme Denuelle. She came to open the carriage door herself, gave me her hand for me to get out, and said, in the most friendly manner, 'Mademoiselle Tristan, we have been impatiently expecting you for a long time. After all that M. Chabrié and M. David told us about you, we are happy to welcome you among us.'

XV

A FRENCH HOTEL IN LIMA

Mme Denuelle showed me into a drawing-room furnished in the French style. I had not been sitting there five minutes when a dozen to fifteen French people came in, all most anxious to meet me. I was grateful for their friendly attentions and chatted briefly with each of them in turn, thanking them as best I could for their warm welcome. Then Mme Denuelle took me to the small apartment that she intended for me: it consisted of a sitting-room and a bedroom.

In Arequipa I had been given a large number of letters to deliver in Lima. Mr Smith, whose kindness to me was inexhaustible, had, when we were still on board, offered to deliver them, so I had given them all to him, and thus it was that an hour after my arrival the people to whom they had been addressed arrived in force in search of political news. They were so eager that a score of questions were fired at me at once. Don Basilio de la Fuente, whom I found living at Mme Denuelle's, wanted news of his wife and eleven children; one lady was in tears over her brother who had been killed; another was worried about her sister who was the wife of General Nieto and who had remained a prisoner in Santa Rosa; and they were all frightened, with some justification, that Señora Gamarra might return to Lima, where she had so many scores to settle.

The people of Lima seemed to me, at this first encounter, even more boastful and more easily scared than the Arequipans. At about eleven in the evening, Mme Denuelle made it clear to my visitors that I must be in need of rest, and to my great relief they all left: I was at my wits' end. Mr Smith told me that when he personally delivered the letter addressed to my aunt, the beautiful Manuela de Tristan, wife of my uncle Don Domingo, then governor of Ayacucho, she had asked him to come back and fetch her, because she wanted to visit me that very evening. She arrived as soon as I was free of the others: I found this very tactful on her part.

After all I had heard of the extraordinary beauty of my Lima aunt, I naturally expected to see a fine looking woman; however, what I saw surpassed all expectations. She was not a human being, she was a goddess from Mount Olympus! A houri from Mahomet's paradise, come down on earth! When I saw that divine creature, I was filled with awe: I dared not touch her. She had taken my hand which she held in hers, and was saying the most affectionate things with such nobility, grace and fluency that I was completely captivated. I feel quite inadequate to describe such beauty. No Virgin of Raphael's had a forehead so noble and so pure, such a perfect nose, so gentle and so fresh a mouth, nor, above all, such a wonderfully beautiful oval face, such a neck, such a bosom. Her skin was white and smooth, with a bloom like a peach; her light brown hair was fine and shiny, and hung in long wavy curls down to her full shoulders. She was perhaps a little too plump, but her figure was tall and trim enough to have lost none of its elegance. Everything about her expressed pride and dignity; she carried herself like a queen. Her clothes were in tune with the freshness of her person.

Her white muslin dress, sprinkled with tiny pink embroidered roses, was very low at the neck and short-sleeved. It had a long bodice which came down to a point in front. This style suited her very well, and it showed off her greatest beauties – her neck, her shoulders, her bosom and her arms. She wore long earrings; a pearl necklace adorned her swan-like neck and a number of bracelets showed off the whiteness of her arms. A dark, sky-blue cloak, lined with white satin, was draped round that lovely body of hers, and a black silk lace veil hid her from the gaze of the curious. When she had finished speaking, I continued to look and to listen, and the only reply I could make to all her offers of assistance, was to exclaim: 'Good heavens, aunt, how beautiful you are!' Now, who can explain the magical power of beauty? For beauty has an irresistible influence which harmonises everything, yet has no definable form of its own. It is an emanation of the divine which gives life to forms and colours, thrills the senses and exhales its own perfume; a magnetic power bestowed by Providence for its own purposes over all created beings who belong to God's hierarchy, right down to the atom which no eye can see. This hidden force which determines our choices and our preferences, which fascinates us, beauty in all its forms, airy, visible or palpable, is to me a benevolent all-pervading influence. I experience it from the song of birds; from the forest giant whose top thrusts upward into the realm of storms; from the savage grace of the untamed beast; from the sight of a man like the captain of *The Challenger*, or of a woman like my aunt Manuela. And when my soul is in the presence of beauty, in the presence of that smile of the gods, it thrills with admiration and pleasure, and ascends towards heaven.

My aunt insisted that I should go and stay with her: I thanked her but refused on the grounds of the inconvenience I might cause her. As it was very late, we postponed the decision until the morrow. When she had gone, Mme Denuelle stayed to chat, so that it was after one o'clock before I was alone.

No later than eight in the morning she came into my room, and soon turning the conversation to the subject of my aunt, she said with embarrassment that, for my sake, she felt that she ought to enlighten me about certain personal circumstances of the Señora Manuela de Tristan. She told me that, for many years past, Manuela had had a liaison with a certain American gentleman, whom she loved and of whom she was extremely jealous. Mme Denuelle spoke in such a way that I could see what lay behind her words: she feared lest I should accept the hospitality offered me, not so much because of the loss of the money I would spend with her, as because of her great wish to have me under her wing during my stay in Lima. If I had not already decided to refuse my aunt's offer, what I had just heard would have been enough to prevent me from accepting. I had learnt enough about the human heart to know that I ought not to go and stay with a woman if I incurred the risk of arousing her jealous suspicions and provoking her hatred, which I certainly wished to avoid. On leaving my uncle Pio's house, I had decided never again to accept the hospitality of any relative. I spoke of this one day to Carmen, who said: 'Quite right, Florita, it is better to eat bread in one's own house than cake at the house of relations.' So I reassured Mme Denuelle, fixed a price with her of two piastres a day and, when my aunt returned at eleven to collect me, as she said, I made it clear that we would each get in each other's way; so it was agreed that I would stay at the hotel. I got the impression that my discretion was much appreciated.

However, my financial situation was enough to cause concern. I had left Arequipa with a few hundred francs. My uncle had indeed given me a letter of credit for 400 piastres, but this was only intended to pay my passage: he had stipulated that I could only cash it on the eve of my departure, thus making it clear that he gave me the money only on the condition that I left the country. There were no ships due to sail, and I knew through Mr Smith that there would be none for two months. To stay for this length of time at the hotel would cost 120 piastres, and in addition I would have to make some modest outlay for articles of clothing. I realised therefore that I should need at least 200 piastres to cover these expenses. I can say that I have suffered every misfortune, except running into debt; the fear of doing so has always been a guiding principle. I have calculated carefully before spending, and so never owed a penny to anyone. When I made this calculation of 200 piastres, and found only twenty in my purse, I was, I admit, very frightened. My wardrobe was, as I have already said, more than modest; however, I began to examine it and, pen in hand, I valued item by item what could be sold of all these rags at the time of my departure, and I saw that it would easily make over 200 piastres. When I realised this, how happy I was! How very happy! When I had left Escudero I had given up all my ambitious plans and wanted to hear no more about politics. I became young and gay again, and completely carefree for the first time in my life. My health had never been better; I was obviously putting on weight; my complexion was clear and fresh; I ate with appetite and slept perfectly; in a word I can say that those two months were the only ones in my life without suffering.

XVI

LIMA AND ITS CUSTOMS

My aunt Manuela was most helpful: she showed me the town and introduced me to society; she declared herself my friend, but this was not on the basis of our having much in common, for I don't think we had. Beautiful as she was, her eyes were not frank, and she never looked straight at one. She sought my company because of a natural interest in a relative from abroad, born three thousand leagues away, of whom she had never heard and who had suddenly appeared. I found in her a vast fund of knowledge of everything I wanted to know. She and Mme Denuelle had similar characters: great intelligence and an ever-sarcastic tongue. She was my main guide; her beauty, my uncle's name and my status as a foreigner quickly opened all doors. I spent whole days with her; I was always delighted with her wit, but pained at the hardness of her heart. Lima was still an entirely sensual city; its way of life had evolved under the influence of older institutions and wit and beauty were the ruling criteria: it was like Paris during the regency of Louis XV. Noble feelings and private virtues could not survive if they were unprofitable, and elementary education had not advanced sufficiently for the upper classes to have much to fear from the freedom of the press.

At my aunt's I met the most distinguished men of the country: President Orbegoso, the English General Miller, the French Colonel Soigne, both in the service of the Republic, Salaberry, La Fuente etc. I met only two women there, the rest having abandoned her society, alleging her flighty behaviour as the reason: these virtuous ladies cleverly concealed under this pretext the aversion they felt to appearing in competition with a beauty like Manuela, next to whom no one looked beautiful. Evening parties at her house were most agreeable. God had showered her with gifts: her singing voice was ravishingly sweet and melodious, and she sang with great skill. An Italian, who had been in Lima for four years, had been struck by the heavenly beauty of its quality and had devoted himself to training it: Manuela had soon outstripped her master. She would sing us the finest arias from Rossini's operas, in Italian, and when she was tired, we talked politics. Like all the ladies of Lima, she took a great interest in politics, and in her society I was able to form an opinion of the minds and the merits of the men who headed the government. Orbegoso and the officers who surrounded him seemed to me to be totally without merit. I also met there the famous priest Luna Pizarro; I found that he was not worthy of his reputation, and far less capable than Baldivia. He was an old man, so virulent that he could be called the Murat of Peru; apart from this, I felt that he had no vision: he showed a passion for destruction, but had no constructive powers. Personal ambition was the motive of all these men; the old priest's aim was to become bishop of Arequipa, and he had become an agitator in order to achieve it. He would have been a mere courtier if that had been the way to achieve his objective. Unfortunately, the nation was too brutalised for true statesmen to emerge, or for those in power to be judged by their merits.

Lima, which then had nearly eighty thousand inhabitants, was built by Pizarro in 1535. I do not know the origin of the name. It had very fine public buildings, a large number of churches, convents and monasteries. The houses were uniformly built, the streets well aligned, long and wide. In nearly all of the latter, water ran in two streams, one on each side; in only a few was there just one stream in the middle. The houses were built of brick, earth and wood, painted in various pale colours, blue, grey, pink, yellow etc; they had only one upper storey and the roofs were flat. The walls came up above the roof, which made the houses look unfinished. Sometimes the roofs could be used, and had tubs of flowers on them, but few of them were strong enough for this. It never rains in that climate. If it were to rain, after four hours the houses would be no more than a heap of mud. The interiors were quite well arranged; the drawing-room and dining-room faced the front courtyard; behind were the kitchen and the slave quarters round a second courtyard. The bedrooms were upstairs, all most luxuriously furnished according to the rank and wealth of the owner.

The cathedral was magnificent. The carvings of the choir-stalls were of exquisite workmanship. The balustrade which surrounded the high altar was of silver, and the altar itself was extremely richly decorated. It was stone built, and so solidly that it had stood up to the most violent earthquakes without any damage at all. The twin towers, the façade and the steps were very fine, and of a magnificence rare even in this ancient Europe of ours, and quite unexpected in a city of the New World. The little side chapels were charming; each canon had one to himself. The cathedral took up the whole of the east side of the main square; the city hall was opposite. This square was the 'Palais-Royal' of Lima. There were arcades along two of the sides, under which there were the finest shops of all sorts; and in the centre there was a superb fountain. All day long there was great activity. In the morning there were water-carriers, the military, processions etc. In the evening, it was a popular promenade, and there were street salesmen with ices, fruit and cakes, and performers amused the public by playing and dancing.

The most remarkable of the monasteries was St Francis: its church was the richest and the prettiest and the oddest I have ever seen. When ladies wished to visit monasteries or convents, they used a curious stratagem: they claimed to be *pregnant*; the good fathers, professing profound respect for the whims of pregnant women, opened all doors to them. When we went to St Francis's, the monks teased us in the most indecent manner. We mounted the towers, and, as I climbed with some vigour, the prior, seeing how slim and agile I was, asked me if I were 'pregnant too'. Flabbergasted by this unexpected question, I was quite nonplussed; my embarrassment provoked in the monks laughter and remarks so indecent that Manuela, who was not shy, did not know what to say. I came out of this monastery very shocked. When I complained, I was told: 'Oh, it's just their way, they're merry fellows; they're the nicest of all of them.' And these are the men whom the people trust. But in Lima, what is not corrupt is abnormal.

I also visited a convent of nuns, the Incarnation. There was, I felt, nothing religious about this establishment: there was no sign of monastic discipline anywhere. It was a house like any other. There were twenty-three nuns, each of whom had her lodging, in which she cooked, worked, brought up children, talked, sang, in a word, did as she liked. We even saw some who were not wearing the habits of their order. They took in lodgers who went freely in and out, and the door of the convent was always open. It is hard to understand the purpose of such a way of life; one is even tempted to think that these women had retreated within these walls in order to be more independent than they would have been in the world outside. One of them was a pretty young Frenchwoman of twenty-six, with her five-year-old daughter. She lived there for cheapness's sake, whilst her husband travelled on business in Central America. I did not see the Mother Superior, who was said to be ill. These new-style nuns struck me as somewhat sluttish. Their convent was dirty and ill-kept, different in every way from Santa Rosa and Santa Catalina. Finding nothing interesting about it, I climbed the tower to get a bird's eye view of the town. That superb city, seen from above, had a miserable look; the unroofed houses looked like ruins and the grey earth of which they were made was of such a dull, dirty colour that they looked like the huts of a primitive people. On the other hand the monasteries and numerous churches built in fine stone stood out boldly, with a solidity which defied time and which contrasted shockingly with the multitude of hovels around them. My instinctive reaction was that the same lack of harmony must exist in the way this nation was organised, and that one day the citizens' houses would be better and the religious buildings less sumptuous. The panorama was a varied one; the country surrounding the town was most picturesque. In the distance I could see Callao with its two forts and St Lawrence Island; all this within the framework of the snow-covered Andes on one side and the Pacific Ocean on the other. What a grand sight! I was so disappointed in this convent that I was not tempted to visit any other. I had gone there in the hope of feeling a religious emotion inspired by selflessness and devotion to a faith, and I had only found another example of the decline of such a faith and the decay of conventual institutions.

The fine Mint seemed to me to be well administered. During the past few years it had been considerably improved. Enormous rolling-mills had been brought from London, and these and the fly-presses were powered by a waterfall. Their coins were not, however, artistically speaking, as good as those in Europe since they lacked good engravers. In 1833 three million piastres worth of silver coins were struck and about a million piastres worth of gold coins.

When I entered the prisons of the Holy Inquisition I felt an involuntary terror. The building was a fine one, like everything undertaken by the Spanish clergy at a time when, having a dominant position within the state, there was no lack of funds to cater for its magnificence. There were twenty-four cells, each about ten foot square. They were lit by a small window which gave ventilation but little light. There were also cellars and secret dungeons which were used for severe punishments and for the unfortunates who were not meant to survive. The trial chamber was beautiful in a way suitable to its terrible purpose. It was very high; two small windows set with iron bars let in only a pale moist daylight. The Grand Inquisitor sat on a throne, and the judges in niches like those intended for statues. The walls were panelled to a great height with beautifully sculptured wood. This hall was so gloomy, so far from human habitation, and the monks who composed this fearful tribunal were so unbending in their attitudes that the poor man brought before them must have been terror-struck as he entered. Since Peruvian independence, the Inquisition had been abolished. The building now housed a showcase of natural history and a museum. The collection consisted of four Inca mummies, which had been preserved intact, but were less well prepared than the Egyptian ones. Then there were a few stuffed birds, some shells and mineral samples, but very little of anything. What I found most interesting was a large number of ancient Inca pots. The Incas made their pots in forms as varied as they were grotesque and decorated them with symbolic figures. The only pictures in this museum were a few daubs, which were not even on stretchers. There was not a single statue. M. Rivero, an educated man who had lived in France, was the founder of this museum. He was doing what he could to add to it; but he was supported by no one, the Republic had allotted no funds for the purpose, and so he had no success. A taste for the fine arts only arises at the advanced state of a nation; when it is tired of wars and political upheavals and has become surfeited with everything, it then turns to the fine arts as a tonic for its chronic disillusionment. The arts, those bright flowers of the imagination, adorn neither the cradle of liberty nor the schisms which follow.

During my stay in Lima, I attended debates in the Congress building on a number of occasions. It had a fine hall, though too small for the new use to which it was put. Oblong in shape, it was previously used for academic gatherings and set speeches by high officials. For the previous ten years frequent plans had been made for a new chamber to be built, but the state funds were absorbed by the War Ministry, and not a piastre was available for useful works. The senators, as they were called, sat in four rows forming a horseshoe with the chairman at the angle. In the middle there was a large table for secretaries. The senators wore no special costume; each one, soldier, priest or citizen, attended the sessions in the garb of his profession. Above the assembly there were two rows of boxes, forming galleries for the use of officials, foreign envoys and the public. Behind, there was an amphitheatre reserved for ladies only. Each time I attended a meeting I saw a large number of ladies present: they were all in *sayas,* reading the newspaper or chatting to each other about politics. Normally the members spoke from their seats; there was however a rostrum, but I only saw it used on rare occasions. This assembly was much more solemn than ours. When a member was speaking, no one interrupted him; he was listened to in religious silence, not a word was lost, each one was audible. The Spanish language is so beautiful, so majestic, the word-endings are so full and so varied, the nations that use it are generally so full of imagination that all the orators I heard sounded extremely eloquent. The dignity of their bearing, their sonorous voices, their well-modulated words, their imposing gestures, everything combined to put the audience under their spell. The priests stood out particularly above the others as orators. A foreigner who judged this nation by the speeches of its representatives would be even more mistaken than if he had judged a book by the publisher's blurb. We all remember that gallant insurrection in Naples, the eloquent speeches of the members of the assembly, their vows to die for their country, and what it all came to when the Austrian army of Marshall Frimond arrived. Well, the Peruvian senators were no better than those whose conduct was revealed to the world in 1822: presumptuous and bold in their words, confidently proclaiming their pompous speeches, all devotion and patriotism, yet each one had only his private interests in mind and not his country, which most of them would be incapable of serving in any case. This parliament was merely a series of permanent conspiracies to appropriate the state funds; this objective was hidden at the back of all the members' minds. Virtue pervaded all the speeches, but base selfishness dictated all the actions. As I listened to those makers of fine phrases, I thought of the monk Baldivia's newspaper, Nieto's harangues, the prefect's circulars, the speeches of the commander of the Immortals, and I compared them with memories of how those people actually behaved, and then I realised how to interpret the speeches of the orators in Congress, and to evaluate how much courage, disinterestedness and patriotism they really signified.

The president's palace was extremely large, but ill-built and badly sited. The interior arrangements were most inconvenient. The reception-room was long and narrow, more like a gallery, and it was meanly furnished throughout. As I went in I thought of Bolivar, and all that my mother had told me of him: he had so loved luxury, pomp, spaciousness, so how could he have borne to live in this palace, inferior as it was to the public rooms of the hotel where he lived in Paris? But at Lima he was in command, he was the leader, whereas in Paris he was nobody, and the love of power is enough to override many an inconvenience. Whilst I was in Lima the president gave neither balls nor large receptions. I was sorry for this, for I should like to have seen one of their state occasions.

The city hall was very large, but contained nothing remarkable. I found the library more interesting. It had fine premises, with large well-kept rooms. The books were displayed on shelves and arranged in an orderly manner. There were tables covered in green cloth, set with chairs. All the local press was available. The majority of the books were in French: they included Voltaire, Rousseau, most of our classics, all the histories of the Revolution, the works of Mme de Staël, travel books, memoirs, Mme Rolland,* etc, altogether amounting to some 12,000 volumes. I was extremely pleased to find all our good authors here in this library. Unfortunately the taste for reading was not yet common enough for many people to profit from it. I saw French translations of Walter Scott, Lord Byron and Cowper, and a number of other translations. There were also a few works in English and in German, and in addition all the best of Spanish literature was there. In short, the library was very fine, for a country so underdeveloped.

* *Translator's note: Sic.* Presumably Mme Roland, 1754–93, the famous hostess during the French Revolutionary period, wrote her memoirs in gaol whilst awaiting the guillotine.

Lima had a theatre, which was very pretty though small. It was tastefully decorated and well-lit, perfect for showing off the ladies' costumes. There was at that time only a bad Spanish troupe, which acted plays by Lopez* and French musical comedies ruined in the translation. I saw there *Le Mariage de Raison, La Jeune Fille à marier, Le Baron de Felsheim* etc. It was such a poverty-stricken troupe that it even lacked costume's. For three or four years there had been a very good Italian troupe which, according to Mme Denuelle, performed all the best operas well and with success. The prima donna became pregnant and departed; this drove her lover to despair and he followed her, and their colleagues were obliged to seek their fortune elsewhere. There were only two performances a week, on Sundays and Thursdays; on the occasions that I went, there was a poor audience. During the intervals, all the audience smoked, including the ladies. This theatre would have been too small if the population had been as keen on drama as on bullfights.

The bull-ring demonstrated, by its enormous size, that this was the dominant passion of the race. I hesitated for a long time before yielding to the persuasion of the ladies of my acquaintance, who invited me to their boxes, so hard did I find it to overcome my repugnance for such butcheries. But if I wanted to study the customs of the country, I could not limit myself to what could be seen from a drawing-room and had to go out and see the people wherever their tastes led them. Therefore one Sunday I attended a bullfight, with my aunt, another lady and Mr Smith. There I found a vast crowd, five or six thousand people, perhaps more, all very well dressed according to their status in life, and happy in the expectation of pleasure. Around the vast arena, the amphitheatre consisted of twenty rows of benches; above there was a gallery divided into boxes occupied by the aristocracy of Lima. The sight of suffering is so distressing to me, that I find it really painful to describe the disgusting and barbarous spectacle that I witnessed. I cannot control the emotion I feel at these scenes of horror, and the pen that would depict them falls from my hands.

* *Translator's note: Sic.* Presumably Lope de Vega is meant.

In the ring, there were four or five men on horseback, each holding a little white flag and a short lance with a sharp steel blade attached. In the middle of the ring, there was a round stockade of stakes close enough to each other to prevent the bull putting his horns between them. Three or four men on foot were inside the enclosure; they emerged only to open the gate for the bull to come into the ring and then to provoke it. They threw rockets on to its back and into its ears and goaded it by a variety of torments: but the moment they were in danger of being tossed, they retreated quickly into their enclosure. I do not think anyone could help being seized with terror at the sight of the bull rushing into the ring and charging furiously into the horses. Its coat bristling, its tail flailing, its nostrils flaring, it bellowed with rage; this convulsive fury was unnerving. Leaping from side to side, it pursued both horses and men, who avoided it with agility.

I can understand the powerful attraction which such spectacles have in Andalusia: there they have superb bulls which need no goading; chargers full of fighting spirit; and those Andalusian *toreros*, dressed in all their finery, sparkling with gold spangles and diamonds, whose agility and grace are magical, who sport with the animal's fury and floor him with one stroke: all this converts the bloody spectacle into something grandiose; the danger is so real and the bravery is so heroic, that I can understand, I repeat, the enthusiasm of the spectators. But in Lima, there was nothing to add poetry to the butchery. In that soft and enervating climate the horses and bulls are feeble, and the men without courage. Ten minutes after the bull was let loose, it was tired; and, anticipating boredom in the spectators, the men in the enclosure, armed with sickles fastened to long poles, hamstrung its hind legs. The poor beast could now only walk on its forelegs, a pathetic sight as it dragged itself along. At this point, the brave *toreros* of Lima threw more fireworks at it, pierced it again and again with their lances, in short, killed it where it lay, like so many clumsy and barbarous apprentice butchers. The unfortunate bull struggled and roared; great tears sprung from its eyes, until at last its head fell into the pool of black blood in which it lay. Then the trumpets sounded, and the dead animal was put on to a cart and removed by four galloping horses. All this time the crowd clapped, stamped and shouted; joy and exultation seemed to have turned everyone's head: eight armed men had just killed a bull, what a fine thing to be enthusiastic about! I found the sight revolting, and as soon as the first bull had been killed I wanted to leave; but the ladies said: 'You must wait, the best sport is always at the end; the last bulls are always the most vicious; they might kill the horses or wound some men.' And they stressed the word 'men' as if to say: 'That would be most interesting.' We were 'very fortunate': the third bull eviscerated a horse and nearly killed its rider; the hamstringers, in their fright, cut all four of its legs, and the creature, panting with fury, fell bathed in its own blood. The horse's entrails were exposed. When I saw this, I left in a hurry, feeling about to be sick. Mr Smith had gone pale, and could only say: 'This spectacle is inhumane and disgusting.'

I took his arm and we walked for some time on the promenade along the river bank. The fresh air revived me, but the thought of the place I had left still depressed me. The attraction felt by a whole nation to the sight of suffering seemed to me an indication of extreme corruption. I was rapt in these reflections when we saw my beautiful aunt's barouche: she called out to me, 'You sensitive girl, Florita, why did you run away at the best moment? Oh, if you'd only seen the last one! What a splendid beast! It was really frightening, everyone got so excited. Oh, it was marvellous!' Poor people, I thought, have you then no pity, to delight in such sights?

The Rimac was very like the river at Arequipa: it ran over a stony bed and amongst rocks. The bridge was quite fine: it was the haunt of idlers who went there to watch the ladies go by on their way to the Paseo del Agua. I shall now pause to describe the costume peculiar to the women of Lima, how they take advantage of it and the effect it has on their customs, habits and character.

There is no place on earth where women are *freer*, where they are more influential than in Lima. They reign supreme, and all initiative comes from them. One might say that the ladies of Lima absorb all of the small quantity

A LADY OF LIMA IN HER WALKING DRESS,
HER *SAYA* AND HER *MANTO*

of energy available to its fortunate inhabitants in that hot, enervating climate. The women are usually taller and sturdier than the men. By the time they are eleven or twelve they are fully developed. They nearly all marry at that age and are very prolific, most of them having six or seven children. They have healthy pregnancies, and easy childbirths, from which they recover quickly. They nearly all nurse their babies, but always with the help of a wet-nurse who supplements the feed. This is a custom of Spanish origin, for there well-to-do families always have two nurses. The women are not generally beautiful, but their attractive faces give them an irresistible influence over men, for no man can see a woman of Lima without a beating heart. They are not swarthy, as is thought in Europe; most of them are very fair skinned; the rest, according to their various origins, are dark, but their complexions are smooth and velvety, of a warm colour, full of life. All their colouring is beautiful, with bright red lips and fine, naturally curly black hair and black eyes, brilliant and beautifully shaped, which express a baffling combination of intelligence, pride and languishment. Their whole charm lies in this expression of theirs. They are fluent speakers, and their gestures are as expressive as their words. Their costume is *unique*.

Lima is the only city of the world where it has ever been seen. Its origin has been sought in vain, even in the most ancient chronicles. It is totally unlike any of the various Spanish costumes, and it was certainly not brought from Spain. It was found locally, when Peru was discovered, but it is also certain that it has not existed in any other city of Latin America. It consists of a skirt, called a *saya*, and a kind of bag which covers the shoulders, arms and head, called a *manto*. I can hear Parisian ladies protesting at the simplicity of this costume; they have no idea how coquettishly it can be used. The skirt is made of a variety of materials according to rank and fortune; its design is so extraordinary that it is worthy of being put on display as a curiosity. It can only be made in Lima, and they claim that one has to be born in Lima to be a *saya*-maker. No one from Chile, Arequipa or Cuzco, they say, could ever learn to *pleat* the *saya*. This claim, which I never bothered to check, shows how unique this costume is. I shall now try to give a rough idea of what it is like.

To make an ordinary *saya* requires twelve to fourteen ells (fourteen to eighteen metres) of satin.* It is lined with light taffeta or very fine cotton. The dressmaker, in return for your fourteen ells of satin, comes back with a little three-quarter-length skirt, which hangs from just above the hips down to the ankles. It is so clinging that at the bottom it is only just wide enough for the wearer to put one foot in front of the other and walk with small steps. So one is enclosed in the skirt as in a sheath. It is pleated from top to bottom, in very small pleats, so neatly that it is impossible to see the seams. These pleats are so strongly made and give the *saya* such elasticity, that I have seen *sayas* that had lasted for fifteen years and which were still pliant enough to show off the figure and allow freedom of movement.

The *manto* is also stylishly pleated, but is made in very light material, and would be unlikely to last as long as the skirt, nor could the pleating stand so long the continual movements of the wearer and the dampness of her breath. Society ladies wear a *saya* of black satin; women of fashion also have them in whimsical colours – purple, brown, green, dark blue, or striped – but never in pale colours, because these are preferred by the 'ladies of the street'. The *manto* is always black, enveloping the whole of the upper part of the body, leaving only one eye uncovered. The ladies of Lima wear a tight blouse only the sleeves of which are visible. These may be short or long, and are in a rich material: velvet, coloured satin or tulle; but most women have bare arms in all seasons. Their footwear is most elegant and attractive, pretty shoes in coloured embroidered satin; when they are of one colour only, the ribbons are in a contrasting colour. They wear open-work silk stockings of various colours, with richly embroidered clocks. Spanish women are always remarkable for the richness and elegance of the shoes they wear, but those of Lima do it so charmingly that they really excel. They wear

* *Author's note:* The satin is imported from Europe. Before the discovery of Peru, the garment was made with a local woollen fabric. Only poor women now use that cloth.

their hair parted in the middle; it falls in two perfectly made plaits ending in a large ribbon bow. This fashion however is not universal. Some wear it curled *à la* Ninon, falling in long wavy locks on to their bosoms, which, according to the custom of the country, they almost always leave bare. For the last few years, the fashion of wearing large crêpe-de-chine shawls has been introduced. This has made their costume more decent by veiling in its folds the bare flesh and the too clearly visible curves. Yet another touch of luxury that they go in for is a very fine linen handkerchief edged with lace. How graceful, how intoxicating they look, these beautiful ladies of Lima, in their lustrous black *sayas* gleaming in the sun, showing off the true figures of some, and the false ones of others – but even the latter are so well contrived that it is impossible to imagine any deceit! How gracefully they move their shoulders, when they pull the *manto* so that it conceals the entire face, after letting a passing glimpse of it be seen! How lithe and supple are their figures, and how they swing and ripple as they walk! How pretty are those small feet of theirs, and what a pity that they are just a little bit too fat!

A lady of Lima is not the same woman when she changes her *saya* for a pretty Parisian dress: one looks in vain for the seductive creature in a *saya* that one met only that morning at St Mary's church. This is why all foreign men in Lima go to church; not to hear the monks sing the divine service, but to admire these unique women in their national costume. Everything about them is full of seductiveness: their poses are as delightful as their walk, and when they are kneeling, they bend their heads roguishly, allowing a view of their pretty bracelet-covered arms whilst their fingers, resplendent with rings, run over their rosary with voluptuous agility and they cast furtive glances which are calculated to turn ardour into rapture.

Many foreign men have described to me the magical effect that the sight of these women has often produced on them. An adventurous spirit had made them face countless dangers in the firm conviction that they would make their fortunes on these far shores. The ladies of Lima seemed to be the priestesses of this hope, or rather these men felt that they had reached Mahomet's paradise, and that God had led them to an enchanted land as compensation for the pains of a long crossing and as recompense for their courage. Such fantasies do not seem surprising when one witnesses how many follies and extravagances foreigners commit for the sake of the ladies of Lima. Their heads are completely turned. They become obsessed with the desire to see the ladies' faces, which are carefully concealed, and this makes the men follow them with avid curiosity. But one must have long experience of *sayas* to follow one successfully, for they all look alike. It needs great concentration not to lose sight of the charming quarry in the crowd: she dodges to and fro like a serpent in the grass; she glides out of sight. I defy the loveliest English girl, with her blonde hair, her eyes which reflect the heavens, her complexion of lilies and roses, to compete with a pretty lady from Lima in a *saya*! I equally defy the most seductive Frenchwoman, with her pretty little mouth half-open, her witty eyes, her elegant figure, her playful manner and all the subtlety of her coquetry, to compete with a pretty lady from Lima in her *saya*! Without fear of contradiction, I can say that the ladies of Lima so dressed would be proclaimed the queens of this earth, if it were only a question of shapeliness, and of the magnetism of the eye to ensure the sway that women are called upon to have over man; but though beauty beguiles the senses, it needs the inspiration that comes from the soul, a moral force, and the talents of the mind to prolong its reign. God has endowed women with more loving, more devoted hearts than men; and if, as there is no doubt, it is by love and devotion that we honour the Creator, woman is incontestably superior to man; but she must cultivate her intelligence and above all become mistress of herself in order to preserve this superiority. It is only in this way that she will be able to exercise all the influence that God intended when he gave her those qualities of the heart; but when she misunderstands her mission, and instead of being the guide and inspiration of man, his moral persuader, she only tries to charm him, to be the mistress of his senses, her influence will vanish with the desires she has provoked. And so it is that when these enchantresses, who have never had any interest in higher things, eventually, after electrifying the imagination of the young foreigners, reveal themselves as they are: blasé, their minds without culture and their souls without nobility, clearly loving only money; then the spell woven by their charm is immediately broken.

Yet the ladies of Lima do dominate the men, because they are superior to the men in intelligence and moral fibre. The cultural phase which the country has reached is still far behind ours in Europe. There is in the whole of Peru no institution for the education of either sex. Intelligence has to develop on its own resources. Thus the pre-eminence of the women of Lima over the men, which exists in spite of the fact they are morally speaking inferior to those in Europe, must be due to the superior intelligence that God has given them. But their costume has been a major additional influence that they enjoy. If they were ever to abandon this costume without changing in other ways, if they could no longer rely on its powers of seduction and yet had not developed the quality of caring for the happiness and improvement of others – and up till now they have been unconscious of the need for such a quality – it is quite certain that they would immediately lose their dominant position. They would descend into a very lowly status, into as miserable a position as any human can occupy. They would no longer be able to indulge in the incessant activity made possible by being able to pass incognito, and would become the prey of boredom, without any means of raising themselves above the generally despised condition of creatures whose only resource comes from the pleasures of the senses. To demonstrate the truth of this, I shall give a short sketch of the customs of Lima society, from which the reader can judge for himself.

As I have already said, the *saya* is the national costume: all the women wear it, whatever their social class; it is respected, and as much a part of the country's heritage as the veil of Muslim women in the Orient. Throughout the year, the women of Lima walk in the streets in this disguise, and anyone who dared to remove from a woman in a *saya* the *manto* which completely hides her face, except for one eye, would suffer public indignation and severe punishment. It is accepted that a woman can *go out alone*;

most are accompanied by a negress, but this is not essential. The costume so alters a woman's appearance, and even her voice, which becomes muffled because the mouth is covered, that unless there is something obvious about her, like being very tall or very short, with a limp or a hump, it is impossible to recognise her. I think I can leave it to the reader to imagine the consequences of this continual state of disguise, sanctioned by time and custom, and permitted or at least tolerated by the law. A lady of Lima wears a French-style négligé at breakfast with her husband, her hair done up just like our Parisian ladies. If she wants to go out, she puts on her *saya* – no corset is needed, since the belt sufficiently supports the figure – lets her hair down, 'covers' herself,* that is to say, she wraps herself in her *manto*, and sets off wherever she pleases to go. She may meet her husband in the street, and he will not recognise her:† she may give him the eye, simper, make provocative remarks, start up a conversation, accept the offer of ices, fruit, cakes, fix a rendezvous with him, leave him – only to start another conversation with a passing officer. She can allow this new adventure to go as far as she wishes, without ever taking off her *manto*. She pays calls on her women friends, and returns home for dinner. Her husband does not ask where she has been, because he knows perfectly well that if she needs to conceal the truth she will lie to him, and as he has no means of preventing this, he takes the wisest course, and does not worry his head about it. So the ladies go unaccompanied to the theatre, to the bullfight, to public meetings, to the ball, to the promenade, to church, and to pay calls on their friends, and this is perfectly acceptable. If they meet anyone they wish to talk to, they do so, then leave them and remain free and independent in the crowd, much more so than the men, whose faces are uncovered. This costume has the great advantage of being economical, very clean

* *Translator's note:* The author here gives the word *tapoda* as the Spanish expression for covering the face with the *manto*. I have been unable to trace this word; *taparse* is the normal expression.

† *Author's note:* A number of husbands assured me that they did not recognise their wives when they met them.

and comfortable, always ready for use without any need of the slightest attention.

There is another practice which I must not omit: when the ladies of Lima wish to make their disguise even more impenetrable, they put on an old *saya*, all unpleated, torn and ragged, an old *manto* and an old blouse; but those who wish it to be known that they nevertheless belong to good society wear good shoes and take one of their finest handkerchiefs. Such a disguise, considered quite 'correct', is called *disfrazar*. A *disfrazada* is held to be completely respectable; for that reason, one never addresses a word to her, and only approaches with caution. It would be out of place and even 'unfair' to follow her. It is rightly assumed that since she has 'disguised' herself, she must have 'important reasons' for doing so, and therefore one ought not to take it upon one's self to pry into her activities.

After what has been said about the costume and customs of the women of Lima, it will be evident that their mentality will be quite different from that of European women who, from childhood, are slaves to the laws, customs, prejudices and fashions – in fact to everything; whilst in her *saya*, a woman of Lima is free, enjoys her independence and has that self-confidence which is born of the ability to act according to the needs of one's personality. The woman of Lima, of whatever social class, is always *herself*; she never undergoes constraint of any sort. As a girl, she escapes from parental control through the freedom bestowed on her by her dress; when she marries, she does not take her husband's name, keeps her own and is always mistress of her own home. When she tires of that, she puts on her *saya* and goes out, just like a man taking up his hat and going where he will. In everything she does, she has the same freedom as he. In any intimate relations they may have, be they frivolous or serious, they always maintain their dignity, although their behaviour in this respect is indeed very different from ours. Like all women they judge the strength of the love that they inspire by the extent of the sacrifices made for them; but because Peru, ever since it was discovered, has only attracted Europeans to come so far simply on account of the gold to be found there, and because gold and only gold, not talent or virtue, has been the standard of value and the motive of every action, and has alone been the gateway to success, the ladies of Lima, quite logically, look for proofs of love only in the amount of gold they are given: the value of the offering determines their view of the sincerity of the lover; and their vanity is satisfied to the extent of the sum or the worth of the valuables that they have received. When one wants to give an indication of how much Señor So-and-so loved Señora Such-and-such, one invariably says something like: 'He used to give her bags and bags of gold; he would buy her the most expensive gifts he could find; he completely ruined himself for her.' Just as we should say: 'He killed himself for her.' A rich woman will always take her lover's money, even if it means giving it to her Negresses if she can't spend it herself. She considers it a 'proof' of his love, the 'only thing' that can 'convince her that she is loved'. Vanity makes travellers conceal this state of things, and when they talk of the ladies of Lima and the success they have had with them, they make no boast of the fact that they had cost them a small fortune, down to the final parting present. Such customs are very strange, but true. I have seen a number of society ladies wearing men's rings, chains and watches.

The ladies of Lima spend little time on household matters, but as they are very active, this is enough to keep things in order. They have a pronounced taste for politics and intrigue. It is through their efforts that their husbands, their sons or other men who interest them, get public appointments: to achieve their ends, the women will overcome all obstacles and suffer all indignities. The men keep out of such business, and rightly so: they would not be nearly so good at it. The women love amusements and parties: they seek company, and play for high stakes, smoke cigars and ride horseback, not in the English fashion but wearing wide trousers like a man. They adore sea bathing and swim very well. As for the social talents, they pluck the guitar, sing rather badly (though a few are good musicians) and dance, quite delightfully, the national dances. They are generally without education, never read and are ignorant of what is going on in the rest of the world. They have much natural wit and understanding, good memories and are surprisingly intelligent.

I have depicted the women of Lima just as they are, not in the way they have been described by some other travellers. It wasn't easy for me, because the warm welcome and hospitality they gave me filled me with gratitude. But as a conscientious traveller I have felt obliged to tell the whole truth.

I have spoken of the theatre and the bullfights, but have said nothing of the show provided by the churches for the benefit of the population of Lima. This is the most popular show of all, attracting crowds daily in their continual search for amusement. Everyone in Lima attends two or three masses a day; one at the cathedral, because of the large number of pretty women one meets there, and the foreigners who go, attracted by their beauty; another at St Francis's, because the fathers serve excellent consecrated bread, the organ is wonderful and the priests all wear magnificent robes; the third mass is at the church of the Child Jesus, in order to enjoy the delightful plumage of the many caged birds there. Beside the altar in many of the churches in Lima there are cages full of many sorts of birds; their song often drowns the words of the priest saying mass. In addition to the various amusements to be found daily in the churches, there are at least two street processions a week; and these are even more farcical and indecent than the ones which had so shocked me in Arequipa. And finally, so that there should be no gap in the ceremonies, no interruption to the edification and amusement of the pious people of Lima, there are midnight services with much ceremonial, where, I am sure, everything is done with the same degree of propriety. How many schools could be founded with the money spent on all these useless rituals! How many useful things could be learnt or done in the time wasted in attending them!

The two main promenades are the Almendral and the Paseo del Agua. The latter is considered the better. It is beautiful, but badly situated. The river along which it runs and the tall trees which adorn it make it unhealthily damp in winter; and in summer it is airless. On Sundays and feast-day evenings this promenade is like the Boulevard de Gand. There are crowded pavements shaded by avenues of tall trees. Almost all the women are in *sayas*, many seated on benches. Their skirts, in this position, show their legs up to the knee. On the roadway there are many barouches, some proceeding at a walking pace, others stationary, so that the ladies inside them can show off their beauty and their finery. People stay for four or five hours here; it would have seemed very long had I not been in the company of ladies, and particularly of my aunt, who had a sparkling wit when she criticised others; and on this *paseo*, there was plenty of opportunity for that.

The Coming-of-Spring festival is one of the great pleasures of Lima: it really is superb. On St John's Day the *amancais* expedition begins, a kind of Longchamp, on which I went with Doña Calista, one of my friends. The entire population was there. There were more than a hundred barouches magnificently decorated, many groups of horsemen and a vast crowd on foot. During the two winter months, May and June, the mountains are covered with yellow flowers with green leaves, called *amancais*;* the effect is springlike, and this has given rise to the holiday and the name of the expedition. The road leading up to the mountains is very wide, and the view at a certain point is enchanting. At various points there are tents where refreshments are available, and where very indecent dances are performed. Throughout the two months of the season, fashionable society frequents these places; the sway of fashion, the desire to see and be seen, makes them put up with their many inconveniences. The road is very bad; the horses sink into the sand up to their knees; the wind blows cold; and in the evening, if one is even a little late in returning, one risks being attacked by robbers, who abound round Lima. Nevertheless, the Limans flock there enthusiastically; they go in parties, take dinner and supper with them, and spend the night there.

Going for walks and visiting buildings were not my only pursuits; I also endeavoured to enter the houses of the

* *Translator's note: Amancay* is the Andean narcissus.

THE COMING-OF-SPRING FESTIVAL OF LIMA
— 'A KIND OF LONGCHAMP'

A VIEW OF THE QUAY AT CHORRILLOS, THE
SEA-SIDE RESORT OF THE PEOPLE OF LIMA

more distinguished inhabitants, in order to study their customs and usages. I had letters of recommendation to several families, and in addition to two of my Arequipa cousins, Señora Balthazar de Benavedez and Señora Inés de Izcué. I was given a warm welcome in these two houses, where I was made the guest of honour at formal dinner parties. There was nothing so boring as these dinners. There was a lavish display of tableware and glass, and especially of food and dainties of all kinds. Lima was remarkable for the progress made in a flourishing art of cookery; for the last ten years everything had been done *à la française*. The region produced very good meat, fine vegetables, all sorts of fish and an abundance of exquisite fruits. It was possible to eat very well at modest expense. These banquets were to me unbelievably tiresome, accustomed as I am to dine in ten minutes. There were two or three main courses, and one had to partake of everything in order not to infringe polite usage. I had to repeat and repeat the same excuses, saying again and again that I never ate soup or meat, and that normally I lived on vegetables and dairy products. We sat for two hours at table, and all the while the conversation flowed about the excellence of the food, and pompous praises were addressed to the host. As at Arequipa, titbits were passed round on forks, but this custom was dying out. The amount of food I saw eaten on these occasions was really monstrous. The result was that at the end of the meal nearly all the guests were ill and in such a state that their feasts were both boring and bad for the health. The profusion of food displayed was the sign of a race which had not yet risen above sensual pleasures. The usual hour for dinner was observed on such occasions. They sat down at three o'clock, the normal time in Lima, but they did not get up until five or six. After that, one had to be sociable with the host and hostess for an hour or two. Such parties, of course, were extremely irksome to me. At all such meals, the best French wines were served, a great burden of expense for everyone.

XVII

A SEASIDE RESORT AND A SUGAR PLANTATION

In my opinion, the place chosen by the people of Lima as a seaside resort was the most barren and disagreeable one on the coast. It was called Chorrillos. The Izcué family had rented a house there for the season, and invited me to stay there for as long as I liked.

Señor Izcué came to fetch me at seven in the morning, and we set off in his barouche. We had four leagues to travel, on sand; however, the road was quite good for the horses: the sand was firm, and they did not sink into it as on the road across the *pampas*. The country varied considerably; after a fertile belt came an arid black landscape, with a few trees here and there. Then we passed through the very pretty village of Miraflor, which was wooded, with charming houses and two towers from which there was a view of the whole countryside, with Lima and the sea, which is a quarter of a league distant. It was certainly the prettiest village I had seen in South America. After leaving it, we continued to pass fields of potatoes and lucerne from time to time, but no wheat. We reached two fine-looking houses, the property of Señor Lavalle, once provincial administrator of Arequipa, where I saw the magnificent gardens belonging to them. There were orange-trees right out in the open, papayas, palms, sapodillas, every sort of fruit. Ten minutes later, we went through El Barranco, a small village set amongst lovely verdure, tall trees and plenty of water. After this oasis, and as far as Chorrillos, there was nothing but a desert of sand. During the whole trip there was a thick, damp mist; I was thoroughly chilled, and so arrived ill. I went to bed after drinking a cup of hot coffee.

I got up only in time for dinner. Seeing that I had recovered, Señor Izcué suggested that we should visit the neighbouring countryside and see a sugar plantation. I was given a horse, and we set off. I had seen sugar-cane only in Paris at the Jardin des Plantes. Those vast forests of cane, eight or nine foot high, so thick that a dog could hardly force its way through, thrust their spears into the air, each with a little spiky flower on top, giving evidence of a fertility in the soil greater than that of our fields of corn or potatoes. Nature, in such favoured climes, seems to be urging man to work, through the rich recompense it gives. I was fascinated, and so next day we went to visit one of the largest plantations in Peru.

Señor Lavalle's sugar mill, the Villa Lavalle, two leagues from Chorrillos, was a magnificent establishment of four hundred negroes, three hundred negresses and two hundred children. The owner was kind and courteous enough to show us round the entire place and took pleasure in explaining everything to us. I was most interested in seeing the four mills for crushing the canes, run by water power. The aqueduct which brought the water to the factory was fine and had been very costly to construct owing to the difficulties of the terrain. I was shown round the great building containing a number of cauldrons, in which the juice from the cane was boiled. We then went into the refinery attached to it, where the sugar dripped out its molasses. Señor Lavalle explained to me his plan for improvements. 'But, mademoiselle,' he added, 'it is desperately difficult to find negroes. The shortage of slaves will ruin all the sugar mills. We lose them in large numbers, and three-quarters of the children die before they are twelve. I used to have fifteen hundred negroes, and now I've only got nine hundred, including the puny children you have seen.'

'But such a mortality is alarming,' I said, 'and indeed casts serious doubts on the future of your undertaking. Why is it that the balance between births and deaths is not maintained? This is a healthy climate, and I would have thought that the negroes would thrive as well here as in Africa.'

'You do not know negroes, mademoiselle. They let their

children die from laziness, and one can get nothing out of them without the whip.'

'Do you not think that, if they were free, their needs would be sufficient to make them work?'

'Their needs are so few in this climate,' said Señor Lavalle, 'that they would have to work very little to supply them. Moreover, I do not believe that man, whatever his needs, can be induced to work regularly without being forced. The Indian tribes scattered throughout North and South America provide me with proof. In Mexico and Peru, it is true, a certain amount of agriculture did exist amongst the natives; and yet we still find the majority of our Indians do next to nothing and live in poverty and idleness. But in the whole of the vast continent of the two Americas, the independent tribes live from hunting, fishing and the wild fruits of the earth; they frequently suffer from famine, and yet this does not make them cultivate the land. They see the advantages that the whites gain from their work, and are keen to enjoy them themselves, yet even this does not get them working. Our missionaries had to use corporal punishment in order to make the Indians in their settlements cultivate the land. The negroes are the same, and you French found the same at San Domingo. As soon as you freed your slaves, they stopped working.'

'I agree with you,' I replied, 'that men, white, red or black, find it difficult to work if they have have not been brought up to do so. But slavery corrupts men, and by making them hate work, they are ill prepared for civilisation.'

'You must realise that slavery with us, as in all nations of Spanish origin, is less severe than in the other American nations. Our slaves can buy their freedom, and are only slaves to their own master. If a slave is struck by anyone else, he may act in self-defence and return the blow. But in your colonies, every white man is his master; he is forbidden, under pain of the severest punishments, to defend himself against a white man. If he is injured, it is true, his master has a right to an indemnity; but the perpetrator is not punished in any way. Your system has added loss of security to loss of liberty.'

'I am happy to agree,' I said, 'that Spanish slavery laws are much more humane than those of any other nation. With you, the slave is not just a chattel, he is a member of the same religion, and the influence of religious beliefs brings about certain modifications. But the root of the evil, the permanent nature of slavery, exists with you as well as in our colonies: for it is impossible for a slave, owing to the fact that he is forced to work continuously, ever to make use of the possibility to buy his freedom. If the goods produced by slave labour in the Americas were to lose their value, I am sure that slavery would become modified in a beneficial way.'

'How so, mademoiselle?'

'If the selling price of sugar, compared to the value of the work required to produce it, were in the same relationship as European products are to their production costs, the owner would have no compensation for the loss of his slaves, and would therefore not push them to work so hard, and would take more trouble to keep them in good condition. The owners are not content to live on the income from their mills, they want them to repay the capital outlay if this is outstanding, or to build up a fortune for themselves independent of their place of residence. Not one of them would ever agree to reduce his crop by a half, in order to allow his negroes to grow more foodstuffs, give them more leisure and improve their lot. At present, in large establishments, the slaves are enclosed in many workshops, are constantly under their master's eye, are ceaselessly harassed, and as a result undergo a moral torture sufficiently acute to make life a burden to them.'

'Mademoiselle, you speak of negroes as one who only knows them through the speeches of your philanthropic orators. But unfortunately the truth is that the only way to make them work is to flog them.'

'If that is so, sir, I admit that I look forward to the day when the sugar mills have all failed, and I think that that day will come soon. In a few years' time, sugar beet will have replaced sugar cane.'

'Ah, mademoiselle, if that's all you have to fight us with . . . ! Your beetroot is a joke. All that root is good for is to sweeten the milk of cows in winter when they are on dry fodder.'

'Laugh away, sir! But with this root that excites your mockery we could already do without your sugar cane in France! Beetroot sugar is as good as yours, and moreover it has the supreme merit, in my eyes, of forcing down the price of colonial sugar. And I am convinced that this is the only circumstance which will make for an improvement in the lot of the negroes, and will lead in the end to the total abolition of slavery.'

'The abolition of slavery? But are you not disillusioned by the experiment at San Domingo?'

'Sir, our revolution, inspired by high ideals, was bound to be filled with indignation at the existence of slavery. The Convention decreed the freeing of the negroes in a fit of enthusiasm, apparently without a thought for the possibility that they might need to be taught how to use their freedom.'

'And then your Convention forgot to pay compensation to the owners, as the English parliament is now doing.'

'That parliament, with the French example before it, has carried through this great act in a more rational manner, doubtless, than the Convention did; but it too has been in too great a hurry to attain its ends. The measures it has passed are too broad and too sudden for any good to come of them in the near future. The disadvantages of simultaneous emancipation are such that it is surprising that a nation as enlightened as the English gave so little thought to the problem, rashly freeing slaves before there was any certainty of their having acquired industrious habits, and before giving them a thorough training in how to use their liberty within our social system. I am convinced that a gradual emancipation is the *only* effective way to turn the negroes into useful members of society. Freedom could have been granted as a recompense for work. The English parliament would have attained its objective more rapidly if it limited itself to freeing annually slaves under twenty years of age, putting them into rural trade schools before allowing them to enjoy their freedom. Every single European colony still has vast areas of cultivable land on which the freed men could be put, and there would also be plenty of work for those who had learned a trade. By this method it would have taken thirty years to reach complete emancipation; every year those freed would increase the working population and consequently the wealth of the colonies; whereas, under the present system, those countries have a long future of poverty and calamity to look forward to.'

'Mademoiselle, your attitude towards slavery proves only one thing, namely that you have a good heart and a lively imagination. These are but fine dreams full of poetry. But in the opinion of an old planter like myself, not one of your fine ideas would ever work.'

Slavery has always made me angry, and I was delighted when I heard of that saintly league of English ladies who refused to use sugar from the western colonies. They resolved only to use sugar from India, although it was more expensive owing to the tax levied on it, until the Emancipation Act had been passed by parliament. Their unity and constancy in carrying out this charitable resolution caused a drop in the value of American sugar on English markets and overcame the opposition to the bill. Let us hope that Continental Europe will follow the example of this noble manifestation of religious sentiment in England! Slavery is ungodly in the eyes of all religions. To be a party to it is to deny one's faith: the conscience of the human race is unanimous on this point.

Señor Lavalle's sugar plantation was one of the finest in Peru; it was vast in extent and its situation was admirable. It ran along beside the sea, where the waves broke on the rocky shore. The tropics are rich in fruit, and Señor Lavalle's orchard had them all. The soil was suitable, and they flourished. The sapodilla trees were so tall that they seemed to be trying to keep out of reach their large green 'apples' whose juicy pulp combined the most delicious flavours. The mango-tree, as high as an oak, bore its oval fruits, fibrous to the taste and smelling of turpentine. How I admired the beautiful dark green foliage of those great orange-trees, bending under the weight of their thousands of round fruits whose colour delighted the eye and whose smell scented the air! It was like a new Garden of Eden. Bunches of pomegranates and Barbadoes cherries held out the cool refreshment of their fruits for the taking, and here and there the banana-plants, bowing under the weight of their fruit, displayed their long, tattered leaves. And this tropical orchard was made even more beautiful by a very varied show of European flowers, reminding one of home. In a delightful spot, full of coolness and fragrance, stood an observation tower, from which the view was magnificent. On one side lay the sea, whose great breakers rolled on to the beach or broke violently against the rocks; on the other were the vast plantations of sugar cane, so beautiful when in flower. Here and there groups of trees provided relief and variety for the eye.

It was late when we returned. As we passed by a kind of barn in which negroes were working, the angelus sounded. They all stopped working and fell to their knees, bending down until their heads touched the ground. The faces of all these slaves were repulsive to look at, full of baseness and treachery; they all, including the children, had a dark, cruel and unhappy expression. I tried to chat with several of them, but all I could get was 'yes' and 'no', spoken with coldness and indifference. I went into a cell into which two negresses had been shut; they had allowed their babies to die by depriving them of milk. They were both stark naked, and were huddled together in a corner. One of them was eating raw maize. The other, young and very beautiful, turned her large eyes on me; they seemed to say: 'I let my child die, because I knew he would not be free like you. I preferred death for him, rather than slavery.' The sight of this woman was most painful to me. Under that black skin there are some proud, great-souled human beings. Negroes have to go suddenly into slavery direct from a natural state of independence; some are untamable souls who suffer torments and die without ever bowing to the yoke.

On the following day we went to see the fishing nets being cast. Their method of fishing was alarming and seemed to me as laborious as it was dangerous. The fishermen went far out into the sea and held up facing the waves the open mouth of a huge net bent round in a large circle. The surge came dashing in furiously, covering them completely, and when the waves retreated the men brought the net back to the shore. There were twelve men involved, and it was only at the fourth try that they caught nine fish. Seeing free men engaged in such laborious work, running such risks to earn their bread, I wondered if there could exist a type of work for which slavery was necessary, and if a country where there were men forced to work in such a way in order to survive needed slaves at all.

I have already said that I could not understand the popularity of Chorrillos with the people of Lima. The word means 'drains':* the village has been so named from the trickles of water which fall from the top of the rocks running along the edge of the sea and which form a pool of fresh water at their foot. Bathing takes place at this spot; the sea is fairly calm there and the waves never reach the lake. Fresh water close by is a great advantage to the bathers, as most of them plunge in after bathing to wash off the salt particles from the skin. Otherwise the place is most inconvenient for bathing; yet it would not be costly to make a bathing establishment as pleasant as those at Dieppe. If Chorrillos remains popular, perhaps the Limans will one day do this.

El Barranco, the charming oasis which I have already described, would have been the right place to turn into a resort for the bathers; it was close to the sea, with fine trees, greenery and water – the same water that formed the trickles at Chorrillos – but the latter village, perched on top of a black, barren rock, had none of these advantages. Nothing could be more depressing and dirty than that huddle of huts: not a tree or a blade of grass to please the eye, and the water was at the foot of the rock. The houses were built of wood; some had unpaved floors. Some were made of bamboo, with no openings except the doors. All were most inconvenient and poorly furnished. All forms of food were scarce, and the market was insufficient for local needs; everything was expensive and of bad quality. It was impossible to walk abroad without sinking up to the calf in black sand which ruined one's shoes and stockings and the hem of one's dress. The wind and sea blew

* *Translator's note:* The Spanish word has no connection with sewage, and is better translated by either 'jet' or 'trickle'.

this black sand into one's eyes, and the sun blinded one. In a word, it was the most hateful place that I have ever been to, and yet it had been growing for the last five years to such an extent that there were some eight hundred houses.

The life led by the bathers in this resort was an exact reflexion of the way they lived in Lima: it consisted in *far niente*, pleasure and intrigue. The women lived like the men, their habits and tastes being similar, and were just as independent as they. They went riding in the surrounding country and bathed with the men; they smoked from morning to night; they played for high stakes (my aunt Manuela lost ten thousand piastres in one evening); they carried on simultaneously four or five intrigues, amorous, political or whatever you will; they went to parties and rustic dances which everyone gave; and yet they spent a large part of the day lying in hammocks, surrounded by five or six admirers. Social life in Chorrillos could ruin the richest families of Lima; they made incredible sacrifices to go and stay there for one or two months. Extravagance on this scale was only to be found at Lima. The climate was partly the cause no doubt, but the lack of fine arts, of any education to occupy the considerable powers of imagination with which this nation is endowed, made the people prey to every folly, swept along as they were by a superabundance of vitality.

After staying at Chorrillos for a week, it was with great pleasure that I returned to Lima. My little apartment furnished in the French manner, and my French-style meals, seemed even more comfortable than before; and I appreciated Mme Denuelle's amusing conversation more than ever.

XVIII

THE EX-PRESIDENT'S LADY

However, despite all the diversions that Lima could offer and the warm welcome of my new friends, I was most anxious to leave. That city, so radiant in the beauty of its climate and the gaiety of its people, was the last place on earth where I would have wished to live. Sensuality ruled supreme there; all the people had eyes, ears and palates but no souls with which to appreciate the sights, sounds and tastes. I have never felt so complete a void or such a barren waste as during the months I spent in Lima. My impatience to return to Europe, which I appreciated and loved all the more since leaving it, made me almost decide at one point to go to Valparaiso where I could hope to find a ship preparing to set sail for Bordeaux; but I soon abandoned this plan because of the strong likelihood that I would come across Chabrié in Chile. I therefore resigned myself to the expense and annoyance of remaining in Lima.

Nevertheless I put off booking my passage for a long time, not so much because I minded the prospect of the bad food on board an English merchant vessel, as because I so strongly desired to travel home via North America. The journey would be a very hard one: M. Briet nearly died of exhaustion when he took this route. Yet I felt strong enough to do it, and would have done so if my means had been sufficient. I admit that I was very disappointed. I wrote to my uncle, telling him how much I would like to know that part of America, and making it clear that only lack of means prevented me from taking the journey. Time and time again I was on the point of writing to ask him point blank for the necessary sum, so strong is my taste for adventurous journeys. However, pride won the day: my uncle's reactions to my plans were such that I feared a refusal, and I did not wish to lay myself open to this.

I booked my passage on the *William Rushton*, of Liverpool, which was due shortly and would be bound direct for Falmouth. I had been away from Arequipa for two months when she sailed into Callao, with Doña Pencha de Gamarra on board, accompanied by her secretary Escudero. Mr Smith brought me the news, together with a packet of letters from Arequipa, containing the results of the latest revolution. Here is a short summary of what I learned.

Señor Gamarra and his wife had arrived at Arequipa on the 27th of April, in order, as was the custom, to supply the needs of their party by extorting sums of money. By means of imprisonments and other enforcements of military law, they levied an enormous tax on the inhabitants, and, either from lack of discipline or lack of will, let their soldiers commit every sort of outrage. All classes of the population became exasperated. The soldiers held private persons up to ransom when they got the opportunity; and they themselves could not go singly into the countryside without risk of being murdered by peasants. One soldier was stabbed to death by a monk from whom he had demanded two *reals*. General discontent seethed throughout the territory occupied by the Gamarra party and rallied the population to Orbegoso: the cry everywhere was: 'Viva Nieto!' Nieto himself, entrenched in the town of Tacna to which he had retreated, was waiting until circumstances called him to play a part once again. The Gamarrists tried once more to exploit his credulity, by sending his brother-in-law to him with a letter from Bermudez, alleging the collapse of the Orbegoso party; but this time Nieto was not to be fooled. He rejected their advances and entered into negotiations with Santa Cruz, president of Bolivia, for assistance.

Such was the situation when, on Whit Sunday the 18th of May, two companies abandoned Bermudez's party. When Señora Gamarra was least expecting it, Don Juan Lobaton, commander of the Ayacucho battalion, took charge of the artillery with two hundred men and raised shouts in the main square of: 'Viva Orbegoso! Viva Nieto! Long live law and order!' The populace, who hated these soldiers, thought it was a trick, and that they were doing it in order to catch anyone who might join them; so they angrily rushed them. Some fifteen to twenty people were killed in the scuffle, including Lobaton, the instigator of the movement.

When the mob saw the casualties, they went berserk. In their rage they attacked the house where Señora Gamarra was staying and sacked it. Doña Pencha had seen the storm coming and escaped the mob violence by hiding in a neighbouring house. In their fury the mob were blindly killing the officers and soldiers who had made the revolution together with the others, and so, to prevent them all being massacred, they had to be sent into hiding. Gamio's house, which San Roman had occupied, was sacked, and Angelita Tristan's, where Colonel Quirroga was staying, was also attacked; but the colonel had escaped.

At the outbreak of the rebellion, my uncle was acclaimed military commander. On the day after, order was restored: the people obeyed the chiefs they had themselves appointed. Their sufferings and the victory which followed had boosted their morale so much that whenever a rumour, false or true, ran round that the Gamarrists were approaching, everyone, even the peasants, took up arms and sallied out to meet them.

Apart from Lobaton, Arismendi, Landauri and Riviro were the instigators of the revolution, leading the mob and expelling the Gamarrists from Arequipa. Several military units which had supported Bermudez lost heart, and one by one they all acknowledged Orbegoso. Nieto returned to Arequipa on the 22nd of May; following the usual custom, he exacted an excessive contribution from the unfortunate property owners of the town. The bishop had to pay 100,000 piastres and the rest in proportion; but Don Pio, who was a member of the ruling group, was on this occasion exempted from any contribution. Gamarra sought refuge in Bolivia. His wife, who was the main target of the public's hatred, stayed in hiding; it was only through my uncle's influence that she was able to find exile in Chile.

Even so, she had to leave at night, in order to escape the vengeance of the mob, who were after her life.

Escudero and Señora Gamarra herself invited me to visit them on board the English ship, from which they were not permitted to land. I immediately went to Callao. When I arrived on board I was greeted by Escudero, who grasped my hand warmly; I returned this mark of affection, and said in French: 'Dear colonel, how has it happened that after leaving you two months ago, victor and master of Arequipa, I now find you on board this ship and forbidden to enter the town?'

'Mademoiselle, we are tossed on the waves of chance if we try to play a role in a country which is prey to civil strife, where there is no political conscience and where each man fights only for his leader. Ah, how often have I thought of you since you left! You were right, and I begin to realise that I could do something better than stay in America. If it had not been for these last events in Arequipa, I might even have returned to Europe with you on this ship. I have thought of it more than once, but it is yet another of my plans that fate has torn from me. I am pinned down here for ever. The poor President's lady is pursued everywhere she goes, her cause is irretrievably lost, that cowardly idiot her husband has gone off to seek refuge with Santa Cruz, and is bound to lose whatever slight chances he has in the future. I cannot abandon this lady: with the help of your uncle's protection, my loyalty made it possible to keep her out of the clutches of the vengeful mob. We escaped from Arequipa by night, like bandits; and we also waited for nightfall to board ship, so murderous was the hatred which pursued her. As Santa Cruz refused to have her in his territory, she is being deported to Chile. I am completely free. Nieto asked me to stay with him, and Santa Cruz asks for me in all his letters. But you, Florita, will see how Señora Gamarra, in her misfortune, deserves my loyalty. So long as she is a prisoner, or in exile and rejected by all, I must follow her to her prison or her exile, and be everything to her.' Escudero was magnificent at this moment. I took his hand and said in a voice which betrayed my thoughts: 'My poor friend, you are worthy of a better fate.'

I would have continued, but at this moment Señora Gamarra appeared on deck. 'Ah, Señorita Florita, how pleased I am to meet you,' she said, 'I am impatient to get to know you. Do you realise, beautiful lady, that you have made a conquest of our dear Escudero? He talks of you ceaselessly, and quotes your words all the time. As for your uncle, all he does is *inspired by you*. Ah, you naughty girl, I was so angry with you, when I found that you had left Arequipa two days before I arrived there. So you wanted to meet San Roman, but were not curious enough to stay for that *grim, fierce, terrible* Doña Pencha? But it seems to me, dear Florita, that if the "bogeyman" of the Arequipans is worth putting in your journal, the big "bogeywoman" of Peru might also find a place there!'

As she spoke, she led me to the far end of the poop-deck, made me sit down beside her and dismissed with a gesture the unwelcome intruders who would have liked to follow us there. Though a prisoner, she was still the president's lady: the way she waved her hand showed how conscious she was of her superiority. Not a soul remained on the poop, although the only shade from the burning sun was under the awning that had been erected there: everyone went below, or stayed on the open deck. Meanwhile, she was examining me closely, and I watched her with no less interest: everything about her showed her to be an exceptional woman, as remarkable for her strength of will as for extraordinary intelligence. She looked between thirty-four and thirty-six, was of medium height and strong-looking, though very thin. Her face, judged by the conventional standards, was indeed not beautiful, but judged by the effect it had on everybody, she was more beautiful than anyone. As with Napoleon, all her power lay in the expression in her eyes: what pride, what daring, what penetration! With that irresistible authority it imposed respect, subdued one's will, captivated one's admiration! The beings to whom the Almighty has given such a gaze have no need of words to exert authority over other humans; they possess a power of persuasion to which all submit without argument. Her nose was long, and slightly turned up at the tip, her mouth large but expressive, her face long, with high, strong cheekbones, her skin swarthy but alive. Her enormous head was crowned with long abundant hair coming down very low on to the forehead; it was dark brown, shining and silky. Her voice was hollow, hard, commanding; she spoke abruptly, jerkily. Her movements were quite graceful, but continually betrayed her thoughts. Her clothes were cool, elegant and very elaborate, making a strange contrast with her hard voice, the austere dignity of her gaze and the gravity of her whole person. She wore a dress of emerald green Indian silk, embroidered in white, the most beautiful pink silk stockings and white satin shoes; a large crêpe-de-chine shawl in poppy red, with white embroidery, the finest I ever saw in Lima, was flung carelessly across her shoulders; she wore rings on every finger, diamond earrings and a necklace of fine pearls of the greatest beauty; under it hung a small scapulary, dirty and worn. Seeing me examine her with surprise, she said in her brusque manner: 'I am sure, Florita, that you, so simply dressed, find me absurd in my grotesque clothes; but I think that having summed me up already, you will have guessed that they are not my own. What you see is my sister's, a kind, poor darling who does nothing but weep; she brought them this morning, and begged me to put them on to please her and my mother and others. These good people have the idea that my luck may turn again if I agree to dress in clothes imported from Europe. I gave in to their pleading, and put on this dress which gets in my way, these stockings which feel cold on my legs, and this shawl that I am afraid of burning or fouling with the ash of my cigar. I like clothes which are comfortable on horseback, for campaigning, visiting camps, barracks, ships of the Peruvian navy: those are the only ones which suit me. I have long been travelling the length and breadth of Peru, dressed in wide trousers of coarse cloth made in Cuzco, my native city, a loose frock coat of the same cloth embroidered in gold, and boots with gold spurs. I like gold, it is the Peruvian's finest ornament, the precious metal to which his country owes its reputation. I have also a large cloak, rather heavy but very warm, which was my father's, and which has been most useful in the snows of our mountains. You look at my hair with admiration,' added this eagle-eyed woman.

'Dear Florita, in a career where the demands, the daring nature of what I had to do, have often been greater than the physical strength I could muster, my position has thereby been compromised; and I have had to compensate for the weakness of our sex by preserving some of its attractiveness, and have used it when necessary to mobilise men's support.'

'And so,' I exclaimed involuntarily, 'you, with all your strength, with all your intelligence, have had to yield to brutal force in order to rule.'

'My dear child,' said the ex-president's lady, pressing my hand with bruising strength, and with an expression I shall never forget, 'my child, be sure that it was because I could not bow my unconquerable pride to brutal force that you see me here as a prisoner; I have been driven out and exiled by the very men who were under my command for three years.'

At that moment I fathomed her thought, my soul mastered hers; I felt that I was stronger than she was, and I could quell her with my gaze. She recognised this, turned pale, and her lips drained of colour. Her expression would have daunted the boldest of the bold, but she was under my spell, and I could read distinctly all that went through her mind. Now it was my turn to take her hand, which was cold and damp with perspiration, and say to her: 'Doña Pencha, the Jesuits said, "The end justifies the means," and it is they who have controlled the masters of the earth.'

She looked at me for a long time without replying; she too was trying to fathom my thoughts. When she spoke it was with the accents of despair and irony: 'Ah, Florita,' she said, 'your pride deceives you. You think that you are stronger than I. A delusion! You know nothing of the ceaseless struggles that I have had to wage over the last eight years! The humiliations, oh! the bloody humiliations I have had to suffer! I have begged, flattered, lied; I have tried everything, I have baulked at nothing ... and even so it was not enough. I thought I had succeeded, that I had at last reached my goal and was about to gather the fruit of eight years of torment, when, in one villainous stroke, I found myself ousted, lost! Lost, Florita! I shall never return to Peru. Ah, renown, at what a cost! What folly to sacrifice one's happiness, one's whole life, to obtain it! It is but a flash, a smoke, a cloud, a will-o'-the-wisp; it is nothing. And yet, Florita, the day that I have lost all hope of living in that cloud, in that smoke, the sun will have ceased to shine for me, there will be no air for me to breathe. I shall die.'

Doña Pencha's expression grew dark with these last prophetic words; her eyes were sunken and swam, as it were, suspended in a globe of tears. She gazed at the calm blue sky above our heads and, rapt in her celestial vision, seemed to be no longer of this world. I was about to continue the conversation, but she suddenly rose; in a trice she had left the poop and called her sister and two ladies, with the words: 'Come here, I feel ill.' Escudero came up to me and said: 'I am sorry, mademoiselle, I am afraid that Doña Pencha is about to have one of her attacks, and when that happens, only I can look after her.'*

'I'm leaving, colonel!' I said, 'I'll come back tomorrow. Go quickly to the poor woman. She certainly has great need of your services and of your affection.'

'Have no fear, Florita, I shall be there till the end.'

I asked my future captain to send me in his launch to the frigate *Samarang*, on board which Mr Smith, Mme Denuelle and others were expecting me. I knew the *Samarang*'s captain very well, as I had met him on my arrival at Mme Denuelle's, where he lodged, and had dined daily with him. He was the exact opposite in everything to the captain of the *Challenger*; he was as ugly as the other was handsome, as gay as the other was gloomy, as extravagant

* *Author's note:* Señora Gamarra was having an epileptic fit. These attacks left her in a terrible state: her features became distorted, her eyes wide open and motionless. She knew in advance when she was about to fall: if she was on horseback, she dismounted quickly; if in a public place, she would retire. As the fit came on, her hair would stand on end, she would cross her hands on the top of her head and utter three cries. Escudero told me that he had known her have as many as nine fits in one day. If she had lived in another age, she could, like Mahomet, have made use of her infirmity to further her ambition, by giving her words the authority of a revelation.

and as untidy as the other was simple and correct. The same contrast was to be seen between his officers and those of the *Challenger*: servants copy their masters; the officers of a warship are a reflection of their captain. The gentlemen of the *Samarang* divided the day into three parts, which they spent as follows: the whole morning they went riding, dressed like rich Mexican brigands; then they frequented the company of women of ill repute. Finally they sat down to dinner, and spent the rest of their time drinking grog and sleeping it off. Apart from this way of life, which harmed only their own health and their own pockets, they were gentle, good-natured and easy-going men. The captain was especially notable for the manners of a gentleman, which he had preserved despite a life of debauchery. His ugliness was not unattractive, as is almost always the case with pock-marked people. I had promised to go and visit his frigate when I went to see my ship. I admit that I expected to find the same slovenliness on board the frigate as I had found in the captain and his officers. What a surprise, therefore, when I stepped on to the deck, to see how completely orderly and clean it was, down to the minutest detail! I had never seen anything like it. The two between-deck areas, the beds, the bearing of the soldiers and of the officers on duty were admirable in their correctness and propriety. As I looked at everything with visible astonishment, the captain smiled and said: 'I am sure, mademoiselle, that you expected to find the place as untidy as you have seen my room when you pass my door.'

'Not quite, captain, but I frankly admit that I did not expect to find such perfect order on board.'

'Let me say, mademoiselle, that I in my turn am surprised that you, always so sensible, had come to such a conclusion on something you knew nothing about. On land I am free of my responsibilities and therefore able to indulge all my proclivities. My behaviour may be criticised by some who are less than frank about their own. I am not conscious that it harms anyone in any way. But on board I am captain of my frigate, and I know what my duties are and how important they are. I have had the honour to serve my country for fifteen years, and I can say that not once have I failed to do the duty to which I was called; and not one of those same officers whom you see me treat at table with so much familiarity and comradeship would benefit from any lessening of my severity for the slightest oversight in the carrying out of his duty.'

Here was a man who, on shore, showed a cavalier indifference to public opinion, yet once on board he was one of the best officers of the English navy, and one of its strictest disciplinarians. There was pride and originality in such a way of life, and also there was a need for great self-control. Both the captain and his officers were completely sober once on board, and worked extremely hard; they allowed themselves no form of amusement. The only reminders that they seemed to keep of their life ashore were the women's portraits which hung in their cabins: there were six in the captain's. All the time I was on board I watched those officers: so solemn, so smart, with expressions contrasting so strangely with those they had worn at Mme Denuelle's. The captain had welcomed me on board with chilly politeness, and all that followed was regulated by etiquette. We left, still amazed at the change of tone and manners we had found in the officers of the *Samarang*, and talked of it all the way to Lima.

I was so deeply disturbed by the conversation I had had with Señora Gamarra, that I could not sleep that night. My head was a jumble of thoughts. By a power of fascination, I had plumbed the depths of that woman's soul. She had long been envied by all, yet her apparently brilliant career had in fact been one long misery. With a shudder I remembered how, for a time, I had planned to occupy the position of Señora Gamarra. So, I thought, were these the torments which would have been awaiting me if I had succeeded in the enterprise I contemplated? Sorrow, humiliations, anxiety: these would have been my lot. Ah! How much better and more noble did my obscure but free life now seem to me! I was ashamed at having for an instant believed in the possibility of happiness in an ambitious career, and that there could ever be anything to compensate for loss of independence.

I returned to Callao. Señora Gamarra had left the *William Rushton* for another English ship, the *Young Henri-*

etta, which was sailing that day for Valparaiso. When I arrived, I found Escudero looking pale and dispirited. 'My poor friend,' I said, 'what's wrong? You look ill.'

'I am ill. I had a very bad night. Doña Pencha had three horrible attacks. I don't know what you had been saying to her, but since you left, she has been in a constant state of agitation.'

'It was my first meeting with Doña Pencha, and it is possible that I said something which, instead of comforting her, increased the bitterness of her grief. If that were so, I should be profoundly upset.'

'As you say, it is possible that, without your knowledge, you wounded her pride, which is extremely susceptible.'

I had been talking to Escudero for about a quarter of an hour, when he was called away. He went quickly below and I remained alone. I went over in my mind the words I had spoken to her the day before, to see if I could guess what might have hurt her so much. But only those who have been in power themselves can understand the pain of losing it and the vulnerable areas which it leaves. I was sorry that I had allowed myself to be so frank, that I had not shown reserve when faced with a suffering which was above the common.

These thoughts were interrupted by Escudero, who tapped me gently on the shoulder, and said, in a tone which pained me, 'Florita, poor Pencha has just had a terribly violent attack. I thought she was going to die in my arms. She is better now and wants to see you. Please be careful what you say to her. One word that upsets her will be enough to set off another fit.' As I went below, my heart beat. I entered the captain's cabin, which was large and very fine, where I found Doña Pencha half dressed and lying on a mattress on the floor. She held out her hand to me, and I sat down beside her.

'You no doubt know that I suffer from a terrible affliction.'

'I know,' I interrupted; 'but is medical science unable to cure you, or have you no confidence in it?'

'I have consulted all the doctors and have done exactly what they prescribed; all to no avail. The older I grow, the worse the disease gets. This affliction has been a great burden in everything I have tried to undertake. Any strong emotion gives me an attack immediately; that alone will give you an idea of how damaging it has been to my career. Our soldiers are so badly trained and our officers such cowards that I decided to take command myself in all important affairs. For ten years, and long before I had any hope of my husband becoming president, I was present on all the battlefields to accustom myself to the firing. Often at the height of the action, I foamed with rage at the sluggishness and cowardice of the men I commanded, and then I would suffer an attack. I had only time to lie down where I was; more than once I have been trampled on by the horses and carried away like a corpse by my staff. Would you believe it, Florita, my enemies used that cruel infirmity against me, so as to discredit me in the eyes of the army? They spread the story that it was *fear*, the roar of the cannon, the smell of gunpowder, that attacked my nerves, and that I fainted away like a society lady in her drawing-room. I admit that these slanders have toughened me: I wanted to show them all that I was not afraid of blood or death. Every reverse of fortune makes me more cruel still, and if . . .' She ceased, and, raising her eyes towards heaven, seemed to be speaking to a Being whom she alone could see. Then she said: 'Yes, I am leaving my country never to return, and before two months have passed, I shall be with You . . .' Only a supernatural power could have given her the expression she wore as she spoke these words. I realised as I looked at her how much she had changed since the day before; her cheeks were hollow, her complexion grey, her lips pale, her eyes sunken and feverishly bright; and how cold her hands were! She seemed ready to depart this life. I dared not say a word to her, for fear of again doing her harm. As I leant over her, my head was above her arm, and a tear of mine happened to fall on it. It was as if an electric spark had touched the poor woman. She came out of her state of rapture, turned abruptly towards me, looked at me, with blazing eyes, and said in hollow sepulchral tones: 'Why are you crying? Are you sorry for me? You think I shall never return from exile? that I'm finished? dead already? . . .' I could find no words to reply. As she had pushed me roughly away from my mattress, I was on my knees in front of her; I folded my hands across my breast with an automatic gesture, and continued to look at her and weep. There was a long moment of silence; she seemed to become calmer, and said in a heart-rending voice: 'So you weep, my dear? Blessed God! You are young, you have life; weep for me, for I am nothing, weep for me, for I am dead . . .' As she spoke these words she fell back on her pillow, crossed her hands on the top of her head and uttered three feeble cries. Her sister ran to her, Escudero arrived, and with loving care everyone gave her the necessary attention. I stood by the door watching her. She lay quite still, not even breathing, and her eyes were wide open and shining.

The captain took me away from this sad spectacle by announcing that his visitors must be thinking of leaving, because the anchor was being weighed. Mr Smith came to fetch me, I wrote a short pencil note of farewell to Escudero and left. As we were about to get into our carriage, we saw the *Young Henrietta* leaving her anchorage. I could see on the poop deck a woman wrapped in a brown cloak, with dishevelled hair; she was waving a white handkerchief in the direction of a launch; it was the ex-president's lady, bidding a last farewell to her sister and her friends whom she was never to see again.

When I reached home, I felt ill; I could not get that woman out of my mind. Her courage, her heroic constancy in the midst of the endless troubles that had beset her, made her larger than life in my eyes; it was heart-rending to see that outstanding woman, victim of the very qualities which made her superior to her fellow beings, forced through the cowardice of a nation to leave her country, her family and friends, and, afflicted as she was with a terrible infirmity, finish her sorrowful days in exile. A lady, born in Cuzco and a childhood friend of Doña Pencha, gave me some details about the life of this extraordinary woman that may be of interest to the reader.

Doña Pencha was the daughter of a Spanish officer who had married a very wealthy young woman of Cuzco. From childhood she was noted, amongst her playmates, for her proud, daring and sombre character. She was very pious, and at the age of twelve decided to enter a convent with the intention of becoming a nun. But her delicate health did not allow her to carry out this plan. At seventeen her parents brought her home so that she could receive the necessary care required by her malady. Many officers frequented her father's house, and a number of them sought her hand, but she declared that she did not wish to marry, being resolved to return to her convent as soon as her health permitted it. Her father, hoping for a cure, made her travel, took her to Lima, introduced her into society and the social whirl. However, she remained unhappy and seemed to have little taste for the pleasures of her age. She spent two years travelling, returned to Cuzco and shortly afterwards, giving up the idea of becoming a nun, she chose for a husband an ugly little officer, quite stupid and the most insignificant of all those who had sought her hand. It was Señor Gamarra, a mere captain, whom she married. Although delicate in health and constantly pregnant, she followed her husband wherever the wars led him: and the continually tough life strengthened her constitution to such an extent that she became very tough and could make the longest journeys on horseback. For a long time she succeeded in keeping secret the fact of her cruel infirmity, which became progressively worse. It was only when, as the president's wife, she came under scrutiny, that the public learned of it through her enemies. Through her efforts and intrigues her husband had been made president. Once she had succeeded in putting him there, she formed a close liaison with Escudero and made clever use of all those she felt capable of helping her. When her rule succeeded that of General Lamarre, the Republic was in the most deplorable state. Civil wars were tearing the country apart. There was not one piastre in the treasury. The military sold themselves to the highest bidder. In a word, it was anarchy in all its horror. Although brought up in a convent and quite uneducated, she had uncommon good sense and will power, which enabled her to govern the nation, which until then had proved ungovernable even by Bolivar, so well that in less than a year order and concord were restored; factions were pacified; trade flourished; the army had regained confidence in its leaders; and, if peace was not yet universal throughout Peru, at least it reigned in the greater part of the country.

At the beginning of her reign, the heroic virtues of Doña Pencha inspired both love and admiration; but she had faults which made this situation short-lived. However brilliant the qualities that God has given us, they are for His own purposes, and not for ours; we may all be perfect in a heavenly context, but none of us is perfect in the context of the social order. Doña Pencha seemed to be made to continue the work of Bolivar for a long period of time, and she would have done so if her womanliness had not stood in her way. She was beautiful, very gracious when she wished to be, and capable of inspiring not only love but adoration. Her enemies spread the most wicked slanders about her. They found it easier to criticise her morals than her public achievements, and accused her of vices to counterbalance her superiority. Ambition occupied too great a place in Doña Pencha's make-up for love to be very important to her: she never took it seriously. A number of the officers of her entourage fell in love with her; others pretended to do so, hoping for advancement. Doña Pencha dismissed them all, not with the indulgence of a woman repudiating a love she cannot respond to, but with the anger and scorn of offended pride. 'What use is your love to me?' she would say curtly. 'I need you only as a soldier. Take your sighs, your sentimental words and your love songs to other young women; I respond only to the roar of the cannon, the speeches in Congress and the shouts of the crowd when I pass along the street.' The hearts of those who loved her sincerely were deeply hurt by such rough language; and those who were merely ambitious and hoped she would take them in tow were equally humiliated. But she did not stop there; she began to hate them, lost confidence in them and took every opportunity to jeer at them, even in public, in the most offensive manner. It is obvious that such behaviour not only lost her all the advantages of her sex, but earned her a large number of implacable enemies. For men always believe the successful to have higher qualities than the failures. Each one planned vengeance against her; a number bruited abroad the claim that they had been her lovers, and that she had only withdrawn her favour from them because they had stopped loving her. These slanders annoyed the proud and masterful president's lady, and sometimes made her cruel. The acts she committed as a result show how carried away she became by anger, and how violently she resented such outrages. One day she went to Callao to visit the military jail underneath one of the forts. The whole garrison was on parade to receive her; she carried out her inspection, and whilst riding along the ranks of one of the battalions, she saw a colonel who had been reported to her as having boasted to all and sundry that he had been her lover. She rushed straight at him, tore off his epaulettes, lashed him three or four times across the face with her whip and pushed him so hard that he fell down under his horse's hoofs. Those present stood petrified. 'That is how', she called out in ringing tones, 'I shall punish with my own hands those who slander the president's lady.' Another time, she invited four officers to dinner, and behaved amiably throughout the meal. During the dessert, she addressed one of them saying: 'Is it true, captain, that you told these three gentlemen that you were tired of being my lover?' The poor man blenched and stammered and looked at his comrades in terror. They sat silent and motionless. 'Well,' she said, 'has my question left you tongue-tied? Answer me. If it is true that you did say this, I shall have you whipped by your comrades-in-arms. But if on the other hand they have slandered you, then you and I together will know how to deal with them.' It was only too true that the young man had said what was reported of him. She had the doors closed, called four tall negroes and forced the three other officers present to whip their comrade with birch rods.

Such behaviour was not in tune with the customs of the country she governed and was bound to create resentment. In fact, in a society in which the two sexes were largely independent, there was no belief in 'virtue' in the sense normally attached to this word when speaking of women, and the Peruvians felt insulted by the actions of the haughty president's lady. In any case, it was not in defence of virtue that Doña Pencha behaved as she did, for she held it in no higher esteem than did the rest of Peruvian womanhood. In private life she would not have been offended by proposals in homage to her charms, and like the other ladies of Lima would not have minded how many lovers were ascribed to her; but drunk with a power that she mistakenly felt to be permanent, she had developed a regal arrogance: she thought herself a superior being, and became as touchy and as imperious as a woman born to sit on a throne. She treated Congress with as little respect as Napoleon treated his conservative Senate. She often sent them notes in her own handwriting without even getting her husband to sign them. It was with her that the ministers worked and to her that they submitted the drafts of laws and departmental decisions. She read everything, crossed out passages she did not like and substituted others; the government was effectively absolute although the constitution was republican. This woman had done great service to her country; her public spirit had earned her great confidence, and she would have achieved stability and prosperity in Peru and made a great queen if, beforc assuming supreme authority, she had seen to it that she could remain permanently in control. She was extremely hard-working and quite tireless; she asked no one's advice and insisted on seeing to everything herself. She knew how to choose able assistants, and used equal skill in dividing up the work and appointing suitable persons to carry out missions. She was economical in her personal expenses but generous to those who deserved her confidence; she treated her staff well, and they were all devoted to her. As a warrior, she was a superb horsewoman who could tame the wildest charger. Her public speaking was as clear as it was dignified. Though possessing all the qualities necessary for wielding authority in Peru as it was at this time, Señora Gamarra had great difficulty in completing the third year of office (the presidential term was three years); her despotism had been so harsh, her yoke so heavy, she had offended so many susceptibilities, that an impressive opposition grew up against her. When she saw that it was not going to be possible to have her husband re-elected, she resorted to a stratagem. Señor Gamarra declared before the Senate that he was not standing for the presidency because his state of health did not permit him to carry out public affairs. Señora Gamarra intended to put up a candidate who was a creature of her own, a slave to her will. Both she and her husband put all the weight of their support and that of their friends behind Bermudez; yet Orbegoso won, as we have seen.

To end the story of Doña Pencha, I can add that on arrival at Valparaiso she rented a very fine furnished house, where she established herself with Escudero and a large staff; but not one lady of the town called on her. The foreign residents who had suffered at her hands all complained loudly against her. Only a handful of her old comrades-in-arms amongst the officers were polite enough to come and see her. Proud and haughty as she was, she must have suffered cruelly from this general desertion, this isolation ringed with hatred. So active a person condemned to inactivity, she must have felt as if she had been buried alive. Having had no letter from Escudero since I left Lima, I can say nothing of what she suffered, but seven weeks after sailing from Callao, she died. This is what Althaus wrote to me about her: 'Gamarra's wife died in Chile six weeks after arriving there. It was said to have been due to an "internal complaint", but I think it was from rage at no longer being *general-in-command*; the poor woman had a sad end. Her only companion was Escudero, who has since returned to Peru and attached himself to Gamarra, with whom he will be up to his old tricks again.'

The day following my visit to Señora Gamarra, I felt ill for the first time since I had lived in Lima. I stayed in bed rather gloomily all day. Mme Denuelle came to spend the evening with me. 'How are you feeling?' she asked.

'No better. I am depressed, and only waiting for someone to make me cry.'

'On the contrary, I've come here to make you laugh. I am sure that it is your visits to Callao that have made you ill. That Doña Pencha, with her epileptic fits, must have got on your nerves; it's enough to upset anyone. They say she was struck down every quarter of an hour yesterday. Thank God we're rid of her. What a wicked woman!'

'How can you tell?'

'Gracious, it's not difficult. She was a virago as bold as

brass, who cuffed her officers, as I might my little negro boy.'

'And why were those officers so low as to let her do it?'

'Because she was the mistress and able to distribute promotions, jobs, favours.'

'Mme Denuelle, an officer who lets his face be smacked deserves it. Doña Pencha knew the men she commanded very well, and if she had no other faults than that of punishing government servants who failed to do their duty, she would still be your president's lady.' Mme Denuelle was tactful enough to change the subject, and when she left, I was almost gay.

At last the day came for me to leave; I had been waiting for it with great impatience. I had seen all I wished to, and the very materialistic life of Lima I now found exceedingly tiresome.

For the last week, I had not a minute to myself. I had to pay goodbye visits to my numerous acquaintances, receive theirs, write countless letters to Arequipa, and sell all the oddments that I wished to get rid of. I carried out all this, and on the 15th of July 1834 at nine in the morning, I left Lima for Callao. I was accompanied by one of my cousins, Señor Rivero. We dined with Mr Smith's agent. Afterwards I had my luggage taken on board the *William Rushton* and settled into the cabin which had been occupied by Señora Gamarra. On the morrow I had several callers from Lima: these were the last goodbyes. At about five, the anchor was weighed and the visitors left. I was alone, quite alone, between the boundless ocean and the boundless sky.

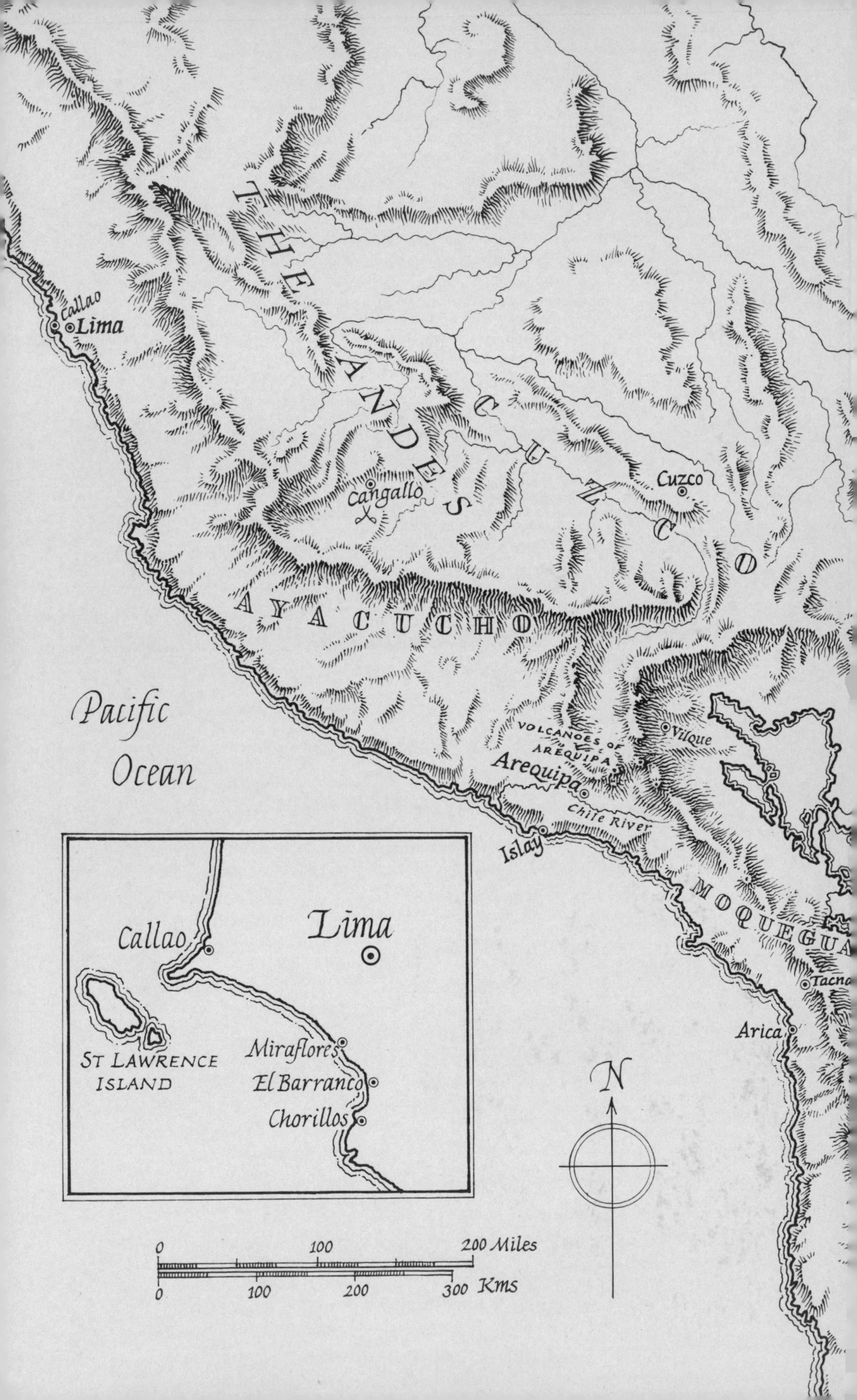

THE ANDES
CUZCO
AYACUCHO
MOQUEGUA
Callao
Lima
Cangallo
Cuzco
Vilque
VOLCANOES OF AREQUIPA
Arequipa
Chile River
Islay
Tacna
Arica
Pacific Ocean
Callao
Lima
ST LAWRENCE ISLAND
Miraflores
El Barranco
Chorillos
N
0
100
200 Miles
0
100
200
300 Kms